A former veterinary science student, Victoria Heywood soon realised that her heart lay in dissecting human nature rather than animals. Since swapping surgical gloves for a laptop, Victoria has worked as a copywriter, journalist and author, both in Australia and overseas. As well as true crime, she has written extensively on relationships, food and travel, and *Every Move You Make* is her 25th book of adult non-fiction.

# EVERY MOVE YOU MAKE

## CHILLING TRUE STORIES OF STALKERS AND THEIR VICTIMS

VICTORIA HEYWOOD

echo

## echo

Echo Publishing
12 Northumberland Street, South Melbourne
Victoria 3205 Australia
echopublishing.com.au

Part of the Bonnier Publishing Group
www.bonnierpublishing.com

First published 2015

Page design and typesetting by Shaun Jury
Cover design by Luke Causby, Blue Cork
Front cover image: © dundanim/iStock

Printed in Australia at Griffin Press.
Only wood grown from sustainable regrowth forests is used in the
manufacture of paper found in this book.

Some of the names in this book have been changed. This is indicated
by an asterisk on first occurrence.

Every attempt has been made to trace and acknowledge copyright.
Where an attempt has been unsuccessful, the publisher would be
pleased to hear from the copyright owner so any omission or error
can be rectified.

National Library of Australia Cataloguing-in-Publication entry
    Heywood, Victoria, author.
    Every move you make : chilling true stories of stalkers and
    their victims / Victoria Heywood.
    ISBN: 9781760063658 (paperback)
    ISBN: 9781760069858 (ebook : epub)
    ISBN: 9781760069865 (ebook : Kindle)
    Stalkers.
    Stalking.
    Stalking victims.

    364.158

Twitter/Instagram: @echo_publishing
Facebook: facebook.com/echopublishingAU

*For Jerome, Charlie and Vinnie*

Writing and reading about crime and criminals, violence and victims is a source of endless fascination – and horror at times – for me. Over the years, I've interviewed rapists and murderers, conmen, safe crackers, drug dealers and more than a few simple douchebags. Some were horrid, some were charming – heck, I still exchange Christmas cards with a few of my contacts and their partners, and would be happy to have them around for coffee.

I've also written extensively about some of the worst crimes Australia has ever seen – from the woman who killed and cooked up her partner for his children's dinner, to the bloke who dismembered his wife and flushed her down the loo, and the teenage Romeo who slaughtered an entire family when the object of his obsession didn't return his love. Horrendous, nightmare-invoking stuff, but somehow bearable when you're just an observer and not personally involved.

This book is different. This time, sadly, I know what it is like to be a victim, even if the reign of fear I endured was just a few short weeks rather than the years that some individuals and families have had to endure, and are still enduring in some cases. I cannot imagine how they have coped – how they have managed to build a life amidst the damage wreaked by their stalkers. For this reason, I dedicate this book to my son, Jerome – may he never again have to live in fear – and to all those who have ever had someone watching every move they make.

This book is also dedicated to my dog – Charlie, the kelpie – for whom stalking is a natural instinct and not the by-product of a twisted desire for control … and also to Vinnie the whippet, Charlie's favourite prey.

# Contents

# Introduction

I always thought that getting stalked was the kind of thing that happened to other people – celebrities in the main, or someone who'd escaped a bad relationship with a revenge-filled ex or had somehow managed to antagonise a random nutcase. As I saw it, stalking was the kind of thing that only happened to a person who was perhaps slightly naive, had made bad choices in their love life or was maybe just too darn attractive for their own good. Given that I was a street smart, overweight, middle-aged mother, living a quiet life in the inner suburbs, the idea that I might attract the attentions of a stalker seemed ridiculous.

Until last year.

Charlie is a slightly older male – still handsome, but getting a bit grey around his chin if you look very closely. He's carrying a few extra kilos, but is friendly, unvaryingly polite to nanas and toddlers alike, and often seen happily making new acquaintances in the park, on the street or at the local cafe. He has the kind of personality that makes him irresistible to everyone from hipsters with Ned Kelly beards to blokes in fluoro vests and workman's boots. He retired young from the family property in the Gippsland countryside, and found a new life in the city when he was still young enough to enjoy its pleasures.

Thanks to Charlie's early life on the farm, he's brilliantly trained and I usually feel free to let him wander behind me and can trust absolutely that he won't raise his nose from my left leg when he's been given the command to 'stay behind'. The joys of a well-trained kelpie.

Mind you, it's a different matter at the shops, when I'll often lift my head from the newspaper at the local cafe to find Charlie lying his head on a stranger's lap – begging for his ears to be patted or a bite of someone's breakfast. He's just as bad at the park, running free, when he'll approach total strangers in the full expectation that they'll throw his ball or tickle his tummy or simply admire his profile.

In short, Charlie is the perfect doggy wingman for a socially isolated writer. Over the years, I've probably chatted to hundreds of complete strangers who've approached me about my dog, or who have been approached by the dog himself. More than a few of those strangers have since become friends. So it was nothing out of the ordinary when the elderly bloke with the walking stick at the neighbouring cafe table one day struck up a conversation about Charlie the dog. It was 28 August 2013.

***

Let's call this man Dick* (mainly because that's the shortened version of what my son and I ended up calling him). Dick was a farmer, down from the country for some medical treatment – a brain tumour, he told me. He was missing his dogs, and Charlie was just so darn handsome and clearly smart that he couldn't resist giving him a pat. Dick and I struck up the kind of conversation common between dog owners. Then it turned out Dick wasn't just any old farmer, but an internationally renowned livestock breeder, exporter of beef cattle to Russia, and an inventor to boot – specialising in a side-shoot of technology that, funnily enough, I knew quite a bit about. Dick needed a website written about his new product. I was a freelance writer who knew about the subject matter. What were the chances of that?

And before you think a cafe might be an odd place to source work, I take the clients where I find them – at various other times, I've been commissioned to write something after a chance encounter with someone at the school gate, on a ski lift and at the Comedy Festival.

Now, if there were such a thing as a standard stalking victim, I would never have classified myself as one. I'm not naive and I have a very well-developed sense of personal safety, honed over years of living overseas and interviewing people ranging from bikers to porn stars, rapists, murderers, common conmen and also corporate bosses with dodgy ethics. Not to mention world famous chefs, actors, marketing gurus, refugees and even, memorably, Stalin's grandson. I used to pride myself on the fact that I could generally tell if someone was having me on.

To give Dick some credit, he had me well and truly fooled at first. And it was only when I called him out on his lies that the real nightmare began.

***

Dick was mad; I'll give him that. Maybe not clinically mad, but he was mad to think that a journalist and writer would accept a brief without employing the journalist's favourite tool, Google, to find out more about the topic under review. That one simple step told me pretty much all I needed to know. He hadn't been president of a noted national institution. He wasn't a famed livestock breeder. And his son certainly wasn't married to the flautist Jane Rutter's daughter. (For the record, Jane Rutter only has a son, currently well below the age of consent in most jurisdictions for anything interesting, let alone marriage.)

Also, Dick's other son had not been murdered by drug dealers in the States and his body left undiscovered for six months – at least, not according to any news reports I could dig up under the name I had been given.

Curious about the technology Dick claimed to have invented, I did a quick patent search too. Nope, nothing under his name there. Then I remembered something: Dick had professed to have been interviewed on ABC TV's *Landline* program about his invention. Unluckily for Dick, my ex-husband was a reporter on that very same program. Access to the archives was the matter of one quick phone call. Nope, nothing. A quick email from my ex to the presenter, Pip Courtney, confirmed this. She had never even heard of the man, although *Landline* had done a story on some similar technology in use in the agricultural sector. (I suspect Dick had watched the program obsessively until he had the details down pat, and could rattle it off to unsuspecting mugs like me.)

Indeed, the only digital traces I could find of Dick were a couple of newspaper articles about his claim to have been abused by priests at a Catholic boys school in Queensland – something he had also talked about in person with me at our chance cafe meeting. According to the news reports, the only problem was that the school had no record of him ever having attended – at least not under the name he was using today. The reporter quoted a representative of the victims of clergy abuse as saying that it was a despicable act to make fraudulent claims, and that it only made it even more difficult for real victims.

As far as I could ascertain, Dick was certainly not who he had claimed to be. None of the facts matched up. However, a search of various professional networking sites turned up a number of people Dick and I both knew. Starting to feel like a bit of a stalker myself, I made contact with these friends of friends, professional acquaintances. Turns out, he'd spun exactly the same story to them and, like me, they'd fallen for it at first then finally blanked him when they discovered the truth. I was merely the latest in a long line of people who'd been taken in by his lies.

I'm still not exactly sure what the point of Dick's fabrications may have been – in other words, what he was hoping to gain from asking me to write a website. It certainly wasn't about striking up a romantic relationship given that at least one of his other targets had been a bloke. Perhaps he was just lonely, frustrated with his lack of career success, or maybe he was simply mentally unwell.

We'd met twice and exchanged a couple of emails by the time I rumbled him, but the moment I knew he was a conman, I no longer responded to his text messages, his emails or the voicemail messages he left. His tone of voice became increasingly demanding. He wanted my bank account details, to arrange another meeting, to find out why I wasn't responding to his requests. He also wanted to borrow money from me, claiming that he had been mugged and lost all his credit cards – possibly the first time I have ever been hit up by a supposedly well-heeled client for a loan! If I hadn't already been suspicious, this request would have been enough to set the alarm bells ringing.

At first, it was simply annoying to see his name pop up on my phone so often, and to have to reject every call. Then one day, the phone buzzed and showed that the call was coming from an unknown contact – common enough when you are a freelance writer. I answered and sure enough, it was him again, obviously calling from a friend's phone or another phone of his own.

'Please don't call me again,' I said, before he had a chance to say anything much. 'I know that you are not who you claim to be, so do not waste my time.' Then I hung up. That would be that, or so I thought. He knew that I knew he was a fraud. Surely he'd just forget about me and move onto someone else?

The next morning I woke up to a voicemail full of obscene and somewhat threatening messages – definitely not worth repeating here.

I thought no more about it, but fired off a quick email to him, explicitly saying that I did not want any further contact with him, and that if he persisted in leaving obscene messages, I would report him to the police. Best to have something in writing, I thought, just in case. And I was right – this is a key step in getting an intervention order should you need one.

***

I'd read about the flight or fight response, but only twice have I ever experienced it at the most visceral level. The first time was in the 1990s when I was living in Russia and a soldier grabbed and attempted to rape me while I was gathering wood for a barbecue in the woods near our apartment. Usually quietly spoken and totally non-violent, I escaped by screaming my head off and repeatedly banging him over the head with a brick lying on the ground nearby. God knows where THAT voice or THAT willingness to brain another human being came from, but I survived the attack and will be forever grateful to an inbuilt survival mechanism that can overcome the best, most polite of upbringings.

The only other time I've experienced such sudden fear was in 2013 when I spotted Dick, the bloke who'd been pestering me by email, phone and text message, around the corner from my house. A matter of metres away from where I lived. It was one thing being cyberharassed – at the time, I didn't quite consider it as stalking – but having him in my neighbourhood was something else entirely. Around the corner from my house, indeed!

I had never given him my address, had never given any indication of where I lived, yet there he was. Despite being middle aged, and not having run more than 100 metres at a slow trot since I was in high school, fear and adrenalin worked their magic. I was home in 20 seconds flat, moved the car (which Dick had seen before and would recognise) to a neighbouring street, and then hovered inside with the doors locked and the curtains drawn. Then when I could see no sign of him out the front of my house through the crack in the curtains, I went to the police.

***

When you're a civilian, with a spotless criminal history (bar some petty milk bar pilfering as a kid), your taxes up to date and only a few parking fines to your name, there's something quite exciting about visiting a police station. (I'm sure many of the people I've written about in previous books feel quite differently.)

From a professional point of view, I was also interested to find out how Australian police treat members of the public popping in for advice and/or help with a stalker, and I have to admit I was pleasantly surprised. I explained the circumstances, played a few of the voice messages I'd been left, and said that the reason I was there today was the fact that I'd seen him near my house (coincidence perhaps, but spooky nonetheless, given that I'd initially met the stalker out of my suburb, and also well away from his.)

Luckily, I hadn't bothered deleting his voice messages, his texts or the numerous emails he'd sent. The police were quite interested in those, as it turned out. They were particularly keen on the emails sent by someone purporting to be Dick's lawyer and threatening me with legal action. I might have been more concerned had the letters not contained a mishmash of spelling errors and dodgy legal terms, and been sent from a person not qualified as a lawyer in any state of Australia. (Yes, I had a friend check.)

I was able to give the stalker's name to the police officer on the front desk – well, *a* name at least, given that there was every chance it could have been entirely false – and also the phone numbers and email addresses he'd used to contact me. I was immediately advised to keep logging all future interactions with him, and to think about taking out an intervention order – something that would mean that if he *did* contact me, then action could be taken against him.

Like me, many are sceptical about intervention orders, given the number of men who flout intervention orders and sometimes go on to commit homicide. As just one example, take the murder of 43-year-old Kelly Thompson in Melbourne in 2014, despite her having taken out an intervention order against her ex, 59-year-old Wayne Wood. Thompson had suffered through months of threats and violence against her, and Woods had openly discussed with people his intention of harming both Thompson and himself. The

Coroners Court was told that Wood had breached the intervention order twice in the weeks leading up to the murder, and Thompson had made 34 worried phone calls to police over that same period. Neighbours called police after they noticed Wood hanging around Thompson's Point Cook home, and were allegedly told to call back if they heard screaming or glass breaking. But it was already too late. After killing Thompson, Wood then killed himself.

I wasn't yet at the point where I thought an intervention order might be necessary for me. But I was almost relieved to hear that when the desk sergeant had done a search on Dick's full name, they'd discovered that he was already 'well known to police' as the saying goes. Call me suspicious, but my next question was whether any of this 'history' involved sexual crimes, or crimes of violence – I certainly wasn't looking forward to being raped or murdered or even bashed as a result of having a friendly chat to an old bloke in a coffee shop. The officer could not say anything more than 'Known to us for similar behaviour.' I was again urged to take out an intervention order. 'Oh, great,' I thought, and went home.

***

At home, the one place on earth where I'd always felt exceptionally safe, every unexpected noise suddenly made me start and wonder – was he outside right now? Had he somehow managed to find his way *inside*? The roller door at the back of the garden was found open – was that him or the wind? The switch from the water tank that controlled the garden irrigation was turned to closed – was that him? But the tapping of a walking stick on the footpath outside my house was the one thing that really set my teeth on edge. Now you might think that Dick being elderly and in need of a walking stick might have been some consolation, but this just made things worse.

You see, I have one old people's home just down the street from my house and another one on the corner. The constant tap of walking sticks past my study window haunted me for months – still does, if I am honest. I was even more unsettled when a friend joked that perhaps Dick wasn't carrying an ordinary walking stick, but perhaps a James Bond-ish cane that actually concealed a sword or a rifle. I'll never look at an old bloke with a walking stick in quite the same way again.

It's the kind of crack I myself may have made before I made Dick's acquaintance, but nowadays, I don't quite see the humour. The thing is, even an elderly bloke with bad teeth and a walking stick is capable of scaring the hell out of someone – even someone much younger, much stronger and much fitter – given the right degree of malevolence. Stalkers come in all sizes, and shapes and degrees of separation, as I was to discover in the course of researching this book.

How people respond varies almost as widely. I sought immediate police help when he turned up near my house, but others choose not to involve the law until it gets unbearable, particularly if they have been in a relationship with the stalker before.

I also chose not to take out an intervention order on the advice of a psychologist friend, who said that given that Dick was a random albeit resentful stranger, there was every chance that he would soon lose interest. If I'd taken out an order against him, then he would have had the opportunity to contest it in court – a process that would perhaps just feed into his sense of injustice and spur him on to further nasty acts.

Most of my friends were curious about the details of what was going on and very supportive, with some particularly keen characters even volunteering to dash to my rescue – any time of the day or night – should Dick turn up near my house again. One was a big, burly, ex-copper; the other was a young, six foot four, insanely fit Irishman who walks his dog at the same park as me. Others wanted to maintain their distance – like being stalked might be contagious. My sister, for one, said it was okay for me to send her copies of emails and voicemails for safekeeping, but she didn't want to know the explicit details.

But there were plenty out there who were downright judgmental: 'What did *you* do to *him*?' was pretty much the gist of it. And also: 'What would you change about your behaviour next time?' from one particularly sanctimonious acquaintance. Like this was MY fault somehow – that my talking to a stranger in a coffee shop, or exchanging pleasantries about a dog meant I was asking for it? It was victim blaming at its most thoughtless, and I soon learned not to talk about the experience unless I knew my confidant could be trusted. How much more difficult must it be for those who know their stalkers intimately – where family and friends will have their relationships and opinions too?

My teenage son was kept informed of what was happening, mainly for his own safety, but I did not share too many of the details of the notes and messages. No kid needs to know that. But it was important that he knew who to look out for (old bloke, glasses, walking stick, bad teeth) and never to open the door or answer the phone without checking who it was first. For weeks, we lived with a big sign on the bench by the phone with emergency contact numbers, and a description of the stalker for houseguests too. There were entire areas of the town that I avoided – particularly the suburb where I knew he lived, and the suburb where I had first encountered him (not mine, thankfully, but home to my favourite cafe). I knew I had to stay away from there when the barista warned me that Dick had started haunting the place, asking about my whereabouts. A few times I'd even spotted him myself when driving through the shopping strip, either tapping along with his walking stick, or deep in conversation with someone at a cafe. I couldn't help a mean flash of hope that he had found a new target.

Thankfully, the stalking was all over within six weeks. 'I think it's time we just went around to his house and nailed his head to the floor,' the desk sergeant told me at what turned out to be my final visit to the station. While half of me hoped she was serious, in the event all it took to make him back off was one stern phone call from the police officer. 'Any more contact with Victoria Heywood and you'll be up on charges,' was the message she gave. Sadly, I wasn't allowed to listen in, but this is what she told me when she reappeared at the front desk, looking rather shaken. 'Well, he's a belligerent one,' was her summation of their exchange. Belligerent, perhaps, but also a bully and like most bullies, scared of authority. I have not heard from him again.

# Who's Stalking Now?

A stalker is a stalker is a stalker right? It seems not, according to international research and some of the brightest brains working with people who 'exhibit stalking behaviours' as the textbooks would have it. Indeed, there is almost as much variation between stalkers as there is between their victims.

The classic image is of a complete stranger watching an attractive young woman (probably blonde and American, if you happen to be watching a telemovie) from a distant vantage point, before swooping in for the kill. However, the reality is far more mundane, if no less terrifying. Most stalkers know their victims – and most of them know them intimately. They are husbands, girlfriends, ex-girlfriends, ex-boyfriends or any other variation on the theme. Stalkers can be colleagues, patients, co-workers, acquaintances – and possibly also strangers. In most cases, the target knows exactly who is stalking them and has had an intimate relationship with him or her.

One American study in 2009 asked victims what they thought had motivated the stalking.[1] Overwhelmingly, 36.6 per cent replied 'retaliation, anger or spite'. A need for 'control' was cited by 32.9 per cent of participants, and 'mental illness or emotional instability' was alluded to by 23.4 per cent. Some thought a combination of factors had driven their stalker's actions. Almost *three and a half million* victims stepped forward to give their views, which is a scary enough figure in itself.

> **Types of Stalkers**
> So what kinds of stalkers are out there? Categories –
> according to Mullen, Pathé and Purcell, the authors of
> *Stalkers and Their Victims* (Cambridge University Press, 2009)
> and used by the UK's Fixated Threat Assessment Authority
> amongst others – include the following:
> - rejected stalkers
> - resentful and retaliatory stalkers
> - intimacy seekers
> - incompetent suitors
> - predatory stalkers.
>
> Of course, some stalkers may combine several of the above
> categories – the incompetent suitor who then becomes
> resentful, for example.

## The Rejected Stalker

The rejected stalker is the man or woman who has experienced the unwanted end of a relationship. This is most likely to have been a romantic relationship, but the end of a friendship, or severing of ties with a family member or even a trusted therapist, could also spur someone on to stalk. As with the end of any relationship, the stalker is likely to feel an acute sense of loss and perhaps anger. But rather than retiring under the doona with a tub of ice cream and a bottle of whisky, like most people would, the rejected stalker instead plots an intricate campaign of harassment.

The stalker may justify their behaviour as an attempt to 'win back' the person who rejected them, although it seems highly unlikely in my opinion that constant threats and harassment would encourage any ex to think, 'Wow – I really must get back with him/her!'

Jealousy, possessiveness and a history of domestic violence are all warning signs that an ex may turn into a rejected stalker.

And it seems that the rejected stalker can be one of the most persistent. Having had their relationship so cruelly terminated, stalking can be one way of maintaining a sense of closeness with their victim. In therapy, the focus is generally on helping the stalker 'fall out of love'. They are encouraged to face up to reality, move on from their obsession with their ex, and accept the sadness of their loss.

## The Resentful Stalker

Resentful stalkers hold a grudge against their victim for some slight or action (either real or imagined). Feeling humiliated or badly treated, resentful stalkers want to 'get their own back', and take delight in scaring and distressing their victim. Sometimes, they may remain anonymous – with the victim having no idea why they are being pursued or perhaps even *who* is after them.

Mark Chapman, who infamously stalked and murdered John Lennon, is a classic case of a resentful stalker. Chapman described himself as the world's biggest rock fan and admired Lennon and all his work, until he read a biography of the musician. Angered that Lennon would 'preach love and peace, but yet have millions [of dollars]', Chapman shot and killed Lennon on 8 December 1980. (See page 155 for more information.)

Funnily enough, stalkers of this kind actually consider themselves the victim – of the system, the business, or the person involved – and resent the power they consider their victim to hold. The motive behind their actions may be spurious – they might just be expressing their rage at someone who, for them, symbolises all those who have hurt or humiliated or otherwise mistreated them in the past.

Retaliatory stalkers are considered a subset of this category. Rather than just swanning around in a dark cloud of resentment for months or even years, retaliatory stalkers will take swift, vindictive action against their victim – perhaps through poison pen letters or a short-lived spate of abusive phone calls. Their campaign of harassment may last only a few days, and once they have vented their spleen, they will stop.

## The Intimacy Seeker/Incompetent Suitor

The intimacy seekers' fancy alights upon a person, often a complete stranger, who they have decided is The One. Many delude themselves that they are actually in a relationship with their victim, as was the case with David Letterman's stalker, who claimed to be married to him (see page 126). This apparently is the one category of stalkers where women far outnumber men.

Intimacy seekers can be downright persistent too. The satisfaction of being in love, even if this is not reciprocated or is actively rejected, keeps them going. Most are socially isolated – they are lonely people just looking for love, and in the absence of other close relationships, reach out to a fantasy figure. (Some, however, are not seeking a romantic relationship, but instead wish to become a close friend or mentor.)

Incompetent suitors, a bit like intimacy seekers, are hoping for a relationship that will satisfy their need for, well, intimacy. However, this type of person is held back not by their irrational belief that their victim loves them back, but by their poor social skills. Some are intellectually impaired; others just lack any social awareness, and are useless at the whole 'courtship' business. (I imagine that those 'How to Pull Any Woman' seminars are filled with blokes like this.)

Given their social awkwardness, it's no surprise that the incompetent stalker's idea of a courtship ritual can be bizarre and frightening. This was seen in 2004 when Britney Spears' stalker jammed her letterbox and inbox with love letters, emails, and photos of himself with scary notes saying things such as 'I'm chasing you' (see page 141).

Perhaps less frightening was the method adopted by Richard Brittain, a stalker I interviewed for this book, who wrote an entire novel about the object of his obsession; see page 232. Richard himself openly admits to some of the delusions that characterise an incompetent suitor: an unwillingness to take 'no' for an answer, and a perverse tendency to take rejection as encouragement. One research study in 2001 suggested that such persistence is encouraged by cultural stereotypes – the pursued offers token resistance, which is finally overcome by the all-conquering lover.[2]

Incompetent suitors can also be led astray by the unwillingness of some victims to cause offence: any ambivalence, even just a polite response to an overture, is taken as a sign of interest and may prolong the pursuit. Both the incompetent suitor and the intimacy seeker have one thing in common: they feel entitled to a relationship with their victim, and are completely blind to the feelings or wishes of the person unlucky enough to have attracted their attentions.

## The Predatory Stalker

Lastly, we come to the predatory stalker: the true stuff of nightmares, and the scenario that most often comes to mind when we think of stalking. Unlike an ex who can't let go of a former partner and whose actions reflect extreme anger or personal distress over the dissolution of a close relationship, the predatory stalker does not target former lovers or intimates, but complete strangers or casual acquaintances. And unlike incompetent suitors and intimacy seekers, their goal is not to establish a relationship, but to exert power and control over their victim. This stalker is often a sexual predator: stalking is their twisted version of foreplay; the real goal is physical or sexual assault. Predatory stalkers gain pleasure from following and gathering information about their victim and from their violent and sexual fantasies, but what really gets them off is the assault itself.

Leaving aside the actual assault, the stalking itself may be sadistic too. Some predatory stalkers take delight in messing with their victim's head by leaving sinister and subtle clues that they are being followed without revealing their identity. But even when the victim is unaware that she (and the overwhelming majority of victims are female) is being stalked, the perpetrator can still glory in the process – deciding how long to prolong the suspense, rehearsing the attack, and fantasising about how it is going to feel.

The surprising thing is how normal predatory stalkers can appear on the outside. They take great care to keep their secret desires separate from their normal lives, often leaving family, friends and colleagues stunned and incredulous when they are finally caught.

Take, for example, 'the Night Stalker' Delroy Grant (also known as 'the Minstead Rapist') who between October 1992 and May 2009, stalked, raped and terrorised elderly women living alone in south-east London, Kent and Surrey in England. Grant was suspected of over 100 offences. The father-of-eight was viewed as a friendly, self-sacrificing neighbour who provided meticulous care for his estranged wife, who was paralysed from the neck down from multiple sclerosis. Grant was found guilty, given four life sentences and ordered to serve a minimum of 27 years in prison.

And then there was American lawyer Danford Grant, a seemingly happily married father-of-three. Described as an ambitious and capable lawyer in an elite Seattle law firm, he was charged with four sexual attacks on three different female massage therapists. The attacks were not only violent and sexual in nature, but were also meticulously well-planned and researched. During one rape-at-knifepoint of a massage therapist in Bellevue, Washington, Grant told her that he had been researching her and to prove it accurately recited her home address, husband's name and other details. In May 2014, he was sentenced to 25 years in prison.

Even more horrifying was James Perry, 'the Mall Rapist'. Over five years, Perry stalked and committed dozens of sexual attacks against children and young women. He specialised in petite young women working alone in strip malls and shopping centres around Madison, Wisconsin, in the United States, and would meticulously plan when and where to attack. After his capture, investigators looked at CCTV footage of him stalking his victims, with one officer describing his behaviour as 'a shark tracking a fish in the ocean'. Perry was a popular member of his suburban community, where he lived with his wife and two young children.

American *ABC News* reported on 26 May 2006:

> It can be argued that Perry's wife, who we'll identify as Joanne, was his first victim. For eight years, Perry completely fooled his family and community. The couple had two young daughters and lived in a family neighborhood near Madison.
>
> 'I was living with pure evil, a manipulator, a liar, pure evil,' Joanne said. 'And I didn't know.'
>
> She said her husband was 'loved by so many people ... You just couldn't help but like the guy ... He was so smart. He really had so much to offer.'
>
> She would not find out until much later that she was the perfect cover for a sexual predator. Her husband lived a double life – deceiving everyone he met. One life was that of the family man. The other was that of a sexual predator who terrorized four states – Wisconsin, Ohio, Illinois and Texas – fondling, raping, then distributing video of his attacks in the dark world of Internet porn.

James Perry, then aged 36, was sentenced in November 2004 to 470 years in prison for creating child pornography, rape, child sexual assault and kidnapping. It was the longest sentence ever handed down for sex crimes in Wisconsin history.

## Are They Nuts?

In real life, as opposed to the stuff you see on television, most stalkers don't suffer from hallucinations or delusions, although many do suffer from other forms of mental illness including depression, substance abuse and personality disorders. Some are erotomaniacs, convinced that they are loved by their victims – even if they have never met. (Hello, the celebrity stalker.) Others are classified as love obsessionals, whose behaviour may be driven by a schizophrenic or bipolar disorder. Most of these stalkers are male. Unsurprisingly, most of their targets are young, female and possibly famous.

A US study back in 1997 looked at psychotic versus non-psychotic stalkers.[3] The researchers found that psychotic stalkers were more likely to haunt the home of their victim, but less likely to send letters (or emails today, one assumes) or to keep their victim under surveillance. I found this surprising, thinking that someone who was 'psycho' was more likely to pop out of the wardrobe wielding an axe.

In fact, the same study found that those who *weren't* psychotic were more likely to be armed with lethal weapons, willing to use violence, and cunning in the ways they were prepared to use this violence – for example, plotting over an extended period of time rather than exploding on the spur of the moment. This may have huge implications for law enforcement and mental health professionals – in terms of how they deal with such a diagnosis – but it has even wider meaning for victims: 'Great! He's psychotic so I *don't* need to be worried?'

Predatory stalkers are a completely different kettle of fish to other stalkers. For one, they are far more likely to have a history of convictions for other sexual offences and to have a diagnosable paraphilia, 'arousal in response to sexual objects and situations that are not part of normative arousal-activity patterns' as the experts would put it.[4] And unlike stalkers who develop delusions that their victim is really in love with them or has committed some imaginary offence, these stalkers rarely have psychotic disorders. They do, however, often have personality disorders.

Given their propensity for sexual violence, predatory stalkers are generally treated within a sex-offender program, with the main focus being on managing the paraphilia that is behind their stalking behaviour.

# The Terrors of Technology

There's no doubt that technology has transformed our lives. But it's certainly not always used for the power of good, as the increasing number of cyberstalking cases demonstrate. Indeed, thanks to mobile phones, social networking, apps, maps, the internet and Google in particular, never before have humans been so switched on, or so easy to find and harass at arm's length.

Gone are the days when you could have an unlisted number, disconnect the landline or simply rent a post office box if you didn't want anyone to know your address, or to contact you directly. These days, a savvy cyberstalker can not only work out where you live, work, holiday or relax – hello Google, TripAdvisor, LinkedIn and Facebook – but can also make sure that you can't make a move without being tracked. Without rigorous privacy settings for your online presence, they're likely to be able to work out where your kids go to school, who your friends are, and even personal details of your family members.

All of which is highly illegal. Stalking someone online has been recognised as a crime in most jurisdictions worldwide. And age, sex or relationship status is no defence. Cyberstalking a girlfriend, boyfriend, colleague, ex-partner, family member, neighbour or anyone else is equally against the law.

Cyberstalking can involve direct or indirect personal threats, or sexual innuendo, and is generally driven by the desire to gain control or to scare you. It includes everything from contacting you on Facebook or any kind of website or forum, or leaving messages on your phone or email account. And with most of us having a mobile at hand all hours of the day, there's little you can do to escape your stalker, short of changing your number and all your digital contact details. Basically, your whole life – should you be lucky enough to keep it.

Two high-profile cases from opposite sides of the globe – those of Simon Gittany (page 61) and Cid Torrez (page 76) – both escalated from cyberstalking to murder (allegedly so in the case of Torrez, who is still awaiting trial). However, there are many, many people out there who are under covert surveillance from their exes or current partners on an everyday basis too. Most of these are women, as stalking is overwhelmingly a crime committed by men against women in Australia and internationally,[5] although there are instances of same-sex stalking, and women who stalk men.[6]

While we tend to think of stalkers as being random strangers, it's actually more likely to be someone known to the victim, and intimate partners are the most common of all. After all, it would be incredibly difficult for a complete stranger to get access to your computer or smartphone in order to secretly install a monitoring app, but for a partner or intimate family member, not too tricky at all.

The same goes for access to your email or social media accounts. No matter how much you love your partner today, would you really be happy for them to still have unfettered access to your digital life in the event of a nasty breakup? The last thing you want is to be tethered by technology to a revenge-seeking ex.

★★★

Cyberstalking is increasingly linked to cases of domestic violence. In a study undertaken in 2013 by the Domestic Violence Resource Centre in Melbourne, a whopping *97 per cent* of the domestic violence workers who took part in the research reported that perpetrators were using technology to monitor and harass women in domestic situations.[7]

The study noted that cyberstalking tends to be a form of abusive behaviour that perpetrators use at the end of a relationship in an attempt to control the victim. However, other studies also show that cyberstalking behaviours are often part of the relationship before the couple separate.[8]

In other words, the person you once trusted above all others doesn't trust *you*. Worse than that, they're prepared to go to any lengths to ensure that not only do they know exactly what you are doing, when and with whom, but also that you feel both frightened and threatened.

Two-thirds of the victims interviewed in the same study said they were made to feel like they were being watched or tracked, yet less than half told somebody about it. Many victims were hesitant to describe their experiences as stalking – possibly believing that the only 'real' stalker is one that is present in the flesh, perhaps standing outside your bedroom window, or following you home from work.

In fact, stalkers no longer have to even get out of bed or leave the house to pursue their target. Technology is increasingly their torture tool of choice, allowing them to invade the privacy of their victim in ways that would have been unimaginable just 10 years ago.

Whether by phone, email, app or internet, technology gives the perpetrator access to their prey 24 hours a day, allowing them to abuse and harass their target easily, instantaneously and from a distance.

Perpetrators are also using technology to create a sense of omnipresence in victims' lives through, for example, the use of GPS (global positioning system) tracking on smartphones, and monitoring of social media accounts. And it can be used as an easy way for offenders to punish and humiliate their targets, most often women.

One woman cited in the 2013 study previously mentioned had her ex-partner bombard her Facebook page with information about how he gave her an STD (sexually transmitted disease) – this information was read by her teenage son's friends, among other people. Another victim had a GPS tracking device secretly installed on her phone, so her ex was able to track her to a women's refuge. And there are plenty more cases like that as the following sections and chapters show ...

## At the End of the Line: Telephone and Text Stalking

Staying under the radar is particularly difficult for those who have had some kind of relationship – romantic or otherwise – with their stalker. I discovered this for myself when the mobile number and email address I'd blithely handed over to a prospective client was used to send me a number of threatening emails and voice messages, including some messages threatening legal action for my failure to respond to his nasty calls and notes.

My ordeal lasted a few short weeks. It was frightening enough to wake every morning to discover a couple of abusive emails and perhaps a drunken voice message or two, so I have real sympathy for the 32-year-old French schoolteacher whose 33-year-old ex from Rhone in the south of France phoned and texted her 21 807 times over TEN months.

Do the maths – that's an average of *73 unwanted contacts per day*. Hell, most of us would struggle to keep up with that number of legitimate emails or calls.

And it wasn't just his ex who had to deal with the barrage of messages. After the teacher finally blocked her number, the man instead began ringing her parents and colleagues at work ... The reason? The couple had broken up in 2011, but the man wanted his ex to thank him – and pay – for the work he'd done renovating their apartment before they split.

In answering the charges that had been laid against him, the unidentified man told the court in Lyons that he'd found it difficult to deal with the loss of his girlfriend, and that he had a history of depression, for which he had previously been hospitalised. And he really, really wanted her to thank him for his handyman skills.

The man explained that he'd vowed to continue the calls until his ex showed some appreciation for his hard work. (In fact, it was only when his ex eventually said thanks, during a meeting organised by a mediator, that the stalking finally stopped.) The renovator conceded that with the benefit of hindsight he could understand that his actions had been 'stupid'. Stupid, indeed, and criminal too.

Regardless of his excuses, the stalker was sentenced to prison for 10 months – six of which were suspended, and was given a €1000 (A$1300) fine. He was also ordered to undertake psychiatric treatment and was prohibited from all further contact with his victim. Perhaps inspired by his time in court, the stalker planned to retrain as a legal assistant, and told the court that he had a 'passion for writing'.

***

It seems that you would be wise to get a character reference for all prospective new lovers – particularly from their most recent partner. This one simple step would have saved a number of Jason Ronald Vaughan's ex-girlfriends from the nightmare that unfolded when their respective relationships with the Australian man came to an end.

Aged 35 when he faced the Brisbane District Court in 2011, Vaughan had bombarded three separate women with sexually explicit emails, obscene phone calls and text messages when they rejected him. Just one year earlier, he had been convicted of stalking a Brisbane artist. This time round, he pleaded guilty to four counts of using a carriage service to menace, harass or cause offence to the three women over a period of time stretching from March 2005 to May 2008.

Vaughan, a scientist working in pathology, obviously had what it took to attract a new partner. One he met on a bus, another at a nightclub. However, when they had the nerve to end a relationship with him, he swung into stalker action.

One ex told the court that Vaughan would leave messages threatening to 'get her'. 'I have ways of getting back at you,' he reportedly said. He also called her derogatory names such as 'fat bitch' and 'slut', and emailed her saying, 'What the fuck was I ever doing with a walrus like you?' and 'I still have plans for you unless you repent and confess your sins to me.'

The girlfriend he'd met at the nightclub in 2007 was bombarded with 15 texts in the three hours after they broke up. (The sheer number of messages doesn't seem too excessive for a couple in the throes of new love, but I can well imagine how it feels to get that volume of nasty messages from a recent ex.) As well as being sexually crude, the messages included insults such as 'Those kids of yours look demented.' He also made threats including 'You vile piece of filth. You will pay for what you have done.' He did not seem to recognise that all she had done was end their relationship – as was her right.

But the scientist was really just warming up. The next girl to call time out on a relationship with him – if several dates could be said to constitute a relationship – spent the next 14 months being stalked by phone. He left sexually explicit messages, called her names, screamed obscenities and in one particularly virulent call, told her that she should 'just fucking die'. Other times, Vaughan simply breathed down the phone into her answer machine or made weird sobbing noises.

The prosecutor, Stuart Shearer, pointed out that it was clear that Vaughan could not handle rejection: '[Stalking] is a course of conduct that is almost routine to him.'

In Vaughan's defence, barrister Aaron Simpson explained that his client had experienced a home invasion in 2007 and had since suffered from post-traumatic stress disorder. He was both depressed and anxious, but was seeking help. He also pointed out that Vaughan had not been in a relationship since. Vaughan cried as he pleaded with Judge Anthony Rafter not to send him to prison.

And it worked. Vaughan was described by Judge Rafter as

'a despicable individual' who had greatly distressed each of his victims. A conviction was recorded and Vaughan was sentenced to 12 months' jail, but released on a two-year good-behaviour bond. I trust the next woman to fall for his charms will Google his name before venturing out on a date.

***

Troy Owen Paterson, from Wagga Wagga in NSW, was an even more prolific phone stalker, if somewhat less personally obsessed with his victims. He'd never actually met any of them, but that certainly didn't stop him repeatedly hounding these strangers to the point where many were in fear of their sanity, scared to sleep and in need of psychological support.

Over the course of just five months between September 2012 and January 2013, 45-year-old Paterson, who as it turns out was born with a brain injury, made more than 29 000 calls and texts to random women. (He clearly had time on his hands and a more generous phone plan than I've ever been able to track down.)

Paterson was charged in the Wagga Local Court with just 21 counts of using a carriage service to menace or harass, but police said that it was possible that there were hundreds of other women out there who were yet to come forward or be identified.

It seems that Paterson found his targets by trawling through the classifieds for females who'd placed innocuous advertisements – perhaps looking for a flatmate or to sell a household item.

One woman who'd offered a reward for the return of her lost cat was asked what else she might be willing to offer him. The implication was clear. If she had sex with the stranger, she'd get her cat back. (I know that many people love their cats, but I can't see many being prepared to shag a random bloke on the off chance that he'd found their missing moggy.)

Another woman was the unlucky recipient of a stream of 282 phone calls and texts from Paterson after simply advertising her car for sale. As a result of the barrage of messages, the victim told police she lived in fear and found going to sleep very difficult.

Many of the messages sent by Paterson involved indecent suggestions, with one reading 'You like sec [sic]. I pay you for sex.' Others threatened violence, or warned the women that he was watching them.

The Harris Scarfe department store was a favourite target, and Paterson logged thousands of calls to stores as far flung as Morayfield, Dubbo, Tea Tree, Launceston, Traralgon, Ballarat and Devonport. He told one staff member that he was going to come into the store and kill her. As reported in the *Daily Advertiser* (2 May 2013), other threats included 'You can run but you can't hide,' 'I'm gonna slit your throat,' and 'I'm going to find and hurt you.'

Unsurprisingly, many of the staff members unlucky enough to pick up the phone to Paterson were distressed by the experience. One woman at the Devonport store – which received around 500 calls a month from Paterson – began suffering anxiety attacks and sought the help of a psychologist.

The court sentenced Paterson to multiple two-year good-behaviour bonds after he pleaded guilty to all offences.

***

As Paterson's case shows, stalking doesn't have to involve a romantic relationship. A Melbourne woman who cyberstalked *American Idol* runner-up and pop singer Diana DeGarmo, was sentenced to 26 months in prison with a non-parole period of 12 months, after wreaking havoc on the Tennessee native's life over a period of three years. And mental illness does seem to play a part in some stalking cases. While Paterson had an acquired brain injury, the *American Idol* stalker, Tanya Maree Quattrocchi, was later diagnosed with Asperger's syndrome and borderline intellectual impairment.

Tanya Quattrocchi of Oak Park in Melbourne's north had become obsessed with contestant Diana DeGarmo after seeing her appear on an American talent show. Armed with a phone and the internet, she wasn't deterred by the fact that the target of her obsession lived thousands of kilometres away. First Quattrocchi posed as a 14-year-old fan so she could join the singer's MySpace site. Then she proceeded to hack into her email account, access personal information and even attempted to blackmail the singer.

Over the course of three months, Quattrocchi sent DeGarmo 570 texts and called her 369 times. (With the cost of international calls, I dread to think what Quattrocchi's phone bill was over this time.) In 2006, this pattern of behaviour saw her sentenced to a community-based order for stalking Ms DeGarmo.

A slap on the wrist and the order that she stay away from any internet-connected device was not enough to halt Quattrocchi's obsession though. A mere six months later she began harassing the star again. She may not have been using her own computer, but records showed that she accessed her victim's MySpace account 700 times from a city internet cafe over six months. This time round, she also widened the net, sending emails to her victim's colleagues and family, many of which detailed explicit – and fictional – accounts of DeGarmo's sex life.

Victorian County Court was told Quattrocchi wrote emails to the star's family and friends stating the singer wanted to have sex with her [the star's] brother, loved older men and – seemingly unaware of the complete contradiction – was a lesbian.

In one email to a male work colleague of the star, Quattrocchi allegedly wrote, 'She said she would love to fuck you … hard. And a lot.' Another email sent to DeGarmo's sister-in-law in November 2007 made false claims about the entertainer's sex life that the judge later described as both 'explicit' and 'disgraceful'. Indeed, even at the time of Quattrocchi's arrest in January 2009, police found her sitting in front of her computer, writing an email purporting to be from DeGarmo's mother, Brenda.

Then aged 23, Quattrocchi fronted court again to plead guilty to four more counts of stalking Diana DeGarmo. While the singer did not appear in the Australian court, she did tender a statement outlining the impact her stalker had had on her life. She said that Quattrocchi had called her nearly every night, had sent messages using her MySpace account, and had sent lurid emails about her to her family. She was understandably deeply angry and traumatised.

'I have moved twice and she still finds me. I cannot have any private or professional life without her infiltrating it,' DeGarmo's statement said. 'No matter what I do I cannot get away from her. She is still to this day stealing my online identity and harassing my friends, family and myself.'

Victorian County Court Judge Lisa Hannan said the offences were serious and that the victims – the pop singer and her friends and family – had reported feeling anxious, stressed, embarrassed and losing sleep. Given that the offences occurred only six months after Quattrocchi had been placed on a community-based order for stalking the same victim, the judge said she had no option but to sentence the serious stalker to 26 months' jail with a non-parole period of 12 months. More damningly, the judge said she was not hopeful about Quattrocchi's prospects for rehabilitation, saying that her offending had become entrenched and was ongoing. The judge told the court that she was particularly concerned to learn that Quattrocchi had told a doctor that she still felt she had been wronged and proposed to write a book about her experience. This had the 'potential to constitute further offending'.

'It is important that you understand the fact you perpetrated your offending using cyberspace does not diminish its significance,' Judge Hannan said. She warned that because of the nature of the stalking, the victims were constantly vulnerable. 'From a victim's perspective you are a faceless stalker invading every aspect of their lives. There is no door to lock, no alarm to activate,' Judge Hannan said.

***

## From Friend to Foe

Revenge, not obsession, drove the stalking behaviour in the case of Allem Halkic and Shane Phillip Gerada. Both were young, male and good mates – that is, until they fell out over a girl. The two had become friends around October 2008, but towards the end of the year, Gerada made some unkind comments about a mutual female friend. Allem told the girl what Gerada had said, and the friendship between the two teenagers swiftly turned nasty.

Gerada wasn't going to take Allem's perceived betrayal lying down. He set out to take revenge on Allem by slandering him to his friends and schoolmates. He also sent hundreds of nasty text messages and messages via MySpace to his ex-friend, threatening Allem and saying that he'd get some well-known local gangs involved in payback as well.

It can't have been a pleasant time for Allem, a previously happy teen and the only child of loving parents, Ali and Dina Halkic, of Altona Meadows, Victoria.

The only real difficulty he'd experienced before was related to his diabetes – keeping it under control was a hassle for an active kid, but nothing that he couldn't handle. This was something different. But Allem didn't confide in his parents, and only a few close friends knew what was going on. They advised him not to react to the barrage of malicious texts, and he seemed to agree that this was the best course of action. However, being constantly bullied by text and email must have been difficult. This was a kid who didn't like conflict at the best of times, and now every incoming beep from his phone or his inbox could signal another attack.

The 4 February 2009 seemed much like any other day. Allem had visited a friend, played a game of poker, and returned home around 9.30 p.m. In a later interview, his parents told reporters that he'd spent some time on his computer, popped downstairs for a bedtime drink and snack, and then returned to his room to watch some TV. His parents soon told him it was time for sleep, and said goodnight.

But sleep was the furthest thing from Allem's mind. First there was a series of vicious texts from Gerada: 'Ur all mouth and no action, wait till I get my hands on u, and I'm telling u now ill [sic] put you in hospital,' said one. 'Don't be surprised if you get hit some time soon. You fucked with the wrong person,' read another. 'It's payback time.'

And Gerada had also taken steps to get his revenge. Allem had recently started seeing a girl, who was still entangled with a jealous ex. Gerada tracked down the ex on MySpace and let him know about Allem. That news did not go down well. At 1 a.m. on 5 February 2009, Allem's girlfriend rang him to say that her ex had phoned her in a rage to say that Allem should watch out.

Ten minutes later, Allem called Gerada to ask what the hell was going on. To this day, no one knows exactly what was discussed except Gerada, and he's not telling. What *is* known is that Allem left the house and made his way to the West Gate Bridge. From the top of the span, just as the sun was rising, he sent a final message to Gerada. 'I need your help. You may not give a fuck about me but just answer your phone tomorrow.' After sending the message, at around 5 a.m., he jumped into the Yarra River, 60 metres below.

Back at the Halkics' house, Allem's parents were woken by their alarm at 6.30 a.m. Going to rouse their son for school, they were shocked to discover his bed had not been slept in, and there was no sign of him. The disappearance was completely out of character – perhaps it was something to do with his diabetes? They called the police immediately to say that their son was missing. It was early days, and he was a teenager, but it was clear that this was no ordinary teenage disappearing act. An hour later, when the police called back and asked if Allem had an insulin pump, and what colour it was, they knew something was very wrong. Their suspicions were confirmed 10 minutes later when a police car pulled into the driveway. They opened the door that morning to the very worst news a parent could ever hear.

The Halkics were haunted by the question: What had caused Allem to take his own life? Allem had taken care to shield them from the fact that he was being seriously bullied online, so it took a few days for police to check Allem's phone and for the cyberstalking to come to light.

As a result, on 8 April, just a few months after a teenage boy saw no way of escaping his tormentor than to jump 60 metres to his death, Shane Phillip Gerada, 21, of Bacchus Marsh, became the first person in Australia to face prosecution for stalking via cyberbullying.

He pleaded guilty and expressed his remorse to the court. 'I did not realise the effect of my words,' he said. He also explained that since the death of his ex-friend, he'd had Allem's name tattooed across his back as a lasting memorial. Perhaps in recognition of his belated realisation of the impact of his actions, Gerada avoided time in prison and was instead sentenced to an 18-month community-based order.

But the magistrate sent a potent warning to other potential stalkers and cyberbullies after the court heard that one-third of young people between the ages of 10 and 18 fall victim to the practice, with some bullies even going so far as to issue death threats.

*The Age* reported magistrate Peter Reardon as saying, 'It just demonstrates SMS messages or internet communication may have severe consequences on intended victims whether it was meant to or not. People really should think about what they are doing instead of just hammering some message of hate or aggression.'

In a prepared statement, the Halkics said that Gerada's prosecution marked progress in the battle against cyberstalkers, and that if they had known what they were letting into their home by providing Allem with a mobile phone and internet access, they may well have thought long and hard about the possible consequences.

They have since gone on to campaign for awareness of the dangers of cyberstalking, and also successfully lobbied the state government for security barriers to be established on the West Gate Bridge.

***

Since its opening in 1978, the West Gate Bridge had become what is referred to as a 'landmark suicide location'. And tragically it is not just adults who have died there. Gabriela Garcia jumped off the bridge with her 22-month-old son Oliver after she used a milk crate to climb over the low-rise railing of the bridge in June 2008. Then, just seven months later, Arthur Freeman murdered his five-year-old daughter, Darcey – on what was meant to be her first day of school – by throwing her off the bridge in front of both her older brothers and shocked commuters. These horrific cases, as well as the tireless campaigning of the Halkics and others, sparked the state government to begin installing anti-suicide barriers on the bridge in 2009 after years of prevarication.

Research from the Coroners Prevention Unit showed that suicides from the West Gate Bridge dropped by 85 per cent in the two years after the barriers were installed without 'any apparent concomitant shift to other Victorian locations'.

***

This was already notable for being the first prosecuted case of stalking via cyberbullying, and further history was made on 20 April 2011 when a hearing was conducted at the Victims of Crime Assistance Tribunal (VOCAT) and Allem Halkic was formally recognised as a victim of crime – this was a landmark decision.

The Tribunal Member made the following finding, detailed on the Bully Zero Australia Foundation website:

It then comes to whether you are related victims of this act of violence, of stalking. Section 11 of the Act talks about this and that is why you are here today. A related victim of an act of violence is a person who at the time of the occurrence of the act of violence was a close family member of a primary victim of that act who died as a direct result of that act.

Later in his judgment Magistrate Capell said, 'It is a recognition that in my view – his death was a direct result of that criminal act of stalking and I'm satisfied in this matter it's one of those rare cases where I would have to say the connection is just inevitable.'

The decision to award Allem's parents under this Act recognised that Allem's suicide occurred as a result of an act of violence. For the Halkics, this decision has allowed them to restore Allem's dignity and to provide recognition that a crime was committed against their son. To his family, all who knew him and the wider community, Allem is no longer a suicide statistic. He is the victim of a stalker.

---

***

It's horrifying to think how cyberstalking destroyed the lives not only of the victim, Allem, and his family, but also the perpetrator and *his* family, who will forever have to live with the consequences of his actions.

The age of the young men involved gives pause for thought too, but there have been other cases of even younger victims. Florida girl Rebecca Sedwick, for example, was just 12 years old when she killed herself after a prolonged period of being stalked by her former best friend from primary school and a slightly older girl – plus a gang of other teenagers, who may not have been the instigators, but who were certainly happy to play along with the bullies.

While police had already discovered why Rebecca chose to

end her life on 9 September 2014, what hastened the arrest of her stalkers was one particularly nasty online post. '"Yes, I bullied Rebecca and she killed herself but I don't give a … " and you can add the last word yourself,' the local sheriff Grady Judd said, quoting a Facebook comment that the older of the two stalkers had made after her victim's death.

It's hard to understand what would drive a teenager to brag about being a bully in a public forum – let alone to show such a lack of remorse about the impact of her actions – but it certainly caught the attention of police, who swiftly arrested the two girls and charged them with stalking. They were later released to their parents, although the sheriff said that he was also concerned about the parenting the two girls had received. 'I'm aggravated that the parents aren't doing what parents should do. Responsible parents take disciplinary action,' the sheriff told the local paper at the time. He was unsure at that stage whether the parents should – or could – be charged alongside their children. At the time, they were considering 'contributing to the delinquency of a minor' as a possible charge for the parents, but this would only work if prosecutors could show that the parents knew what their kids were up to, and did nothing about it. Difficult to prove, one would think.

According to police, the stalking started when the 14-year-old, unnamed girl began dating Rebecca's ex-boyfriend. You'd think stalker girl would have been happy to have 'won' the bloke from her competitor, but no. Nothing would do but for Rebecca to be publicly humiliated and threatened with physical violence as well. And access was easy; all three girls were in the same grade at primary school together, even though there was an age gap of two years between Rebecca, her former BFF and her other tormentor.

I can't help but suspect that stalker girl had watched the 1988 cult black comedy *Heathers* – starring a young Wynona Ryder, Christian Slater and Shannen Doherty – where one high school girl kills her popular friend by giving her a drink liberally laced with bleach. (Unlike the girls, the results were not pretty.)

**Tips for Victims**

Phones are an essential part of modern life, keeping us connected to family, friends, work, and the wider world via the internet, in the case of smartphones. Most of us would find it hard to live without our pocket friend, so what can you do when your phone is being used as a weapon against you?

Firstly, it is an offence for a person to use a 'carriage device', such as a telephone, to menace, harass or cause offence (penalty: three years' imprisonment), or make a threat to kill (ten years) or cause serious harm (seven years).

Everyone also has the legal right to tell another person either to not call them at all, or to restrict when they can ring. For example, an ex could be told only to ring you when they wish to arrange access to the kids, and only on Sunday nights between 7 p.m. and 9 p.m.

If the person breaches the restrictions, it may be considered harassment or stalking, and legal action may be taken. Charges may be laid, or the harassment may be used to support taking out an apprehended violence order.

For more information, visit the website of the Australian Stalking Information and Resource Centre (www.stalkingresources.org.au).

Rebecca was in grade six at Crystal Lake Middle School when her stalker/classmate told her 'to drink bleach and die' according to newspaper reports at the time of the arrest. Somehow, the 14-year-old also managed to win over Rebecca's 12-year-old BFF to her cause and the two girls set about making Rebecca's life hell, calling her names, beating her up and repeatedly bullying her both online and in person over a period of two years. Fifteen other girls were also allegedly involved in tormenting Rebecca before her suicide.

At one stage, she attempted suicide by slitting her wrists and was hospitalised. Not long afterwards, her mother removed her from school and began teaching her at home instead. Then she started at a new school, and appeared happy and content. But the relentless barrage of messages continued – on Kik Messenger, Instagram and

Ask.fm – all examples of social media apps that seem to be essential to teenagers today.

After two years, Rebecca had had enough. A search of her computer records after her death showed some of the pain she had gone through. As well as search queries such as 'What is overweight for a 13-year-old girl?', police found that she had been Googling ways to commit suicide. She changed one of her online names to 'That Dead Girl' and one of her screensavers showed a photo of her with her head on a railway track. The last message she sent was to a boy she vaguely knew. It said simply, 'I'm jumping.' And then she did – making her way to an abandoned cement factory and throwing herself off the top of a tower.

More than 250 people mourned the death of Rebecca Sedwick at a funeral in her hometown. Many wore bright green shirts – Rebecca's favourite colour – plastered in anti-bullying messages. A large sign on display read, 'Everyday, more and more kids kill themselves because of bullying. How many lives have to be lost until people realize words do matter?'

Neighbours were less than complimentary when asked by journalists about the 14-year-old stalker. It seems that she was known locally for being rough with younger children and was often left to roam unsupervised. Newspapers also reported that the family lived in a mobile home and owned a pit bull – perhaps playing to public opinion that the type of home and dog could explain how a child could stalk another child so persistently that a 12-year-old could consider death as the only way out.

The two main perpetrators were charged as juveniles with third-degree felony aggravated stalking. Under Florida law, they could also have been charged under a number of other laws, including battery and bullying (such as the *Jeffrey Johnston Stand Up for All Students Act*, which was named after a teenager who killed himself after being harassed by classmates). Given the young ages of the girls, the charges were later dropped; however, both were suspended from school and required to attend counselling.

# The Social Media Minefield

Okay, most of us have done it at some stage. Peeked at someone's Facebook page to see what they have been up to and who they've been seeing. But when does a desire to stay up-to-date with a friend or ex's life become menacing? When does checking facts about a stranger become sinister? When does simple human or romantic interest cross the line and become stalking?

Much has been written about the addictive power of social media, and many of us have experienced it firsthand. Throw some jealousy or spite into the mix and it seems that social media is a powerful tool for those who want to exact revenge or simply make someone's life hell.

The ex factor is particularly destructive. Indeed, a recent British study concluded that the more time you spend checking out your ex on Facebook, the more psychologically damaging it is for you, the more you'll desire your ex and the harder it will be to move on to more fish in the sea.[9]

The results from participants in the study showed that those who unfriended their exes – and their ex's family and friends – were shown to recover from a breakup more quickly. Oh, and also to avoid the chance of being charged for stalking.

Melbourne man, Karl Le, for example, should doubtless simply have unfriended his ex, a British university student, once their relationship broke down. Instead, the 44-year-old Le turned to Facebook to besiege her with emails and text messages. In a further nasty twist that would usually involve celebrities and tabloids, the jilted lover then posted a home video of her performing a sexual act onto a website he'd created specifically for that purpose. A link to the website was then sent to her friends, her family, her classmates and even her university lecturers. The most intimate of moments was now very public property.

Appearing outside the Ringwood Magistrates' Court in August 2012, where Le pleaded guilty to one count of stalking his former lover, he admitted to a news crew that he had done 'a shameful, reckless and stupid thing'. He also admitted that he thought his actions were no different to those involving celebrities such as Lara Bingle and Paris Hilton, who'd had their privacy breached online in a similar fashion.

It can be tempting to think that celebrities are 'asking for it', for the sheer fact that they are public figures and often court publicity. (Indeed, it's probably true that some celebrity sex tapes have been leaked in order to drum up news interest and reignite a flagging career.) The court heard that Karl Le's victim, far from being fodder for a trashy celebrity magazine, was convinced that he would kill her if she did not respond to his messages, and that she'd lived in fear of the ping of an email coming into her inbox. Le had also described the video as 'insurance'. He was found guilty of stalking and initially sentenced to one year in prison with a minimum of four months.

While stalking on Facebook doesn't involve a physical threat such as being followed or put under surveillance, the emotions that are likely to be stirred up are very similar and are equally as real. Just as it is frightening to be followed home from work, or around town, it can be unsettling and scary to find that someone is watching your every online move – to know they are reading your every comment or update, or looking at every photo you post.

Of course, there is a clear difference between friends and family looking at your page to see what you are up to and stay abreast of your news. They'll read your posts and then move on to other pages and people. To them, you are just one of a circle of friends.

### How Not to Be a Facebook Stalker

- Don't give into the temptation to stalk your ex – or anyone else – on Facebook, Twitter or any other social media platform. Taking a quick squiz once or twice is probably understandable, but if you find yourself checking regularly or becoming addicted to seeing what they are up to, your alarm bells should start ringing.
- Think of the benefits of *not* staying connected. Do you really want to know that your ex had a great dinner out with a hot date or to watch their relationship status change from single to not?
- While you're at it, unfriend your ex-in-laws and ex's friends as well because there is every chance you'll hear something about your ex on the grapevine from them too.
- It's commonsense, but don't post public comments about your ex or your subject of interest. If you want to confide in a friend, do it in a personal message or email. The relationship is broken – that's why it's called a breakup – so focus on your future instead. You should be aiming to reduce the time you spend ex-watching and ex-bashing.
- Avoid the temptation to 'friend' your ex's new partner on Facebook. It might seem a great way of keeping tabs on your ex, particularly if you are no longer connected personally, but it will only prolong your pain and is unlikely to end well.

This kind of social browsing is entirely healthy, and exactly what Facebook and other social media sites were designed for.

Research undertaken by University of Missouri Professor Kevin Wise divided Facebook users into 'social browsers' as in the previous example, and 'social searchers'.[10] With social searching, the viewer doesn't just browse, but focuses in on one person – their wall posts, pictures, updates, etc., and does not balance this with viewing or interacting with other people.

In his research, Wise wired up a number of undergraduate students to facial EMG sensors that measured when they responded favourably to stimulus. Worryingly, Wise discovered that people gained the most pleasure from social searching. In other words, the addictive quality of stalking someone on Facebook is directly linked to its function as a pleasure-stimulating activity – your Facebook stalker really does get off on checking out your profile.

Of course, some Facebook stalkers are known to their victims; others are complete strangers. Some lurk in the shadows, simply observing you. But possibly the most frightening of all is the one who targets you specifically, often reacting to every online step you take – either with hatred or obsessive admiration. This type of Facebook stalker is likely to be 'out to get you' – either wanting revenge for a breakup or slight, or wanting to become a closer part of your world. Blinded by their obsession, it's possible that the innocuous comment you posted may be misconstrued. Judging from the stalkers I've interviewed, even a simple comment about going on a picnic on a lovely day could be read variously as a covert invitation (They want me to come along …) or an insult (Go on, rub my nose in it …). Either way, they're taking your comments personally.

Ironically, one of the most famous people to have been Facebook-stalked is Facebook founder, Mark Zuckerberg, who was forced to take out a restraining order against 31-year-old Pradeep Manukonda in 2011. Gossip website TMZ claimed that the Facebook top cat had filed legal papers saying that the stalker had tried to 'follow, surveil and contact Mr Zuckerberg using language threatening his personal safety'. He had also made contact with Zuckerberg's girlfriend, now wife, Priscilla Chan, and his sister, Randi.

According to *Time* magazine, Manukonda went to several of Facebook's offices in Palo Alto, California, looking for Zuckerberg so he could ask him for money for his family. On 24 January, Facebook security also caught Manukonda as he was about to climb the front steps of Zuckerberg's home. He sent flowers and several handwritten letters as well as stalking Zuckerberg on Facebook.

TMZ posted excerpts of some of the messages Manukonda had

## Signs You Have a Facebook Stalker

If you suspect you are being stalked on Facebook, ask yourself the following questions:

- Has the person failed to leave you alone despite your requests for them to stop messaging you, leaving you wall comments, or sending you things like links and Farmville gifts?
- Do they leave lots of comments suggesting that you spend more time together, perhaps even the rest of your life?
- Do they use threatening or sexually explicit language?
- Have they posted unkind comments, or perhaps private information about you online? Or about people close to you?
- Are they constantly harassing you with updates, messages and comments? Even if the content is not spiteful or threatening, constant contact is a sign of obsession.
- Do you *feel* that you have a stalker? If you feel that someone is obsessed with you, either because they really like or really hate you, chances are you are probably right.
- Are you getting irritated, frustrated, upset, scared or overwhelmed by their constant messaging and posts? This is enough of a reason for you to block them, unfriend them or – if necessary – delete your profile.

sent to Zuckerberg, with one message reading: 'Please mark [sic] ... time is really running out for me ... please help me. I really need your help ... please respond in time before it's too late for us ... I owe my entire life at your service ... please help me, then i am ready to die for you.' In an interview, Manukonda claimed that he just wanted advice from Zuckerberg and was a 'peaceful' guy. The court did not agree, and Manukonda was barred from online contact, and from getting within 300 yards of Zuckerberg, his sister, or girlfriend.

Manukonda later returned to his home country of India, and in a bizarre move filed a suit in an Indian court accusing Zuckerberg of being behind a number of physical attacks on him. TMZ reported that Manukonda claimed that he had been 'stabbed from the back side' and that Zuckerberg had set up a fake Facebook page saying that Manukonda was a member of al-Qaeda.

## The Evil Cyber Killer

I grew up in a house without television. Not because of my age or religion or poverty – thanks for your concern – but because of the sheer stubbornness of my parents, who believed that books were better for developing young minds than TV. Who knows, they may have had a point. Today, as the parent of a teenager myself, I feel a bit the same way about letting my child use the internet. Sure it's a great tool and means for communicating, but there's a lot of mind-numbing trash on it and it's also pretty much an open gateway into our home through which *anyone* could enter.

Nothing illustrates this more than the case of Garry Francis Newman, the evil Victorian sexual predator who hid behind online identities to lure and murder Adelaide Hills schoolgirl, Carly Ryan.

\*\*\*

Imagine this: It's 2006, you're a 14-year-old girl, and you've been chatting online via your MySpace webpage with a 20-year-old guy for months. He's cute, charming, funny and a musician. He's also a bit exotic, being American by birth, and he's into the emo subculture too, just like you. Result.

Meeting your soul mate online is all the sweeter too, after the rough time you had last year when some older teens encouraged you to drink and you ended up in hospital having your stomach pumped. Then came the inevitable lecture about choosing your friends more carefully.

You swore off alcohol and drew away from the kids who caused you so much grief, but found a new outlet in chat rooms on the internet. And that's where you met Brandon Kane, a Texas-born, Victorian-raised emo, who plays guitar and thinks you are 'hot'. He's smitten and you're so giddy with love that even your mother is excited for you.

Except that everything about the guy you've fallen in love with turns out to be a cold and calculating lie.

This is exactly what happened to Carly Ryan. Born on 31 January 1992, Carly Ryan was just 14 years old when she first made contact with 20-year-old Brandon Kane. Carly was living with her mother, Sonya Ryan, in the Adelaide suburb of Sterling, and had a bright and bubbly personality, despite her liking for grim emo music.

The two clicked instantly and romance was born. So when Carly was planning her 15th birthday party, to be held on Australia Day 2007, the one present she really wanted was a visit from Brandon. Brandon had to decline as he was going to be in the States for Christmas and then travelling to Paris, but he did suggest that his father, Shane, come across from Melbourne in his stead.

Carly's friends weren't so keen on the idea – Carly had been talking online with her boyfriend's father, Shane, too; her friends thought there was something dodgy about him, particularly the way he'd ask whether they liked kissing other girls and whether they were bisexual.

Even without knowing this, Carly's mother wasn't so sure it was a good idea for Shane to attend the party. But Carly talked her mother round, saying that Brandon's dad was a security guard – an SAS commando who had worked as a bodyguard for Marilyn Manson (the heavy metal superstar singer who chose his stage name by combining those of Marilyn Monroe and Charles Manson, the serial killer).

Shane was given the go-ahead to represent his son at Carly's 15th. But the man who arrived at the Ryans' home in January

2007 for Carly's birthday party was not Shane, not a former SAS commando, and certainly not the father of Brandon Kane.

There is a famous *New Yorker* cartoon from the 1990s entitled 'On the Internet, Nobody Knows You're a Dog' and showing a real dog logging on for a chat with no one being the wiser. Like most really good cartoons, it has a bitter kernel of truth. The dog in this case was Garry Newman, a 47-year-old father-of-three, who had moved back in with his mother after a nasty divorce from his wife and who'd had little to do with his sons since. Neither Shane nor Brandon were real – they were just some of the many pseudonyms used by Garry Newman to chat with innocent young teenage girls.

***

The birthday visit started badly, and ended worse. For a start, Shane was nothing like Carly had imagined her boyfriend's father to be. He was short, overweight, had thinning hair and crooked teeth and walked 'hunched over like an ape', as Carly's mother later described him. He certainly didn't look or behave like an ex-SAS commando.

Carly disliked him on sight, and was creeped out when he took her shopping and then peeked at her over the top of the changing-room door as she tried on different outfits. Worse still was the way he hung around her and her friends, encouraging them to kiss while he watched. At the party, he monopolised her time and reminded her of 'Brandon' any time she spoke to a boy. He was finally kicked out of the Ryan house when Carly's mother found out that he'd slipped into her daughter's bed after the party, whispering that he loved her and would never let anything happen to her.

Shane returned to Victoria, furious with Carly's mother for standing in his way and still obsessed with the now 15-year-old Carly. Sonya Ryan warned him off in no uncertain terms, and he retaliated with a string of vicious emails.

It was then that he tried to enlist the help of his oldest son to win back Carly; the son was horrified and refused to help. Then Newman turned to his youngest son – a boy of 17 who'd barely spent any time with his father throughout his childhood, but was now living with him. This son was more amenable to helping his father, and travelled with him across to South Australia. There, using the Brandon construct once again, the father convinced Carly to go to the beach with him and his son, on 19 February 2007.

On 20 February 2007, the body of Carly Ryan was found by passers-by at Horseshoe Bay, Port Elliot. She had been viciously bashed, choked with sand and her body then tossed in the water. Shortly afterwards, Sonya Ryan was told the news that no parent ever wants to hear.

***

Police quickly connected 'Shane' and 'Brandon' to Carly Ryan's death, and colleagues in Victoria swooped on the man they now knew was actually Garry Newman. When they turned up to question him, he was found seated at his computer, logged in as Brandon and chatting with a 14-year-old girl in Western Australia.

As it turned out, 'Shane' was but one of 200-plus fake identities used by Newman. Others ranged from the tame 'kuruptkoala' to the unprintable. His computer hard drives were filled with child pornography and vampire trivia.

His personal profile on his MySpace site – the site with which he had communicated with Carly as Shane – read:

I may not be a kid anymore, but i tend to act much younger than i am, and NEVER EVER call this a mid-life crisis. To me there is no such thing.

All throughout our lives we are going through changes, even people in their late teens and early 20s do. It's called evolution.

I am very forthright and self opinionated, and this annoys some people, but they can either live with it or hate it. Either way they are not going to change me.

I have my left ear pierced twice, and also my nipple and tongue pierced. I also have some tats. There will be more piercings over the next few months.

I am more a baggy jeans and t-shirt person, and am more comfortable at a live band venue than a nightclub/disco. I was in the military for a number of years and left there as a commando.

I have worked in a number of jobs which have included sales, marketing, hotel bouncing, and have recently had a go at web design. But the effort required for what people expect to pay for a website has meant i have put a hold on that for the time being.

I am about to get my security licence back, and work at that for a year whilst i get my life back in order after some financial disasters and several years travelling the world.

I am divorced, and have custody of a beautiful and loving 18 year old son.

He has been my life for many years after i was awarded custody of him, and he always will be my life. No one will ever change that!

More To Come …

From forensic examination of Newman's internet accounts, it was later discovered that Newman had pursued a 14-year-old girl in the United States in 2002 and 2003, referring to her as his 'princess' and his 'wife'. He had also had numerous online exchanges with a 14-year-old girl in Singapore, under the pseudonym 'Nash'. When she failed to turn up for a planned rendezvous, Newman had been incandescent with rage. He had bragged online that the girl 'would pay' for her behaviour and that he would use 'a young guy' to lure her out of her home. He told an online buddy that she was going to end up 'looking like that packaged meat you get at Safeway'.

Newman and his younger son were charged with murder and extradited to South Australia to stand trial in the Supreme Court in October 2009. Both pleaded not guilty.

***

Both Newman and his son's names were suppressed for the duration of the trial. So too was any information relating to Newman's pursuit of other teenagers, Justice Trish Kelly ruling that such evidence was inadmissible and prejudicial. Jurors would have to make up their minds purely on the evidence that was presented to them about the murder of Carly Ryan.

Prosecutors alleged that the duo had used the 'cyberspace alter-ego' of Brandon Kane to attempt to seduce the then 14-year-old. When Carly rejected the advances of the father and son, they had then used their 'internet construct' to lure her to Port Elliot in South Australia in February 2007. There, Newman was alleged to have beaten Carly about the head, pushed her face into the sand and thrown her in the water – all in front of his son.

In court, Garry Newman wept over her death, claiming that he was 'like a stepdad' to the girl and that he only had the 'greatest respect' for her. He denied having any sexual interest in her, and claimed that he was essentially asexual, with very little interest in sex at all. (The collection of pornography on his computer certainly suggested otherwise ...)

He did admit to being obsessed with social networking websites (having 200 accounts at www.ratemybody.com under false names) and he said that he and Carly were very close friends. The last time he'd seen her was on the beach at Port Elliot, where he and his son had taken her to a party. Here, his story differed markedly from the prosecution. Rather than killing her, Newman claimed that Carly had refused a lift back to Adelaide and they had simply left her there. The first they'd heard of her death was three days later.

By the end of the trial, Newman looked a mess – he was shaky, unshaven and on suicide watch. Much of his time in court had been marked by heated exchanges with prosecutors and his son's own lawyer. Both, he said, were trying to paint him as a 'sicko predator'. He also offered contradictory evidence – first trying to blame his son for the whole affair, and then denying that either of them had anything to do with it. Twice, Newman's own lawyer tried to ditch his client, claiming 'irreconcilable differences'.

In the end, it took the jury 10½ hours to come back with their verdict: Newman was guilty of murder; his son was not. Throughout their deliberations, the only question the jury had had for the judge was whether it was possible to find the son guilty of manslaughter. Yes, they were told, but only if they were convinced that he had participated in a plot to do harm to Miss Ryan – resulting in her death – or had encouraged his father to harm Miss Ryan in a fatal way.

The one option that may have suited the jury best – that the son had assisted an offender – was not available to them, as prosecutors had never charged the son with that crime. It was murder, manslaughter or nothing.

Newman showed no reaction when the jury found him guilty of murder, but the son was visibly relieved with his acquittal verdict.

Newman was jailed by the South Australian Supreme Court for a minimum of 29 years for the murder of the 15-year-old who had rejected his sexual advances (a sentence he later unsuccessfully tried to appeal). At the same time, Justice Trish Kelly lifted a long-running suppression order on his identity, allowing his name and image to be published for the first time. (The son's name or any identifying information has never been released.)

In passing sentence, Justice Kelly said Newman's plan was an incredibly cruel thing to do to a beautiful and suggestible child:

I say child because that is what she was, in love with the idea of the handsome, musically inclined and rather exotic Brandon Kane who spent Christmas in the United States and was coming home via Paris to be with her. The real man, instead, was an overweight, balding, middle-aged paedophile with sex and murder on his mind.

The judge expressed significant concern with two key aspects of Newman's behaviour. First, that the fingertip of a latex glove had been found at the scene, which indicated premeditation. Second, that even after murdering Carly Ryan, Newman had simply returned and continued chatting to other teenage girls as if nothing had happened.

In a statement to the press on the day of Newman's sentencing, Carly's mother released a statement saying, 'Nothing can give Carly her life back but I will endeavour to honour her by moving forward, helping to prevent such an awful crime happening to another child.'

Sonya Ryan later started the Carly Ryan Foundation, named after her daughter, the first child to be murdered in Australia by an online predator. In 2012, Sonya Ryan was awarded the title of South Australian of the Year, the state's top honour, in recognition for her work promoting cybersafety. She now regularly lectures students, parents and teachers on the dangers of online predators. Many instances of suspect online contact have been referred to the police as a result.

Sonya Ryan has also continued to push tirelessly for legislation to make it illegal for adults to lie to a child online about their age, and to attempt to arrange a meeting with that child. However, 'Carly's Law' has yet to be passed.

## The Facebook Predator

Fake Facebook profiles are something that happens more often than Facebook is probably likely to admit. But in their most recent annual report, they do concede that somewhere between 68 and 138 *million* personal accounts are either duplicates or false. Some of these accounts are doubtless created for benign purposes – such as when people set up a number of personal accounts for different audiences, or create a full account rather than a page to promote their business or even give their dog a social media presence.

Facebook's terms of service prohibit users from providing any false personal information or creating an account for anyone other than themselves, but in reality, it is virtually impossible for the organisation to check the veracity of every individual account.

Of course, many fake profiles are created for the purposes of spamming, but a few – as was seen previously in the case of Carly Ryan – are specifically set up so that predators can stalk their prey from the shadows, alone in front of their computer.

The thought that she was putting her life at risk is probably not something that crossed 18-year-old Nona Belomesoff's mind when she accepted a friendship request from a 21-year-old man named Christopher Dannevig on 20 February 2010. Like most of us, she probably took a peek at his profile photo (blond hair, blue eyes, Buzz Lightyear features) clicked 'Accept' and thought no more about it. (You can still see his profile on Facebook today, but unsurprisingly, he appears to have few friends.) If she'd known a little more about the man, she may well have thought twice about striking up a friendship. Dannevig, as it turns out, already had form, and on the day he first contacted Nona had only just been released from jail on parole after having been jailed for a serious personal violence offence.

Court records from August 2012 state the following:

[Dannevig] had been sentenced in the District Court on 17 December 2009 in respect of an offence that occurred on 15 November 2008. Upon the latter date, the offender and the victim, a 16-year-old girl, had recently met. They caught a train to Ingleburn railway station then proceeded to walk along a bush track ostensibly to retrieve the offender's bag that he claimed that he left in that area. The offender approached the victim from behind and physically restrained her. At the time he was holding a knife, it is unnecessary to recite here the full details, other than to say that the sentencing judge noted the seriousness of the offence, that he had been on conditional liberty at the time of that offence and that he had occasioned extreme fear in the victim. In that sentencing hearing, Dr Jeremy O'Dea, a forensic psychiatrist, noted the offender's developmental history, intellectual disability and the problems with anger and treatment for a diagnosis of ADHD. However, Dr O'Dea did not diagnose the offender as suffering from a major psychiatric illness.

It seems that Dannevig was not only fond of knives, he was developmentally delayed, showing a degree of mental retardation, and was prone to anger – an explosive combination.

And that wasn't all. Some years even before that incident, on April Fool's Day, 2005, Dannevig had attacked another woman – a stranger who'd done nothing more foolhardy than choose to go for a stroll in bushland by herself. Armed with a knife, Dannevig had 'severely' threatened and cut the woman, who only managed to escape when Dannevig was scared off by the arrival of other walkers in the area.

If Nona had known any of this, it's unlikely she would have friended him in the first place; however, without this vital information, the two began corresponding online. Nona shared what was going on in her life – her love for her family and animals, how she'd graduated from Canley Vale High School in 2009, and was still living at home with her parents in Sydney. She was a homebody at heart. She also told him that she was studying a class called 'Work in the Animal Care Industry' at the Sydney Institute TAFE, New South Wales. She loved horses in particular, and was determined to build a career saving and looking after animals, possibly even becoming a vet.

Then on 15 April, her new Facebook friend, Dannevig, disappeared back into the ether. She was not to hear from him again.

She did, however, accept a friend request from another man – Jason Green. He was a team leader, employed by the Wildlife Information Rescue and Education Service, also known as WIRES, and seemingly shared many interests with the animal-mad young girl. They began chatting online and several weeks later, he offered her training for a job at WIRES. The two arranged to meet near the Leumeah train station on Wednesday, 5 May. Nona was delighted at the thought that she'd soon be working in the career of her dreams, and her family was happy for her. She also wrote about the great opportunity both in her diary and on her Facebook page.

The first meeting went well, with Nona and Jason Green walking a short distance from the train station to a nearby bush track in Smiths Creek Reserve, where the training was to begin. Located between the suburbs of East Campbelltown, Ruse and Leumeah, the reserve is approximately 85 hectares in size and has seven kilometres of creek flowing through it. Although the park is only 100 metres wide in places, in other parts you can almost imagine that you are in the middle of the bush, kilometres from anywhere. It's full of magnificent natural bushland and home to a surprising number of native animals – a great spot for some training in wildlife spotting. Green set Nona some tasks, and graded her on her performance.

The two met up a further five times over the following days for more training at the same location. On the last occasion, something happened to worry Nona enough that she talked it over with her cousin.

It was supposedly part of a demonstration of self-defence, with Green offering to show her what to do if someone ever tried to kidnap or rape her. Green then blindfolded the young woman, tied her hands behind her back, and pushed her to the ground and lay on top of her. 'What would you do?' Green reportedly asked. Finding it difficult to breathe, and being scared at the turn of events, Nona begged him to get off, but Green refused, saying that he was serious. It was only when Nona began to cry that Green relented and let her go. She was clearly shocked, and Green took out his phone and appeared to make a phone call. He even offered to call an ambulance, but Nona declined. All she wanted to do was to go home to her family.

There was just one training session left to go as part of her recruitment into WIRES, and this one was going to involve an overnight camp in the bush, again at Smiths Creek Reserve in the Leumeah area. Nona told her mother that she was expecting to be paid for the training, and that she'd given Green her bank details so that WIRES could make the transfer. She'd also told Green her PIN number – based on the date of her birthday. She noted in her diary for that date 'camp night – double pay after 5 p.m. – get paid'.

At 9 a.m. on Wednesday, 12 May 2010, Nona Belomesoff left her family home to meet up with Green. She had never slept overnight by herself, or anywhere but a friend's house, but was determined to finish her training. She told her father that 'if she didn't go, she would lose her job, and this job was her dream'. She would never return home or see her family again.

***

At 9.40 p.m., on Friday, 14 May 2010, two days after she'd set out for her final training session and a full day after her distraught parents had reported her missing to police, the body of Nona

Belomesoff was found face down in a creek in the middle of Smiths Creek Reserve. It was a remote part of the park, where it was unlikely many members of the public would venture. Nona had been vulnerable and far from help when she died.

She was fully dressed, wearing a white shirt and – oddly enough – a fabric sleeping mask, and although there were signs of some bruises and trauma, she hadn't been battered or stabbed or shot. It was immediately assumed that she had drowned, given that her mouth and nose were underwater, and an autopsy later established that there were indeed features suggestive of drowning, although a definitive cause of death could not be determined.

It wasn't long before the police caught up with her killer. Firstly, Nona's parents had reached out for official help as soon as Nona had failed to make their arranged rendezvous at the Leumeah railway station the morning after the campout. Her father had also called WIRES directly to find out about the training, and to his consternation, had heard that they did not run overnight training sessions of any kind. What's more, the WIRES employee who took Mr Belomesoff's call was able to confirm that no person called Jason Green was employed at the organisation or indeed known to anyone there. Nona Belomesoff's parents went to the Liverpool police station that night and reported their daughter as missing. So who was the mysterious Jason Green, had he killed Nona, and what had happened to him?

Checking Nona's bank account details, police discovered that a man had made a withdrawal at the ATM near the Leumeah train station at 5.24 p.m. on 12 May. He had first submitted an account balance enquiry before withdrawing the maximum amount possible, $170. They had footage of the likely killer, but now they needed to identify him.

The next break in the case came with the discovery of a 'grading sheet' – obviously associated with some kind of training – found at the scene of the crime. Fingerprints were found and these were soon matched – not to Jason Green, but to Christopher James

Dannevig, whose fingerprints were already on file after his two previous attacks on women. It was enough for police.

At 12.30 a.m. on 14 May, police officers turned up at Dannevig's door and demanded an explanation. First, he explained that yes, he did know Nona Belomesoff, and yes he had met up with her on both Tuesday and Wednesday, the day of her death. He admitted that he knew she was dead, but claimed to have suffered a blackout and could not explain how she had ended up face down in the creek. He also admitted emptying out her bank account – something that would have been hard to deny given that he'd been caught in the act on camera.

But that wasn't all he had to confess, although it took several interviews to get the facts out of him. Dannevig was Jason Green – Jason Green did not and had never existed. Dannevig had created the false Facebook account under Green's name in late April 2010 once he had learned of Nona's interest in animal welfare. It was all an elaborate ruse to entrap her online and force her acquaintance – with what end in mind, only he knew. He'd tracked her down, baited the trap with the promise of Nona's dream job, and then he had sprung it.

Dannevig was arrested and imprisoned, pending trial, but unbeknownst to him, several of his fellow prisoners were actually undercover policemen. They learned from him that he'd pushed Nona over, before knocking her down onto a bed of rocks, grabbing her and forcing her unconscious, then holding her down in the water until she drowned. This contradicted his earlier statements of having no memory of events, and simply fleeing the scene when he came out of his 'blackout' to discover her dead in front of him.

\*\*\*

Christopher Dannevig pleaded guilty to the murder of Nona Belomesoff in a Supreme Court hearing on 31 August 2011. Almost one year later, on 3 August 2012, Justice Peter Hall heard

Dannevig's case and pronounced sentence. In his summing up, he said:

> I am satisfied on the evidence beyond reasonable doubt that the offender killed the deceased, probably by drowning. Injuries suffered by the deceased and detailed in the autopsy report, I note, are consistent with her having fallen in a struggle and hitting her head on rocks before entering the water and that the deceased died by drowning.
>
> The offender's actions in bringing about the death of a completely vulnerable and defenceless young woman in this way involved brutality of a high order that makes this offence a most heinous crime.

The judge noted the grief and distress of the Belomesoff family, and expressed sympathy and compassion for them, on behalf of the community. Justice Hall said Dannevig had never given an account of what he intended to do or why he murdered her, but it was clear that once in the reserve he formed the intent to kill.

But Justice Hall said Dannevig displayed a 'complete understanding of what he was doing' and used a 'strategy of deception and lies' to lure her to bushland away from the public.

Justice Hall imposed a minimum sentence of 21 years with a parole period of seven years to allow intensive monitoring of his progress once allowed back in the community. Dannevig will be locked away until 7 August 2032 at the very earliest.

---

# Sex, Spies and Videotape

It seems that there are few depths to which a stalker will not sink in order to keep an eye on their victim – including the illegal use of work tools in the case of an obsessed father who used council CCTV to stalk his ex-wife and her new partner.

Runnymede Borough Council employee, Scott Thompson, 43, from Frimley Road in Ash Vale in the UK, was employed to look after the borough's CCTV cameras as part of the Safer Runnymede program. However, instead of using them to *prevent* crime, the man used them to commit one – stalking.

Thompson had split from his wife, Susan, and understandably, things between the soon-to-be-divorced couple were stressful. There were the usual tensions – access to their two young kids, finances, parenting decisions, the house ... Thompson was left without a home, and a wife, and soon he was to lose his job as well.

On 3 March 2013, Susan Thompson, her new partner Phil Dunne and the kids went out for a family breakfast. That's when she noticed the CCTV cameras were swivelling to follow her movements. According to the local paper *GetSurrey* (4 December 2014), Mrs Thompson told the court at the trial of her ex that she 'looked up at the camera and saw it was fixed on us' as she, Mr Dunne, and her children walked down Woodham Lane, New Haw. At the time, she was also on the phone to her ex, who was supposedly hard at work fighting crime at his office in Addlestone.

'My conclusion was he was using the camera to track my movements and make it very clear he knew exactly where I was and what I was doing,' she told the court. 'It's very upsetting.

On that occasion I felt very intimidated and felt I had no control over him watching me.'

The Staines Magistrates' Court was also told that on one occasion Thompson had used the cameras to 'observe Mr Dunne's car for five hours' and that he was 'exploiting his position' in order to determine whether Mr Dunne was visiting his ex, and how long he might be staying. Susan Thompson made a complaint to council about her ex's behaviour in April 2013 and Thompson was unceremoniously suspended from his job.

This move obviously did not go down well with the embittered ex-husband. On 30 June in the same year, Thompson was seen standing outside his victim's New Haw home staring 'intensely' into the house. The prosecution explained that because he could no longer monitor her movements on CCTV, he'd resorted to doing it in person. On his access visits with his children, he also grilled the kids about their mother's new boyfriend and referred to him as 'the new daddy'.

None of this impressed the district judge William Ashworth. Neither did the argument from the defence team, who claimed that the complaint was malicious and it was all a ploy from the ex-wife to get financial assistance during their divorce proceedings. Plus, there was no way he could have been on the phone to Susan at the time she claimed, thanks to the poor reception in his office. As a final attempt, the defence counsel argued that maybe Thompson had accessed the cameras in an attempt to check on the welfare of his children. Or perhaps it was one of the other CCTV operators employed by the council.

Again, the judge wasn't buying it. He dismissed Thompson's evidence and said that he had not found him to be a 'credible witness'. 'You repeatedly argued when you were in the witness box and were not believable,' he said.

Instead, the judge suggested that Thompson was obsessed with his estranged wife and her new relationship:

Targeting the family and the making of calls at the same time – you were obsessively using the camera and phone not only to watch her, but to let her know she was under observation.

I'm sure you became obsessed at the time of the divorce and abused your position of CCTV operator to watch and wait for Mr Dunne as you wanted proof he was in the house. Your conduct was clearly harassing Mrs Thompson and must have had a profound effect on your two innocent children.

The use of the cameras and trying to get information from your youngest daughter characterises, in my view, as stalking.

Thompson was convicted of stalking, fined and received a five-year restraining order at Guildford Magistrates' Court, forbidding him from going to Woodham Lane or contacting either Mrs Thompson or Mr Dunne, except to arrange child contact.

## The Dance of Death

You'd have to have been living under a rock, or overseas, to have missed the tragic story of how Lisa Harnum was thrown off the balcony of her 15th-storey apartment in Liverpool Street, Sydney, by her fiancé Simon Gittany in July 2011.

Lisa Harnum died almost instantly as a result of injuries sustained in the fall, and the question raised at trial was: Was it suicide, an accident or murder? The prosecution – drawing on the evidence of one key eyewitness to her fall as just one part of their case – contended that Gittany deliberately lifted Lisa over the balustrade and then 'unloaded' her over the edge – like a bag of rubbish. (Indeed, the eyewitness says he initially thought it was a large black suitcase being dropped over the balcony. Not even knowing that it was a person, rather than a piece of rubbish, the sight and implications for anyone on the ground below so disturbed the witness that he voluntarily contacted police to report what he had seen.) The defence in turn said that Lisa climbed over the balustrade of her own accord and either slipped or allowed herself to fall off the awning on the other side.

The trial of Simon Gittany was lengthy and made headlines around the nation, but in the end NSW Supreme Court Justice Lucy McCallum – who presided over the judge-only trial – delivered a verdict of guilty. Gittany was sentenced to 26 years in prison, with a non-parole period of 18 years, for Lisa Harnum's murder.

In handing down the punishment, she said that jailing Gittany for life would be disproportionate, but also said that Gittany had no prospects of rehabilitation. During sentencing, Justice McCallum described the cruelty of the crime. 'Ms Harnum must have been in a state of complete terror in the moments before her death,' she said.

Sadly, this is but one of many appalling examples of a woman being murdered by an intimate partner, with at least one woman each week suffering the same fate (if not the same dreadful means of death) according to the Australian Institute of Criminology.[11] But it was what went on *before* Lisa's death that makes her case so unusual, with Simon Gittany monitoring everything she did. She was stalked by her fiancé even inside the apartment they shared, with the aid of not one but two wall-mounted video cameras. I include her story not only as a memorial to a beautiful, bright, vivacious young woman who dreamed of love and making a new life for herself in Australia, but also as a warning that the definition of stalking needs to be broadened to include those who are stalked within an ongoing relationship.

***

Lisa Harnum moved to Australia from Canada in 2004, settling first in Melbourne and later in Sydney. After moving to Sydney, she undertook a hairdressing course at Australian Hair & Beauty near Bondi Junction, where she also worked part-time to help pay for her course fees. An ex-dancer, petite and pretty, Lisa Harnum (also known as Cecilia, her middle name, by Gittany) had a long history of bulimia, but few of her friends knew about this. Around January 2010, she met Simon Gittany and shortly afterwards moved into his apartment in Pitt Street, central Sydney.

The honeymoon period did not last long, and when Gittany signed a new lease on the apartment in Liverpool Street, Lisa was seriously considering not moving with him. A series of text messages to her mother in Canada, to whom she was very close, included the following:

Same as usual. Walking time bombs x any minute boom explosions!!!

I feel trapped, like I have to watch everything I say do feel, everything. I got in trouble yesterday because I said that I felt cold. So stupid.

However, Lisa did make the move to The Hyde apartments, and it wasn't the only change she made. Lisa also stopped working at the hairdressing college – Gittany claimed after her death that she had had a personality clash with some of the other girls, but the prosecution argued that it was part of his growing desire to control every aspect of her life.

Possibly the most striking example of this is the fact that towards the end of 2010, as their relationship was deteriorating, Gittany had not one but three surveillance cameras installed in the apartment at The Hyde. One tiny pinhole camera – so small as to be almost undetectable – was mounted outside the front door, and the other two were *inside* the apartment. These looked more like motion sensors than cameras. At his trial, Gittany denied that these were for the purposes of stalking Lisa, but who was he kidding? Who has surveillance cameras installed in their home if they are not for the purposes of monitoring the residents? Who has surveillance cameras at home anyway?

It was a sophisticated system – fully integrated and with video footage from the cameras feeding into a computer in the study, and also an external hard drive *hidden in the ceiling*. This bloke was serious about wanting to know what Lisa got up to at home when he wasn't there to watch in person. (It would make for pretty boring viewing if you were to try this at my house, let me tell you.)

Lisa's mother gave evidence that around the same time – towards the end of 2010 – Lisa had told her that she was no longer allowed to wear dresses. A text message sent by Lisa Harnum to her mother further stated that they had decided not to go out to clubs any more after that night because Gittany 'gets so uptight' and 'gets uncomfortable with all of the guys around'. The same day, Lisa Harnum also wrote:

> … Time for me to grow up and wear big girl pants now. This relationship sure has changed me a lot! I'm much more calm than I was before, domesticated, conservative, and dainty. I have nails now too […] quite long and now I have natural French manicure! Bought a whole bunch of flat and casual shoes and no more cleavage I'm afraid. Simon is terrified of summer and the beach. He said we seedling [sic] to have to find the burka bathinsuit to wear. Hehe xoxo

Her mother saw the changes in her daughter in person, when Lisa returned home to Canada for Christmas – without Gittany in tow. She wore no make-up, her clothes were in dark colours and designed to hide her body, not show it off. She also made it clear that Gittany did not want her to catch up with any of her old friends back in her hometown. Her mother was keen if not desperate for her to stay, but Lisa insisted on going back to Australia – and Gittany – at the end of her time away.

On Lisa's return to Sydney, Gittany strongly suggested that she see a counsellor – after all, it was *her* problem, not his. The notes from the one and only consultation that took place were shown in evidence in the later court case:

> She feels she is losing herself. He takes her keys, won't let her wear heels to the shops, tells her what to wear and had her stop work. She talks back to him and he does not like this. He won't let her have her own opinion. He wants her to be submissive. He uses words like 'evil', 'poisonous', a 'snake' to refer to her. Tears. 'Is that what a good relationship looks like?' Asking if it is her fault. She is doubting herself.
>
> There is no physical abuse, no substance abuse, she is not thinking of harming herself. Discussed whether it was her fault or that Simon was like this. She speaks to her mother in Canada and she tells her to come home. I told her she needs professional support and offered to see her pro bono if she could not afford the fee.

In early February 2011, Gittany signed up for a service that would allow him to download an app that would monitor all of Lisa's text messages. This was done without her knowledge, as Gittany freely admitted during his trial. His excuse? That Lisa had said that she had a shameful secret (perhaps the fact that she was bulimic?). Gittany claimed that he was desperate to know the secret and for several weeks he read her text messages, but on finding nothing of importance kind of lost interest. The judge was not convinced:

> I do not believe the accused's evidence on that issue. There is no reference in any of the text messages in evidence to any festering conflict over a closely-guarded secret. I think it was a pretext put forward by the accused in order to excuse an inexcusable breach of trust.

Gittany's newfound ability to stalk Lisa's digital life gave him access to every thought she shared with close friends, and her mother –

every text and email and probably also the content of her every internet search or article view. Maybe he knew from this that she was getting bored and frustrated at home without the stimulation of work, but in any event he arranged a job for her at a friend's hairdressing salon. However, it was not a hairdressing role that was on offer, but that of a receptionist – the kind of role that would limit her interactions with customers to the bare minimum, if one wishes to put a malicious slant on it. From the trial report, it also seems unclear whether Lisa was actually getting paid for this work or not. She did not stay there long, and things were deteriorating on the home front too. It probably wasn't helped by the fact that Gittany now had the tools at his fingertips to know pretty much everything about her life.

***

On 29 March 2011, Lisa Harnum complained to her mother that she and the accused had 'domestics' and that he had said some very hurtful things. And he didn't limit his anger to his fiancée. After intercepting a text message from Lisa's friend Rebecca Triscaru where she advised Lisa she should 'do what her heart tells her to do', Gittany rang and blasted Rebecca. He told her that he didn't want her speaking to Lisa any more.

Lisa was becoming increasingly isolated, and the smallest thing could set Gittany off on an abusive rampage – even something so minor as having her hair down:

> Who the fuck do you think you are walking around the house like you own it or coming & going without my permission?! Again I waited for you to apologize for your disgusting comment but you walk around like a peacock with your hair out & too proud to apologize. You lied to me & promised you would listen to me at all times. Obviously, you're still the proud person & nothing has changed!

Gittany and Harnum were known amongst their friends and family for their tempestuous bust-ups and passionate reconciliations, yet few were surprised when Gittany popped the question in front of a crowd of family and friends on the occasion of a surprise party he had thrown for her 30th birthday. However, the ups were becoming increasingly rare and the downs were catastrophic.

Even within a week of their engagement, the two were arguing again. In a message shared with the court, Gittany wrote:

> Cecilia [Lisa's middle name, and the one by which Gittany commonly called her] you are my fiancé [sic] & I love you but we both know you have some problems that effect [sic] the mood of our relationship at times but you refuse to admit it. Please pray to God so he can help you get rid of these habits. I love you & want a future for us. Please get rid of them! Words from my heart.

Lisa replied, voicing her doubts:

> I love you too Simon and I do pray every single day for God to make me a better person. Simon no one is perfect and I may have things about me that I need to work on but it breaks my heart to think that instead of helping me in a constructive way you resort to yelling and telling me to get rid of my faults or we won't work. My whole life all I wanted was to be accepted. You know the worst part of my childhood was girls surrounding me at school and telling me to change or they would make my life hell. I didn't even know what I did wrong. I don't feel sorry for myself Simon. I have nobody left to make feel that way. There are things we obviously need to think about before we go any farther with this. Neither if [sic] us want to make a mistake.

Gittany's response came through almost instantly:

Ok so you want me to help you get through this in a constructive way? Sure no problem. Btw, I didn't like your last few lines, don't use fear of loss on me Cecilia! I'm the one asking you to fix things before we go ahead but without the fuckin [sic] games.

The following day, Lisa texted a friend in Melbourne, Giselle Pratt, and asked about coming to stay. In a follow-up call, where Lisa was crying so hard that her friend could barely understand her, she explained that it was over with Simon and she needed a bolt-hole. She was still unaware that her phone was being monitored, however. Simon now knew of her plans and was swiftly on the phone to Giselle to demand that she *not* let Lisa come and stay, and to tell her not to go to Melbourne, but to stay with Simon in Sydney. He made it clear that Lisa was not to know of this conversation. Giselle, however, stuck to her guns and told Gittany that she would never turn away a friend in need. However, later that night, Lisa rang Giselle directly and said that she would not be coming to Melbourne after all.

Lisa's world continued to shrink. Now she only saw her personal trainer Lisa Brown – who Gittany had arranged to come to the apartment complex – and a new female counsellor, Michelle Richmond. She'd even given up her gym membership, although she and Gittany had once been regulars.

Gittany claimed at his trial that Lisa enjoyed staying at home in the apartment, but it seems that fear may have been driving her indoors. Thanks to the video, Gittany was always able to check if she was there. She told her counsellor that one time when she had ducked out to the shops, Gittany rang her on her mobile and demanded that she return to the apartment.

The counsellor also explained that Lisa couldn't work out how Gittany always knew what she had talked about with her mother. 'She was very careful about the things that she said to her mother because somehow he would know and even come back and repeat the conversations back to her. That made her feel isolated and shut down and concerned,' the counsellor told the judge.

Lisa trusted Michelle Richmond, and in one session they discussed her options for leaving Gittany. On Thursday, 28 July, after Gittany had left for a meeting, Lisa met up with her trainer Lisa Brown, whom she also trusted, and gave her a couple of pillow cases full of items she had smuggled from the apartment. She also sent a text to Michelle Richmond to tell her that she'd taken the first steps towards freedom.

But Gittany had the monitoring program recording all her messages, and shortly after coming home, he was aware that his fiancée was making plans to escape. In the judge's full verdict, she explained what happened next:

> At about 7 p.m., Ms Richmond received a call from Lisa Harnum's mobile telephone number. She said that nobody spoke on the other end. She then called the number back and the accused answered. She pretended she did not know who the call was from, saying, 'Hi, I just received a missed call from this number.'
>
> Ms Richmond said that the accused said to her, 'Michelle, you fucking bitch, if you ever come near Cecilia again, try to contact or meet her, have anything to do with her, I know where you live. I will fucking harm you.'
>
> Ms Richmond stated that he continued with that monologue until she hung up because she could not cope with the abuse. She said that he was angry and was screaming and that there were no gaps between the words, that it was 'just a monologue of abuse'.

It seems clear that Gittany now wanted Lisa to stay away from her only two remaining friends and supporters – Brown and Richmond. Her mother recounted one of her final conversations with Lisa, as reported in the verdict:

Mrs Harnum said Lisa told her that Simon had made her call both Lisa Brown and Michelle Richmond and tell them that she hated them and did not want to have anything further to do with them. Lisa told her the accused had started yelling at her and telling her that she shouldn't embarrass him, that she was to do as she was told, that she should submit and he had her on her knees in front of him. He had her kneel in front of him.

Lisa and her mother also discussed the possibility of Lisa hopping on the next plane to Canada. But it was another phone call from Lisa to her personal trainer that helped unravel what had been happening behind the scenes. Without wanting Lisa to know that he was bugging her phone, Gittany needed some way of explaining how he knew that Lisa had removed items from the apartment, so he blamed the trainer. Lisa, naturally enough, was very upset that her friend could have betrayed her confidence. When the coast was clear, she rang the trainer to vent her anger, and was doubtless surprised to hear that no such thing had happened. How had Gittany known what she was up to? It was probably this question that lead to Lisa taking a closer look at the home computer, and discovering files that showed Gittany had been stalking her electronically.

Naturally, her mother was the person she rang for advice:

Mrs Harnum said that, during that last call, Lisa Harnum told her that she loved her and Jason [Lisa's brother] with all her heart. Mrs Harnum said, 'What's wrong?' Lisa Harnum was very upset and said that she was going to try to leave. She said, 'Mommy, if anything happens to me, please contact Michelle.' She made Mrs Harnum take down Michelle Richmond's details and read them back to her. Mrs Harnum described her as 'frantic' ... Mrs Harnum said Lisa told her that she would contact her as soon as she could, however she could, the next morning. Lisa Harnum then said that she was going to go to sleep. They said their goodbyes. That was the last time Mrs Harnum heard from her daughter.

No one knows exactly what transpired between Gittany and Lisa Harnum over the course of that night. However, it seems clear that Gittany knew from his surveillance that Lisa was planning a flight back to Canada, and that she had discovered that he had been monitoring her. The idea of losing control over Lisa must have enraged him – and then Lisa had made a run for the door and the elevator.

At 10 a.m. on the morning of 30 July 2011, the neighbours reported hearing banging on their door and, with the banging, a woman's voice screaming, 'Please help me, help me, God help me.' She said she knew it was her front door that was being knocked on because, as she heard the banging, she approached the door and could see it shaking. She heard a man's raised voice yelling. She could not discern any words. As reported in the verdict:

> Mrs Glanville said that, as she was walking towards the door, there was silence. The screaming and yelling lasted for just a few seconds and then it stopped dead. She locked the door.
>
> Mr Glanville also heard banging on the door and screams. He said it was a lady screaming ... in a very distressed manner. He walked to the corridor where his wife was. The screaming had stopped by that stage. He said that it stopped suddenly. He did not open the door.

Footage from Gittany's own pinhole camera showed Gittany grabbing Lisa, covering her mouth and pulling her back into the apartment. Sixty-nine seconds later she was dead. This is Gittany's version of events, given in an interview with police:

> We had a fight last night. We just worked out it was better for her to go home to Canada. Sometimes it is me who wants to

break up with her, sometimes the other way. I woke up this morning and she was packing her bags. I said, 'Let's not break up.' She said, 'No no.' I know it is just an act. She always wants me to beg when she gets the upper hand. Neither of us slept last night and we were talking. She said, 'You told me to leave, and I'm leaving.' She grabbed her black handbag and went to leave through the front door. I stopped her. She started to raise her voice, and she was yelling. And I yelled back, 'Shut the fuck up.' I was in the kitchen. I saw her pass towards the balcony. I remember thinking, 'What is on the balcony?' I saw her step over the railing onto the little cliff face. I ran towards the railing and I can't remember. I was just trying to hold her from falling. I was just grabbing at her, I don't know, I might have had a handbag or jacket and then she was gone.

At the trial, much was made of Lisa's mental state and whether she was so desperate that she took her own life, as Gittany claimed. However, the judge did not buy it:

Lisa Harnum was trying to leave the accused on the morning of her death. He stopped her with an act of serious aggression. There is no doubt in my mind that he was in a state of rage at that point and that he had lost control of his temper. According to the accused, after dragging her back into the apartment, he let her sit down, made some insensitive remarks and went to make her a hot drink. The proposition that he was able to bring himself under control so quickly after the struggle at the door is inherently implausible and I reject it. I do not accept his evidence that Lisa Harnum climbed over the balustrade. I do not entertain a reasonable doubt about the accuracy or reliability of the evidence of [the eyewitness]. I cannot know exactly what happened in that apartment in the minute or so following the struggle at the door, but I think it is likely that Lisa Harnum was at some point rendered unconscious. Based

on my assessment of all of the evidence, I am satisfied to a
point of actual persuasion and beyond reasonable doubt that
the accused maintained his rage and, in that state, carried her
to the balcony and unloaded her over the edge. It follows that
I am satisfied beyond reasonable doubt of the elements of the
offence. I find the accused guilty of the murder of Lisa Cecilia
Harnum.

Gittany will spend the next 26 years behind bars, but at least he
has his life – oh, and a new fiancée, at least for a while. Bearing a
striking resemblance to his murdered fiancée, Rachelle Louise first
met Gittany when she was 19. She maintained an impassioned
defence of her killer boyfriend throughout the trial and beyond –
a decision perhaps sweetened by alleged payments of $150000
from Channel Seven for participating in a two-part interview. Their
engagement has since ended and they are now 'just friends', the
*Sydney Morning Herald* reported on 6 May 2015.

***

About the only good thing to come out of Lisa Harnum's death
is a new smartphone app for victims of domestic violence, released
by the Lisa Harnum Foundation in November 2014. It looks just
like an ordinary news service app but hidden inside are some smart
controls to trigger a panic alert in case of emergency.

When the app is opened, it immediately displays a range of
news, entertainment news, sports news, local news, and so on.
This is updated constantly through Google, so it is always current.
But should the user press the help button, she is taken to a secret
page where she can store her safe contacts. This also holds national
numbers to support women and families in domestic abuse. Best
of all, there is also a function where she can store a pre-written

message – something like 'Need your help now!' If in distress, the victim simply has to open the app, swipe the top bar from left to right (which brings up the safe contacts) and then hit 'send'. Immediately, the pre-arranged message will go out to her safe contacts, with links to her exact geographic location.

The idea behind the app was for victims to have instant access to help when under threat, given that domestic violence often remains hidden behind closed doors. And because the app is not obviously a domestic violence helpline app, it is hoped that perpetrators – who may well be monitoring their partner's phone – will assume that it is a simple news app.

The app is available free of charge for anyone who needs it. And there are plenty of victims out there – including those who are being stalked – who do.

Domestic violence in Australia is common and widespread. Nationally, surveys have found that anywhere from one-quarter to one-third, or even up to one-half, of Australian women will experience physical or sexual violence by a man at some point in their lives.[12] A study by VicHealth in 2004 found that among women under 45, intimate partner violence contributed more to their poor health, disability and death than any other risk factor, including obesity and smoking.[13]

We know that a woman is more likely to be killed in her home by her male partner than anywhere else – or by anyone else. We also know that most women do not report violence to police; they are even less likely to report violent incidents to police when the perpetrator is a current partner.[14] Having access to other sources of help is therefore even more critical.

## There's an App for That

As the case of Lisa Harnum shows, apps that are supposedly marketed so that helicopter parents can keep an eye on their kids, or bosses can check up on their employees, can also be used for more nefarious purposes. Increasingly, stalkers are using mobile phone spyware to monitor their victim's texts, calls, photos, emails and web history. Meanwhile new technologies such as GPS trackers help stalkers keep track of their victim's every movement – with many reports of women fleeing domestic violence being tracked to refuges via this technology.

Mobistealth was the app used by Simon Gittany to monitor Lisa Harnum's every move. In researching this book and delving into some areas of the internet and the world that made me feel like I had been bathing in slime, I found that the product's website encourages potential buyers to 'get the answers you deserve'. It's a tagline designed for stalkers and vengeful exes if I ever heard one.

One online review explains how the app works:

> Mobistealth is a powerful yet easy to use spy software that allows you to secretly monitor the cell phones of your employees, spouse, kids or any family member. Mobistealth cell phone spy software provides a robust set of features that allow you to get all of the current information that you desire from the target phone.
>
> Once installed, it will silently record all the activities on the phone and send the data to your online account. With the help of Mobistealth, you can now easily monitor phone surroundings, text messages, email, GPS locations, call details, photos and videos, browser history, instant messenger chats and more. In addition, Mobistealth works in stealth mode which means that the phone user won't even notice that the spyware is already on his smartphone.[15]

So, this is a *good* thing?

And here's a list of all things that Lisa Harnum was totally unaware that Gittany knew about her – taken straight from the app maker's website. It makes for chilling reading if you think about it from the 'target's' point of view ...

1. View Sent/Received SMS – You can monitor all details of sent and received messages on cell phones.
2. Application List – This feature allows you to view details of all apps installed on phone so that you can filter out inappropriate apps.
3. Spy Contacts and Appointments – You can monitor all details of contacts stored on phone as well as the details of calendar and appointments.
4. Monitor Chat Messengers – You can remotely monitor chat messengers on cell phones and computers.
5. Monitor Web Browsing – You can monitor internet browsing history of target phone and computer.
6. Location Tracking – Mobistealth makes it possible to monitor location even if GPS is not present on phone.
7. Monitor Emails – You can monitor emails send and received using phones as well as computers.
8. Monitor Pictures and Videos – Mobistealth makes it possible to remotely monitor pictures and videos.
9. Keylogging and ScreenShots – You can log keystrokes as well take screenshots remotely of target computer.

Oh yes, and even swapping SIM cards won't help the unwitting victim – the company also offers a SIM change alert, which notifies the watcher of the new number, and simply tracks this instead.

## The Bodyless Murder

Simon Gittany is not the only man whose use of such spyware eventually led to murder. In the US in 2012, police discovered that Mobistealth was also the app by which Cid Torrez of Florida spied on his estranged wife, Vilet, and learned that she had a new boyfriend. The two had been married for 13 years.

Vilet was last seen on 31 March 2012 in the suburb of Miramar, when video surveillance from her townhouse community's gate-house showed her returning from a date at 5.21 a.m. Torrez, her estranged husband, was waiting at her home with their three children, although he usually lived elsewhere and was meant to be looking after the kids for just that one night. He is sticking to his story that she never came home – and that she must have disappeared somewhere between the gatehouse and the house. He reported the then 38-year-old woman missing two days later. No trace – apart from the footage of her arriving in her car near her home – has ever been found of Vilet Torrez. A post on the Missing Persons of America website stated:

Vilet Patricia Torrez, 38, from Miramar, Florida was last seen leaving a friend's home last Friday night.

Her company car was found in the parking lot of her apartment complex and she did not show up for work at her job as a bath remodeling specialist on Monday.

Cid Torrez, Vilet's estranged husband said he last saw her on Friday afternoon when he picked up their three children for the weekend.

'Our relationship, as far as when it comes to the kids, she's a great mother. As for her and me, we did have our little differences right at the end, but when it comes to our kids, everything was very, very close. My kids need their mother,' said Torrez. The Torrez's separated about two months ago after 15 years of marriage.

Torrez said that Vilet had a new boyfriend who he had met. Vilet went to dinner on Friday night, but the police are not revealing whom she went to dinner with.

The search continue[s] for Vilet, who her brother, Javier Blanco calls 'a beautiful human being, a hard-working, religious woman and, mostly, a devoted mother'.

The police said they have no persons of interest in the case and everyone has been cooperative.

If you have any information as to her whereabouts, please call the Miramar Police Dept. at 954-XXX-XXXX.

As the days passed, the family grew increasingly worried, going so far as to set up a Facebook page in an attempt to draw public attention to the case:

> This weekend is bittersweet as two of Vilet's children are having birthdays. It has taken too long already but the family won't give up! Thanks for coming over. Search parties will be organized soon. We need to continue spreading the word, printing and handing out flyers whenever possible, posting and re-posting her information, physically looking for her. The smallest lead from the most unexpected place could be the one that leads the detectives and family to her. Don't think you can't help. You can make a difference in her children's lives and give them the one gift they most desire. Spread the word. Let's make it known that Vilet will be found! God is on our side!

Despite the absence of a body, about nine months after Vilet Torrez vanished, on Thursday, 21 November 2012, a grand jury from Broward County, Florida, indicted her husband, then aged 39, on a first-degree murder charge. He pleaded not guilty and was initially held without bail in the Broward Main Jail. Torrez is still in prison awaiting trial at the time of writing.

But there were more charges yet to come. On the day of Torrez's 41st birthday, he was charged with an additional crime – that of installing spyware on his wife's mobile phone when he began to suspect she was 'cheating on him'. Torrez appeared in court to face the new charges wearing a striped jumpsuit, according to reports at the time.

(I'm sure it's not just me who finds it distinctly unnerving that even though Torrez's relationship with Vilet was over, he didn't want her seeing anyone else.)

In the public Facebook page set up in the days when Vilet first went missing and when the family had first reached out to the community in the hope of new leads, the family commented on the news that Torrez had been monitoring his ex's every move:

This was reported last night on CBS4 news. Very telling and very sad: 'In a new, lengthy police report just released in July we discover that in the months before Vilet disappeared in March 2012, Cid had the ability to locate Vilet's phone anywhere she was. Investigators say he used the service often.

'The report says "he received approximately 175 notifications. However, all 175 inquiries made by Cid were made prior to Vilet's disappearance. This service was not utilized once Cid reported that his wife was missing."

'Vilet's family wonders why Cid would not have told police that he could track her phone once she vanished from the Miramar home she shared with the couple's three children.

'"If somebody was looking for somebody and they had this technology available why didn't they provide this information to the police," said [Vilet's brother, Javier] Blanco.'

Of course there will be tons of excuses made by his attorney. But really …

It seems that Cid Torrez had been bugging Vilet's mobile phone – the one given to her by her employer – and had been logging her emails, phone calls, text messages, as well as having the ability to track her location at any given point in time.

Contemporary news reports say that bank records show Cid Torrez had been shelling out for the spy service for many months before Vilet disappeared – from 9 August 2011 to 9 June 2012, a police spokeswoman said. If this was indeed the case, I'm not surprised Vilet's family were shocked. This bloke knew her movements, was being kept informed of every step she took, but didn't think to mention this to the investigating authorities?

Even more damning was evidence from one of Torrez's clients, who said that Torrez had told him that he was monitoring Vilet with some spyware, and used to check her phone activity from his computer at work. A report on 25 January 203 in the *Sun Sentinel* claimed, 'The murder case pivots on circumstantial evidence that portrays Cid Torrez as an abusive and jealous estranged husband who had asked a friend about obtaining a gun, how to dispose of a body and said: "Either she's with me or she's dead."'

Torrez is yet to face court on either the surveillance or murder charges, but remains on remand in prison. His three children now live with members of their extended family.

---

★★★

Of course, few app makers publicly brag that they have created a tool for stalkers. Instead, they claim that their software is entirely legal – you know, so mum can keep a watchful eye on her teenage daughter's whereabouts or an aged and demented relative can be tracked when they go walkabout (providing they remember to take their smartphone, that is).

But no matter what the marketing materials might say, companies are making a lot of money out of selling covert surveillance apps. In 2013, the US makers of the surveillance app mSpy announced internal survey results: 50 per cent of its clients were using the product to spy on a romantic partner, and 74 per cent of its clients were male. At the time, they had just signed up their millionth customer. A quick Google search turns up a plethora of similar apps – Highster Mobile, FlexiSpy, Spyera, mCouple, the list goes on …

The covert nature of these tools is the real problem. Unlike normal apps, which appear on the smartphone menu for anyone to see, surveillance apps generally operate invisibly in the background.

The real question is: If the app is being used for legitimate purposes, you'd expect that the target would have consented to having their phone monitored. If this is the case, *why does the app need to be hidden from them?*

While it would be nice to think that most of this massive and growing market is made up of caring spouses, parents and bosses, the reality is probably far more sinister.

Think about it. The technology behind the app allows the stalker to see who their target is contacting. When they are making contact. How often. Where they are going. And the consistency with which they visit certain places.

Yes, these apps may have been designed to help worried parents or employers make sure everything is okay. They can help jealous partners discover if their loved one is cheating. But they can also be used by people with less pure motives. They can be used by people who want to control and monitor who the object of their obsession is talking to, and where they are at all times of the day and night. In other words, these apps are tools that are perfectly designed for stalkers.

Videos about these products on YouTube are enough to make you think twice about ever getting romantically involved with anyone ever again – particularly an American man, if the mSpy ad is anything to go by. While the company's spokesperson talks about legitimate uses in business and for monitoring children, not one but all three testimonials are given by blokes who had been searching for ways to spy on their lovers and found the solution in the mSpy app:

> So I had a sneaking suspicion that my girlfriend was cheating on me. And instead of having numerous confrontations and having her right in my face, I went to mspy.com … Basically you can track phone calls, applications, text messages, photos, videos, key strokes, multimedia, anything you want to track you can. If she's going to a dating website you can find that out as well

… And it got to the root of the problem. I figured out she was cheating, and I saved a lot of time.

Worryingly, he concludes, 'I'm going to use mSpy in the future too …'

The second bloke is not much better. Sounding rather chirpy for someone who's talking about heartbreak, he says:

The reason why I got it, a while back I was dating this girl and I thought I was in love with her. And out of the blue, one week, she started acting strange. She was always texting and I'd ask her who it was and she'd say it was her friends or her sister or her family or whatever. But she was being really secretive about it, acting really weird.

Again he concludes by gloating how mSpy solved his girlfriend problem by letting him know who she was talking to, and what she was getting up to behind his back. You know, rather than actually having a real-life conversation …

***

What's particularly worrying about the information that the apps can provide to a stalker – whether male, female or GLBTI (gay, lesbian, bisexual, transgender or intersex) – is that often victims are trying to escape the control of their tormentor. As seen in the case of Lisa Harman, most stalking and/or domestic violence victims will reach out to others before leaving an emotionally or physically abusive relationship. And even when they do cut the ties to their ex, they will still need to be online in some way. Our lives are increasingly digital, and any person who can access the things we share via email, text, voice calls or search for on Google will essentially know everything about us.

Those escaping an abusive partner, or even just getting out of a dead-end relationship, might need somewhere to stay. They might be dead broke and need to talk to their bank or the local Centrelink office. They will almost definitely want to reach out to friends and family for comfort, if not for practical advice about what to do next. The digital eavesdropper will soon learn everything from the state of their bank account to where they are planning to move, and perhaps even how they are coping with being stalked.

It's complicated by the fact that sometimes it takes ages to make the decision to leave. A lot of research can go into that final move. There might be a lot of talking oneself into it, and out of it, and into it again.

Apps such as Mobistealth and all the rest allow the abuser to uncover their partner's plans, and block them before they have had a chance to put them into play. Or to wait until they do leave, and then track them down to what they'd imagined would be a safe location. This is clearly a huge invasion of privacy, not to mention a breach of trust. The results can be deadly, but the technology is available to anyone with the cash to pay for the service – concerned parents, micro-managing bosses and cyberstalkers alike. There is no mental health check for those who buy these apps and monitoring services, and no means of determining whether the person installing the app means no harm, or plans on inflicting it.

**\*\*\***

In a promising move that heralds hope for victims of cyberstalking, the manufacturer of the StealthGenie app was arrested in the US in September 2014, the first prosecution of its kind. The *Washington Post* reported on 29 September 2014 that federal officials said that the manufacturer of the app had broken the law by enabling users 'the ability to secretly monitor phone calls and other communications in almost real time, something typically legal only for law enforcement'.

For $100–200 per year, StealthGenie allowed purchasers to follow most of the movements and communications of their targets. The app and other digital tools like it are most often marketed as a way to monitor children or 'suspicious employees'. However, activists working to prevent domestic violence say that this type of surveillance software is more often used by people who mistreat their partners, and have been advocating for federal officials to take a tougher stance regarding the 'high-tech tools' employed by abusers.

In November 2014, the app's creator pleaded guilty in court and was fined US$500 000, but avoided jail time. The maker was also ordered to hand over the software's source code to the authorities.

Like its many competitors, StealthGenie required users to gain physical control of a target's phone so that the app could be installed, but it would operate in secret after that. The *Washington Post* reported that Cindy Southworth of the National Network to End Domestic Violence commented, 'The fact that it's running in surreptitious mode is what makes it so foul. They work really hard to make it totally secretive.' This is why it is vitally important to control who has access to your phone.

The *Sydney Morning Herald* reported (19 October 2014) that according to solicitor Alex Davis, smartphones are a factor for 80 per cent of the clients she sees at the Women's Legal Services NSW – women seeking legal assistance in family law, domestic violence and sexual assault issues.

The paper also detailed that women seeking shelter at a North Melbourne Berry Street family violence service are told to switch their phones to flight mode when they first present for assistance. Manager Sharon Clark said that in early 2013 the service changed its standard introduction questionnaire to include such queries as: 'Who set up your phone? Who set up your Facebook account? Who has access to your passwords?'

Victims and even police and community workers may not know

**Tips for App Security**

- Lock your phone with a code and do not share it with anyone.
- Turn off the GPS on your phone.
- Turn off Bluetooth on your phone when not in use.
- Avoid buying or letting anyone give you a 'jail-broken' phone (i.e. one that has had the manufacturer's restrictions removed) as this will be much more vulnerable to spyware.

If you think a stalker is monitoring you, even if it is your partner or ex:

- Don't change your normal way of behaving, such as suddenly deleting your history, or they may suspect something is up.
- Use an anonymous device – such as a work or library computer – to communicate with people who can help you, or work out an escape plan.
- If you think your phone may have smartphone spy software installed on it, the best and only way to remove it is to restore your phone to the factory default settings. Just make sure you back up all your contacts and photos before you do this.

how to use smartphones safely, and may not realise that different accounts, such as email, mobile and Facebook, may be synched. Obtaining funds and creating programs to educate people in these matters remains a challenge. Another difficulty is that the technology is changing so rapidly. The *Sydney Morning Herald* reported that the Women's Services Network received a phone call 'about a woman who was being sent videos of herself in her lounge room by a former partner. He had been hacking her smart TV.'

Another app that has been banned is one that was made in Brazil called Boyfriend Tracker, which tracked the phone user's movements via GPS. But while the law is moving slowly to combat the sale of stalker apps, there are also plenty of non-covert apps out there that can allow a stalker to track you down.

Take the app Time to Split, for example. Split is basically designed to help you avoid people you'd really rather not run into – like your ex, or perhaps your boss if you are taking a sickie.

The app uses location technology to track down those you deem 'undesirable' and alerts you when they are nearby. It can even tell you who the person you want to avoid is with and suggest a possible escape route.

Split uses data from Facebook, Twitter, Instagram and Foursquare to chart the whereabouts of people on your 'Avoid' list. Another similar app is called Cloak. The problem is, the very same app could be used by a stalker to keep tabs on their victim – right down to where they are and with whom they are socialising.

Even seemingly innocuous mobile messaging platforms such as WhatsApp can be compromised, so that a stranger can check any user's status updates and whether they are online or offline. The stalker can also check out their target's profile pictures – even if the target has their privacy setting set to 'nobody'. WhatsApp has 700 million monthly users, many of whom are children. The implications are seriously creepy.

# Love (or Not) Online

When I first started dating – many, *many* moons ago, I distinctly remember that technology played a relatively minor part in the whole process. The kit I needed was very basic: a fixed line home phone (for which I had to fight my sister and parents for access) and a cassette player for creating nausea-inducing romantic playlists (taped directly from the radio, and so often marred by mum calling me to dinner, or our dogs barking in the garden).

Technology has also transformed the world for stalkers.

Back then, if you wanted to stalk someone, you had to get off your bottom and physically follow the person around. Or just walk slowly past their house over and over and over again, as one of my friends did to a very cute and slightly older boy who lived a couple of doors down from our house. (Yes, Janet, I am talking about you.) Janet took every twitch of the curtains as a sign that he was watching her watching him, and took great pleasure in the idea, but I still maintain that it was more likely to have been his mother, wondering whether or when she should call the police.

Stalking in those days took real effort and just wasn't possible at the click of a keyboard. However, the reality of modern dating involves not just the mobile, but mobile apps, Facebook, Skype, and also Spotify or MOG playlists. And then there is the whole online dating scene, which gives lots of lonely hearts and possible stalkers a whole new digital world to explore – or exploit.

***

My smug married friends aren't the only ones to question whether online dating is the answer to the single person's prayers in the second decade of the second millennium. I'm certainly not the poster girl for success, having dipped my toe in those murky waters once or twice over the years – and still flying solo.

But given the growing number of people in Australia today who classify themselves as single (never married, divorced, married or even 'it's complicated'), there's no doubt that a huge proportion of those are also hoping to find love (possibly again) one day.

Looking for love online is increasingly the pragmatist's choice – and particularly so if you are female. Six out of Australia's eight states and territories are currently experiencing a man drought, according to McCrindle Research – and there are almost 100 000 more women than men. If female, your chances of meeting a bloke at your local bar or a friend's barbecue are slimmer than ever before. Meanwhile, the internet offers an anonymous way to see who is out there from the comfort of your couch, and possibly reach out to those who ring your bell. If you're looking for more fish in your pond, then online dating certainly has appeal, but while it delivers fish, it can also deliver some fishy characters.

The key problems: Are you talking to the person to whom you think you are talking? What happens if you do meet up? Do they match your 'ideal'? And even if they do, what happens if it all goes terribly wrong and you end up with Mr or Ms Stalker rather than Mr or Ms Right? It does happen, as the following cases show.

***

Noodling around on the internet in the name of research – in other words, Googling all sorts of combinations of the words 'online', 'dating' and 'stalker' can deliver some unexpected nuggets, such as the couple of brief news stories on Genoveva Núñez-Figueroa that appeared in the American press.

In a (rarely) humorous example of the thousand and one ways

in which online dating can go horribly wrong, police were called to a house in Thousand Oaks, California on 19 October 2014, after neighbours heard screams coming out of the chimney. Stuck two metres down inside the chimney was Genoveva, a woman who had met the homeowner on an internet dating site and was clearly keen for further contact.

The rescue effort, involving two hours of hard yakka from the fire brigade, partial demolition of the chimney, and the application of huge quantities of liquid soap, finally saw her being freed at 8.15 in the morning.

The house belonged to a man who told reporters he wished only to be identified as 'Lawrence', no surname thank you very much. He'd met the woman on an internet dating site, and had taken her out a couple of times before deciding that perhaps she wasn't right for him. Genoveva obviously felt differently. It wasn't the first time she had turned up at his house, or tried to access it from the rooftop. 'Which just goes to show you, you have to be careful who you meet online,' Lawrence told CBS Los Angeles. In another interview with Fox 11, Lawrence said that the short relationship was 'just a fatal attraction, man. I didn't think it was going to get this bad. It got bad real quick. Real quick.'

Núñez-Figueroa was arrested on suspicion of illegal entry and giving false information to a police officer. No Google searches have turned up anything further on her, or how her love life is currently going, and believe me, I've looked.

*** 

Stalking, of course, is nothing new to the City of Angels, as tragic cases such as that of Rebecca Schaeffer (see page 158) demonstrate. Perhaps it is the proximity to Hollywood and the concentrated presence of so many high-powered and impossibly attractive celebrities – many of whom have their own dedicated stalkers. But the first person to be convicted of cyberstalking in California – just three weeks after the law was introduced – could not have been further away from the movie world. He was a 50-year-old Los Angeles security guard named Gary Dellapenta, and the object of his obsession was Randi Barber.

Randi had met Dellapenta through a mutual friend, and was just 28 years old to Dellapenta's 50. So perhaps it's not surprising that Randi rejected his repeated advances for three years. Dellapenta persistently followed her despite getting no encouragement, and even joined her church. The harassment became so bad that Randi managed to convince the church elders to ban him from attending services or participating in the congregation in any form.

In revenge, in 1998, Dellapenta began frequenting sex-related chat rooms and posting advertisements under her name, saying that she fantasised about being raped by strangers who showed up at her apartment. Should men respond to the advertisement, Dellapenta would send a reply from an email address purporting to be hers.

What makes it even worse is that Dellapenta not only emailed 'interested' parties details of her real address and phone number, but also instructions on how to break into her home and bypass her security system. In the end, six different men showed up at her apartment saying they were there to rape her, but fortunately she was never assaulted. Many more rang her for a 'chat'.

At first, Randi Barber had no idea why this was happening, but when she finally learned about the ads on the web, she placed notes on her door explaining that the ads were false. However, Dellapenta then placed *new* ads saying that the notes were part of the fantasy. He was only caught when the victim's father pretended to respond to the ads and traced their origin. (Since Randi did not own a computer and never used the internet, it was abundantly clear that she had not posted the ads or sent the emails.)

Dellapenta was arrested on charges of cyberstalking. He pleaded guilty to one count of stalking and three counts of solicitation of sexual assault and was eventually sentenced to a six-year prison term.

\*\*\*

When a hopeful lonely heart logs on to an online dating service looking for love or companionship, the last thing on their mind is the possibility that they may be inviting a potential stalker into their life. But sadly, it is impossible to tell from a carefully curated selection of photos and a well-crafted profile whether or not you've clicked on – or clicked with – a nutter. The person on the end of the internet connection could be a far cry from their pictures or who they claim to be – a very obvious pitfall to meeting potential new partners in this way.

Profiles can be very clever works of fiction, hiding the truth of a sometimes very disturbed personality. Photos can be harder to fake although the use of Photoshop and filters is apparently rife. (I've often wondered why would you completely fake a photo when the end goal, I guess, is to actually meet a real live person. Surely that person is going to notice the discrepancy between the photos posted online and the missing hair or extra 20 kilos in real life?)

However, it seems that up to one-fifth of online dating profiles – including the photo – may be completely fabricated, according to one 2013 survey reported by Sky News on 3 August 2013. A poll of 2000 people found that 18 per cent admitted to lying about their age, 28 per cent exaggerated their financial status, while 10 per cent admitted to faking where they lived. (This survey was carried out in the UK, but I can't imagine Australians being any more honest.) Online dating websites say they are taking all steps possible to try to stop scammers and fraudsters from misusing their services. However, many people have already fallen prey to those online who are masquerading as a better looking, more educated or more appealing version of their real selves.

Englishwoman Mary Turner Thomson, for example, was left with £200 000 of debt and a broken heart after falling for a man named William on an online dating site. She married him and had two children, but in April 2006, she received a phone call that blew her life apart. The woman on the other end of the line told her that Will Jordan, Mary's husband and the father of her children, had actually been married to *her* for 14 years and that they had five children together. It later emerged that Will Whatever-his-real-name-was had fathered 13 children with six different women in total. He'd been deceiving women for 27 years, and spinning a convoluted web of lies to cover his tracks for all that time. I'll bet none of that had been mentioned in his dating profile. Turner has since written a book about her dreadful experience: *The Other Mrs Morgan* (2007), retitled *The Bigamist* in 2008 (Mainstream Publishing/Random House, UK).

In Australia, at least, it seems that some dating sites *are* on the lookout for fakes. Tara Moss, the author and genetically blessed model, met her now husband, the poet Dr Berndt Selheim online in 2007. Moss, not wanting to attract the wrong sort of attention, created an anonymous profile with no photos to give the game away. After she struck up a rapport with Selheim, she eventually sent him a picture of herself (I'm sure he must have been delighted), upon which the dating site promptly shut her profile down. They had seen the photo of 'Tara Moss' and incorrectly assumed that she was an imposter.

## Own Goal

As the case of Tara Moss shows, it can be surprising who chooses to turn to an internet dating site in the search for love. Most girls would be pretty pleased to a) find and b) attract the attentions of a former professional soccer player on such a forum, but the girl who fell for Matthew Ghent, a former Aston Villa and England youth goalkeeper, soon realised that this relationship was not one that dreams are made of. The very opposite, in fact.

After first making contact on the UK-based dating website, the two had a stormy six-month relationship. Throughout it all Ghent had been very controlling, prosecutor Julia Barnett later told the Northampton Magistrate's Court. But having finally kicked the former soccer star out of her life, the woman was then subjected to a relentless campaign of harassment that left her suicidal.

The court heard that in an attempt to win her back, the once well-known soccer player booked a holiday for the pair, without her knowledge. When she refused to go on the trip, the stalking began in earnest. Ghent bombarded her with 70 emails and text messages and transferred money into her online PayPal account – unasked. He even turned up at her work (as a parole officer!) and refused to leave until the woman's colleagues threatened to call the police.

In a victim impact statement the 30-year-old woman said she had been left feeling alone and with nowhere to turn. The impact on her is one that many victims of stalking will find familiar:

> I have gone from being a safe, independent and confident woman to someone who is constantly looking over their shoulder.
>
> I have never felt so trapped and isolated while in the relationship. Everything I did and said was in an effort to placate Matthew and to avoid situations of confrontation and aggression. I was constantly treading on eggshells, left feeling confused, in fear for myself, my friends, my family and my pets.
>
> I was downtrodden and broken, lacking confidence and spark and I always seemed vacant and distracted.

Her statement added that she was receiving counselling, had considered killing herself and had been prescribed anxiety drugs to help her get through each day.

She was left constantly 'looking over her shoulder' and, almost a year on from the ordeal, she was considering abandoning her career and moving abroad for a fresh start. (I'm not so sure that moving abroad would necessarily have provided her with any solace; one Australian victim I was told about, but who did not want to be interviewed for this book, had been stalked in person by an ex-colleague for three years, then for a further four years by electronic means after the stalker had moved to Singapore for a new job opportunity.)

The defence team claimed that Ghent, from Tamworth, in Staffordshire, admitted sending the emails and text messages, but also denied that they were threatening. Whatever the intent of Ghent's communications, there's no doubt that the victim was right to be worried. It was also revealed that Ghent had prior form for harassing an ex-partner. In 2006, he had been imprisoned for three months for assaulting and stalking his then girlfriend, Maria Morris. The court at that time heard that Ghent had throttled Maria and kicked her in the stomach – did I mention she was pregnant with their son at the time? – purely because he disliked the way she had decorated their Christmas tree.

Ghent, who retired in 2008 and was selling hair and beauty products online at the time of his arrest, once had a promising future as a footballer, but never made a first team appearance. He later appeared for Barnsley, Lincoln City, Solihull Moors and Tamworth – the minor leagues after his hopeful start. His failure to achieve his footballing dreams played a part in his difficulties, the defence claimed.

The *Daily Mail* (13 May 2013) reported his counsel, Mark Moore, as saying, 'He has suffered from difficulties since his career ended, but he has always participated fully in courses ordered by the courts. There is now a degree of openness about his behaviour, which is perhaps more difficult to admit in the macho world he is from.'

A Facebook photograph, posted just weeks before Ghent had to appear in court, suggested a man happy in that macho world. According to the *Daily Mail*:

Just weeks before he admitted the charges in court, he posted this photograph on his Facebook page, showing himself sitting in a bathtub full of cash, cigarette in one hand and a glass of wine in the other.

He even gloated that he had hidden the £50 notes underneath the £20s to avoid being too ostentatious.

He wrote: 'Because I can. Go **** yourself,' adding: 'The bottom layers were actually 20s/50s. I thought it was too "bling" to put 50s on top.'

Nice.

At the conclusion of his court case, Ghent was handed a 10-week suspended prison sentence. He was also given a two-year supervision order, ordered to take part in a domestic abuse education program, handed a restraining order banning him from contacting the victim and told to pay her £750 (around A$1145) in compensation.

In sentencing the ex-footballer/now hair-product purveyor, Deputy District Judge Elizabeth Harte said Ghent was guilty of an 'exceptionally unpleasant case of true stalking behaviour'. The judge followed up with a stern warning: 'If you fail to moderate your behaviour, you will go to prison for a long time.'

Should this happen, one hopes his ex-girlfriend is not appointed his parole officer.

## The Reject Pile

One of the biggest problems encountered by those looking for love online is rejection. But it's not your own rejection you should probably be most concerned about – it's the reaction of those whom you reject. After all, rejection is a prime stalker motivation.

Take, for example, the case of the South Australian butcher who stalked a woman he met on a dating website. Duane Edward Cremer, 49, pleaded guilty to stalking the woman between 21 January and 2 February 2012 with the intention of 'causing her serious physical or mental harm or of causing her to fear such harm'.

The pair had met on a social website and after exchanging texts and then meeting up, the woman made it clear she wasn't interested in further contact. As you might well do.

Cremer, meanwhile, had other ideas and hopes. *The Australian* reported (17 January 2014) that his lawyer had said that Cremer had only given the woman one kiss on the cheek and that while he had pleaded guilty to stalking, this had only involved seven text messages. The lawyer admitted that the text conversation had perhaps been 'too forward'.

In a victim impact statement read to the South Australian District Court, the woman said those seven text messages from Cremer had terrorised her. 'I feared for my and my family's life,' she said. She had gone from being a trusting, cheerful and relaxed person and now had nightmares and was scared to answer the phone, especially when it was from an unidentified number.

I've no idea of the content of the text messages, but my mind immediately went from the word 'butcher' to the thought of 'knife' and all that might imply.

The Adelaide court was told that Cremer had had a difficult childhood, and had become a ward of the state after his father murdered his mother. Cremer had also previously stalked an ex-partner after the breakup of a difficult relationship, and had actually been convicted of that offence in 2007. Being rejected by another woman – this time from a dating website – had tipped him over the edge yet again.

***

This kind of begs the question whether online dating sites are doing enough to protect women from being targeted by stalkers (and men who have previously been convicted of domestic violence). In the UK, one in five dates now starts via the internet, and there are hundreds of sites operating in the UK. The industry is now worth £300 million a year.

**Online Rejection: Firm but Fair**

- Tell them immediately that you do not feel a connection.
- Let them know you are not interested in pursuing a relationship or friendship with them, and wish them all the best. Be precise, and use these exact words or something very similar.
- If you are vague, you may give them hope that there is still the possibility or chance for a relationship with you. Do not be too indirect, too flowery, and don't sugar the pill. Just say it how it is.
- Copy and save all chats, messages or emails, in case they don't get the point and you need to take further action. Then you will have your proof that you *told* the stalker that you were not interested.
- After you tell them to stop contacting you, make sure that you ignore them completely. Do not respond to any emails they send or engage in any form of communications with them – no matter what they threaten or what they say. These communications should be saved or shared with the police if they continue, and not deleted.

The UK's anti-stalking charity Paladin was set up in 2013 to offer counselling to stalking victims. A number of women who had met men online – and seen them transform from Romeo to Rottweiler – have contacted the charity for urgent help. At least three of these cases included threats and actual violence, according to *The Guardian* (7 September 2013).

Paladin told *The Guardian* that in all these cases the men were found to have previous histories of violence against women. Most dating sites do not require a lie detector test or provide a checkbox where members can tick 'yes' to having a nasty streak, mental health issues or issues with control or jealousy. There is nothing to warn dates about the propensities of their potential new love interest. Likewise, there is no regulation to prevent abusive men from joining new dating sites, or even old ones under a new nom de plume. The anti-stalking charity believes that anyone 'found to be involved in stalking or violence should be barred from all dating agencies and the matter referred to the police'.

One case study highlighted in *The Guardian* article involved a woman they called June*, who met her former partner on a dating website, unaware that he had two prior convictions for assault causing actual bodily harm. Just four weeks into June's new romance, he became verbally and emotionally abusive, threatening to share naked pictures of her on Facebook and also with her employer. He never physically abused her, but showed signs of a rotten temper – chucking crockery and other items around.

June told *The Guardian* that she believed dating sites need to offer 'panic buttons' where users can report concerns about the people they meet. Rather than having an automated response, sites should offer 'a human sitting there and taking your concerns seriously'.

★★★

There are, of course, potential dangers associated with the formation of any new relationship – whether formed through an introduction from a friend, a family member or via meeting at any of the usual places – the more recent evolutions of which apparently include hot yoga, salsa dancing, the school gate and the supermarket aisle. However, online dating also offers unique risks and challenges. First is the forum itself. Many of those who venture onto these sites have been hurt in the past, and may unwittingly present as vulnerable and/or lonely – a prime target for a stalker.

As for the stalkers themselves, a computer screen affords the ideal hiding place for those afflicted by emotional insecurities or mental health problems. They can browse potential partners/victims confident in the knowledge that they are anonymous. Profiles of prospective partners are carefully scrutinised and they may target someone who gives the impression of a kind and caring nature. And if the potential date appears vulnerable due to disappointments in other relationships and loneliness, they may be the perfect choice. Then there are those who simply won't take no for an answer.

Chat rooms abound with such stories, like the following query posted online in an internet dating forum:

A little while ago, I joined this online dating service just for fun. Right off the bat, I met this guy who was 47 years old (I'm 30, so that's a little old for me!). He seemed nice at first. For about a day or so:) Then it became clear he has some issues (other than the ones he told me about) like maybe he was very childish, controlling, and narcissistic (for instance, he once sent me an email which said 'Am I the only one who thinks about me, or is it just me?' I had to laugh at that one!:)) He said things like that all of the time, and then he had the nerve to insult me. So I banned him on that dating service site from messaging me (but he could still speak to me in the chat room), and I banned him from emailing me on one of my email addresses. Somehow he found out my private email address and continued his barrage of insults. Not only that, but I found out he had been spying on me in the chat room under a different name, and wanted to know 'why I was "invisible" on AIM' (which I wasn't).

Eventually he apologised and we got back to talking for a whole day before his insults started again. Now I'm afraid. I have him blocked everywhere I can think of, but he always finds a way through. This has been going on for a month now I think. He hasn't threatened my life or anything like that, but he knows vaguely where I live and he lives fairly close. I mean, he could take the train here if he wanted. If he got mad enough. Do you think he could?

So far it's just insults like him telling me that I'm immature because I like scrapbooking (which happens to be an adult hobby, by the way ... :)) and I sing. What's wrong with

99

that? My Grandmother sang to me. My mother sings. My aunt and dietitian are in choral groups and they are older than me. So anyway, his accusations are totally unfounded. I have asked those around me, just to be sure.

Is there anything else I can do to keep him away, or do you think I am safe?

★★★

---

## The Pizza Pest

Some dating websites market themselves at those looking for a long-term relationship; others at the slightly more seamy end of the business target those looking for a casual hook-up, or perhaps even paid sex. Delivery driver Theofillus Sugiaman's marriage had broken down, and he was on the hunt – not necessarily for a new partner, but for some fun.

That hunt for fun resulted in what Brisbane District Court Judge Michael Shanahan described as 'one of the most serious examples of the offence of stalking'. And it all started in March 2012 with a date arranged over a website between a 41-year-old father-of-three and a 21-year-old female, who had reportedly been working as a prostitute according to news reports. The two became casual lovers, but when he discovered that the unnamed female was also seeing other men, he snapped and began a truly frightening campaign of harassment.

Sugiaman had showered the young woman with money and gifts, but when he became suspicious that he was not the only man in her life, he installed monitoring software on a mobile phone that he then gave to her as a gift. This meant he was able to access her address book, and also see with whom she was talking. His stalking was not confined just to his 'girlfriend', but extended to the other men she was seeing, her friends, and even some complete strangers.

Tens of thousands of threatening phone calls and text messages were made or sent to more than 15 targets.

In many of these communications with victims, Sugiaman told them he knew where they lived; he sent countless unwanted taxis and pizzas to their homes, and also threatened them with violence and death. In the case of the young woman, he called her 10 636 times over a six-week period, averaging 240 calls a day. Police later determined that 87 of these calls were menacing or harassing, and 24 threatened violence, between 20 October and 2 December 2012. Between December 2012 and May 2013, she personally had to put up with more than 100 unsolicited pizza deliveries. Unsurprisingly, the young woman told the police that her life had been made hell.

When the young woman, the main target of his obsession, moved house and new residents moved in, he started stalking them too. Don't forget, these were people *she* had never met and that he'd never met either – it was enough that they were living in the house where his former crush had lived.

One man, whose contact details Sugiaman had found on the young woman's phone, attracted his particular ire. He was the unlucky recipient of 4214 threatening phone calls and 475 menacing texts between October 2012 and May 2013. The texts were particularly worrying because they indicated that Sugiaman knew his home address, and had clearly been observing the property, and knew that he had recently installed sensor lights – perhaps as a reaction to the stalking. 'Your stupid sensor lights won't save you,' one text message read.

Sugiaman also went so far as to damage the man's car – the repairs for which cost $1200.

Sugiaman used online software not only to hide his real phone number, but also to make it seem as if the 21-year-old woman (and some of his other stalkees) were making the abusive calls and sending the vicious text messages. But he slipped up when he used the fake phone number dodge to make it look like his victims were making bomb threats and fake calls to emergency services.

Now police officers might not get too enraged by a dodgy pizza delivery or two, but hoax bomb threats and false triple zero calls are another matter entirely. A series of bomb hoaxes at the Brisbane and Gold Coast airports, Jupiters Casino and at shopping centres chewed up the time and energy of more than one hundred police officers over the course of several months.

One text message to the Police Link number and an unnamed member of the public read, 'I've planted a bomb at Forest Lake shopping centre, it will go off in one hour.' Sugiaman was also behind warnings to aircraft carriers that there were explosives on board, and a bomb threat at the Brisbane Airport that told of a kidnap victim in danger on 6 December 2012. Australian Federal Police also treated as credible a threat from Sugiaman that there were explosives at the Gold Coast Airport on 9 April 2013.

Police were desperate to find the hoaxer, and tracked the messages back to the phones of the young woman and some of the other stalking victims. They were put through hours of grilling about their involvement in the bomb threats before Sugiaman's 'sophisticated' scheme was unveiled.

In court, Sugiaman's barrister, Andrew James, explained that his depressed client had suffered from the breakdown of his marriage and, at the time of the offences, had recently lost custody of his children and became delusional. He tendered a psychological report and references from his children and two pastors.

He said his client had been working two jobs and consuming lots of energy drinks when the stalking offences took place against a background of long-term depression. He said Sugiaman believed he had not been paying for sex, but had been giving the woman money to help her stay in the country.

In sentencing the serial stalker, Judge Michael Shanahan said Sugiaman's conduct had lasted over a nine-month period in 2012 and 2013. He said the conduct was aggravated by the fact many of the victims were initially investigated by police as possible suspects in the bomb threats. The *Courier Mail* reported on 1 August 2014 that the judge said:

> You used that access to commence a whole scale course of harassment and threatened behaviour, not only against her, but against any person that she came in contact with. That included two other clients of hers, that conduct may well have been motivated by jealousy, but it seemed that it extended quickly to all other people she had contact with and indeed some people who she had no contact with whatsoever.

Theofillus Sugiaman, 41, was sentenced in the District Court in Brisbane to a maximum of seven years of jail. The judge said that his large-scale harassment had not only disrupted lives but had also tied up police resources. The judge also placed restraining orders preventing Sugiaman going near his victims for 10 years.

Judge Shanahan ordered that Sugiaman be eligible for parole after one-third of his sentence had been served on 15 September 2015. He took into account 442 days served by the prisoner in pre-sentence custody since his arrest on 16 May 2013.

---

## The Warning Signs

Okay, there is probably no one sure-fire way of spotting a potential online dating stalker-to-be, but there are certainly some red flags. Online interactions can have an entirely different flavour to the real world. Things move more quickly in cyberspace and cyberstalkers, like pretty much anyone wanting to attract someone, can initially present as intelligent, charming and persuasive. They may also appear to be very interested in their target – which can be extremely flattering at first. However, a trawl of the internet, and advice from specialists in the field, suggest a few common themes:

- They're constantly in contact over the course of a day, and are very quickly very keen to move from the dating site to private email, texting or telephone calls.
- They want to know lots of personal information – about school, work, hobbies, family, favourite cafes, etc. They listen very attentively to their target because they want to be able to win them over – not forgetting that any information could also be used against the target later on, of course.
- At first, they may be overly agreeable too, and perhaps make overly romantic comments like 'I feel we were meant to be.' They often present as too interested, too soon.
- They keep changing their own story about themselves, may be vague about the details of their life, or somehow what they say just doesn't add up.
- They become increasingly demanding or controlling, wanting to know details of what has happened since the last contact, why the target has been offline, when they can finally meet up and so on.

Possibly the most worrying sign of all is if they begin to talk about things that have not been personally disclosed – this suggests a degree of research or perhaps background monitoring. Omnipresence is another warning sign too – consistently showing up in forums or online at the same time as their target. They may even make up stories about dates or experiences that have never taken place.

***

Even if an internet contact turns out to seem okay in the early stages, there are still things that daters can do to minimise someone's opportunity to inflict harm later on.

Step one in my personal acid test would be to refuse a date with anyone who says they like long walks on the beach at dusk – a predilection that possibly could be perfectly innocent, but also happens to be in my top three things not to do with a man you've just met on the internet, along with strolls down dark laneways and picnics in remote bushland. Along with this, I'd also add not giving them your phone number, home address, work address, or *anything* that you don't want your mother to know and that could come back to haunt you later. That includes sending intimate pics, obviously.

It should be noted that I say this from the perspective of a woman who agreed to meet and interview a double murderer *at his home*. I also interviewed one of Australia's most wanted criminals in the car park of a remote national park for one of my previous books, *Love Behind Bars* (2013). Let's just say, it ended safely, and Joe remains one of my all-time favourite interviewees. The chainsaw and spade in the back of his ute were for professional, park-rangery purposes only.

But it's important to remember that personal safety needs to take precedence over enthusiasm. You don't want to arm a potential stalker with all the information they need to make your life hell.

- Create a separate email address for all your online dating correspondence.
- Never give away personal information such as your full name, workplace, work or home address, home phone number or birthday, until you know someone relatively well.
- Do a reverse Google image search on photos of profiles to check for authenticity – or check the person out on Facebook (or LinkedIn if they have given you details of their profession and full name). By the way, this isn't stalking; it's called taking precautions and checking your facts – and it's how I discovered that the man who stalked me was a fraud.
- When you meet somebody for the first time, pick a public place, tell a friend or family member where you are going and keep the first meeting brief – coffee is perfect.
- Don't let someone you only know through a dating site pick you up or drop you at your home.

- And never, ever, *ever* send money to someone you've only ever communicated with online or over the phone. No matter how good their backstory – serving with the armed forces overseas, a Nigerian prince fleeing national conflict, or a spy – you don't want to end up with an NSTD (non-sexually transmitted debt).

# Watching the Windsors

Even as a child, I was never one of those girls with a fantasy of a) discovering I'd been adopted and in reality was heir to a throne or b) growing up to marry a prince and so becoming a princess. Now, after learning that Kate Middleton personally has an estimated 220 stalkers, I'm even less inclined to want to don that crown.

Of course, the appeal of the royals' numerous, very nice homes around the United Kingdom and their pots of cash – held in the counting house, according to the old nursery rhyme – might help to soften the blow of the stalker threat somewhat. But even Prince William's estimated personal net worth of US$40 million only puts him roughly on par with movie star Jennifer Lawrence (and way behind lots of other celebrities).

On the other hand, Charles, the Prince of Wales, is the next male heir to the throne and earns about $30 million *annually* from a 200-square-mile (518 000-hectare), $1.2-billion real estate holding known as the Duchy of Cornwall. King Edward II established the land holding in 1337 to make sure that his own son and all future Princes of Wales had a reliable income.

For that kind of money flowing into my husband's bank account each year, would I be prepared to put up with the constant threat of being stalked? Perhaps not.

Royal stalkers – of which there have been many over the decades – often claim to be in love with or in an intimate relationship with a member of the royal family. However, they are generally not motivated by the contents of the royal bank accounts, but by various forms of mental illness, including schizophrenia and hallucinations. Indeed, scientists who studied more than 20 000 incidents of people who have stalked the royals found that 80 per cent of them could be classified as psychotic and in need of psychiatric treatment.[16] This is in contrast to stalkers of everyday folk, for which the figure is just one in five who are technically psychotic. (As a commoner and victim of stalking myself, I'm not so sure that I am comforted by these statistics.)

The study mentioned was sponsored by the UK Home Office and led by Dr Paul Mullen, a forensic psychiatrist at Monash University in Melbourne, Australia, and the Victorian Institute of Forensic Mental Health, and Dr David James, a consultant forensic psychiatrist at the North London Forensic Service. The results were first made public in 2008, although the results were known earlier and kept secret for a while, probably because of their sensitivity.

The team studied data contained in files on 8000 people kept by the UK's Metropolitan Police between 1988 and 2003. Just under half were nuisance correspondents – people who wrote repeated threatening, amorous or obscene letters. By the time the scientists had made their way through all the files, about 250 of the 8000 were judged to be true, serious, life-threatening dangers to the House of Windsor. That said, over the 15 years covered by the study, 600 people had managed to get close to a member of the royal family, and there had been 17 attacks on staff, bodyguards (or protection service personnel, as they are more formally known) or royal property.

As a result of the team's findings, a new strategy was put in place that involved the establishment of a Fixated Threat Assessment Centre (FTAC), a joint effort by London's Metropolitan Police, the UK Home Office and the Department of Health. As well as wanting to protect their own royal family, the establishment of the FTAC recognised that the main danger of death or serious injury to other public figures also came from mentally ill outsiders, who had usually signalled their intent by sending repeated warnings in the form of inappropriate, harassing or threatening communications or approaches towards the politicians in question.

In previous times, stalkers of public figures had simply been removed from the scene if they were acting in a threatening or unusual way, but officials had not gone so far as to offer treatment that might prevent them from doing something similar in the future. Following the establishment of the FTAC, psychiatrists employed by the centre now assess the stalkers, and refer them on to mental health services if they are deemed in need of treatment. And it's not just about protecting the high and mighty – it's also about helping people with obsessions who have mental illnesses that might otherwise have gone untreated.

From one of the fathers of the FTAC, Dr James, himself:

> [The FTAC] provides an avenue for improving the assessment of cases of possible threat to public figures and for employing specific forms of management, as well as opening some possibilities for prevention and early intervention.[17]

In other words, it's all about preventing harm and facilitating care, as the strapline of the centre itself says. Think too of the others who are intimately involved. Supporting the approach taken in the UK, research from the US shows that in fact those most at risk include the families, colleagues or even neighbours of the person who is mentally ill. It's not the public figure (or their bodyguards, should they have them) but those who are closest to the stalker in real life.[18]

## Taking Precautions

The public doesn't know exactly what has gone on behind the scenes of the FTAC in the years since it was first established, and what threats the FTAC has had to deal with. However, it's not hard to guess that in the lead-up to the birth of Charlotte Elizabeth

Diana, Prince William and the Duchess of Cambridge's second child, in May 2015, things would have been pretty busy down at Stalker Central in the UK.

In response to a Freedom of Information request from the *Daily Mirror* (UK) to the FTAC, it seems that specialist security officers were closely monitoring up to 220 stalkers or high-risk fanatics, who could pose a possible threat at the time of the royal birth – to the royal bub or either of its royal parents, or their extended families.

As reported in rival newspaper *The Express*, prior to Charlotte's birth, psychiatric officers and psychiatric nurses were busy making visits to 'fixated persons' in order to carry out welfare checks. In other words, they wanted to make sure that all known threats were continuing to take their medication. The FTAC, which employs nine detectives, three nurses and a community support officer, also reportedly combined resources to identify potential fanatics online.

Each time Kate gave birth – to Prince George in July 2013 and Princess Charlotte in 2015 – hundreds of media professionals and well-wishers (and probably more than a few stalkers) gathered outside the Lindo Wing of St Mary's Hospital in London.

With so many stalkers of her own, Kate must have some idea of the difficult road ahead for her expanding family. And like any other mother, she's doubtless concerned about the welfare of her children. At the age of one, Prince George himself reportedly already had two stalkers of his own.

In October 2014, lawyers for Prince William and Kate Middleton issued a warning to a freelance photographer who was allegedly 'harassing' Prince George. (Stalking by paparazzi is obviously much more than just a sore point for Prince William, given that his mother, Princess Diana, died as a result of injuries sustained in a car crash in the Pont de l'Alma road tunnel in Paris on 31 August 1997. The media blamed the paparazzi following the car, although an 18-month French judicial investigation found that the crash was actually caused by the driver, Henri Paul, who lost control of the car at high speed while drunk.)

Without even going into all the conspiracy theories that also surround Princess Di's death, the idea of any child of his being relentlessly pursued by snap happy snappers or any kind of stalker must not weigh well for Prince William, who was only 15 years of age when his mother died. (Prince Harry was 12.)

Since that time, there has been a long-standing agreement between the British press and the royals. Unofficial photos of royal children are almost never published, unless there is a compelling reason (and not just, 'How cute! Prince George had a temper tanty when Nanny tried to put him in the stroller!').

In any event, according to a 30 April 2015 article in *The Week*, William and Kate were worried that the paparazzi had been pursuing Prince George during his outings with his nanny. One man, who attempted to photograph Prince George at Battersea Park, was particularly concerning. He was known to palace security, having already been spoken to by royal protection officers on a number of occasions in the previous five years. Officials believed that the man may have been 'stalking' Prince George for some time, by placing him under surveillance and taking note of his daily routines.

A statement issued from Kensington Palace said that 'the Duke and Duchess of Cambridge were prompted to take action after the man was spotted near the young prince'.

*The Week* reported, 'The duke and duchess understand the particular public role that Prince George will one day inherit but while he is young, he must be permitted to lead as ordinary a life as possible.' I trust this will include visits to the dress-up box to try on that crown, and that *Cinderella* is not banned from the royal reading list.

## A Right Royal History

While stalking has only been recognised in recent times, it is a phenomenon that has haunted the British royal family for decades, if not centuries – from the teenager who nicked Queen Victoria's knickers to the man who crept into Queen Elizabeth's bedroom for a midnight chat.

Most recently, the skeletal remains of Robert Moore, who had sent thousands of parcels and letters to Queen Elizabeth II were found near Buckingham Palace in late 2011. His body may have been undiscovered for around three years – a sad end for any human, but also a reflection on how Moore's obsession with the monarch destroyed his life. He'd spent 15 years trying to make contact with the Queen, sending numerous letters in the first instance, some of which ran to as many as 600 pages. (As someone who takes months to churn out 240 pages for a whole book, I'm in awe of someone who can churn this number of pages out for a mere letter.) More seriously, I can't think of a more obvious pointer towards serious psychiatric issues.

Along with the letters/bricks, Moore also sent Her Majesty a selection of obscene photographs, the details of which unsurprisingly have not been made public, along with boxes with labels warning of hazardous substances and – less threateningly – a photocopy of his passport. A handy clue for investigators, one suspects.

Robert Moore (no relation to Roger Moore, who once acted on Her Majesty's Secret Service in the James Bond movies) was an American by birth. He arrived in the UK in 2007, and somehow made himself a home on a small island in the lake in St James's Park in the middle of London. While the island is officially closed to the public and pretty much inaccessible unless you have a boat or are prepared to wade out, this inconvenience did not prove much of an obstacle to the fiercely determined/insane Moore. After all, the island afforded him a direct outlook of the palace, the Queen's main place of residence, including views onto the palace's balconies. Who knew when she might pop out to wave to her loyal subjects, and her number one fan?

Moore was in his late sixties at the time he set up house opposite the object of his obsession. And somehow his presence remained unknown, despite the fact that every year millions of Londoners and tourists visit St James's Park, according to the Royal Parks website.

Moore's precise cause of death was never determined, but it is thought that he had problems with both alcohol and, ahem, his mental health (see previously for my view on people who write letters that run to 600 pages).

Erotomania was one of the explanations given for his obsession. As described earlier, erotomania is a type of delusion in which the affected person believes that another person – usually someone who is of higher status or famous – is in love with them, *even if they have never met the person*. In other words, Moore thought he was in with a chance with the Queen.

More seriously, this illness often occurs during psychosis, especially in those suffering from schizophrenia, bipolar mania or delusional disorder. This results in the person believing that their secret admirer (the Queen in this instance) is sending secret messages declaring their affection. Sometimes these messages are delivered by 'telepathy', at other times by secret signals, special glances, or messages through the media. The Queen's Christmas speech was doubtless a highlight of Moore's year.

On 'getting the message' from their victim, the recipient then returns the perceived compliment with gifts, visits or even 600-PAGE-LONG LETTERS. Secure in their delusion, the stalker also finds it hard to believe that their gifts or other offerings are unwanted. Any lack of acknowledgement or negative reaction is dismissed as being a ploy to conceal the forbidden relationship from the rest of the world.

Robert Moore had a precedent for royal stalking in the case of a woman named as Léa-Anna B in a noted paper written by the psychiatrist Gaëtan Gatian de Clérambault way back in 1921 (The erotomania syndrome is also known as de Clérambault's syndrome.)

The patient who inspired de Clérambault's paper, a 53-year-old French milliner called Léa-Anna, somehow became convinced that the then King of England – George V – was passionately in love with her (and this despite the fact that he was doubtless unaware of her humble existence on the other side of the Channel). She made a number of trips to London, which was probably no small deal on a milliner's income, and would wait patiently outside the gates of Buckingham Palace awaiting a signal from him. She believed that the closing of the curtains – at 4.30 p.m. every day – was the sign that he loved her.

De Clérambault was only deluded in thinking that the delusion that now bears his name was something that only ever affects single women. The case of Robert Moore proves it, as does the case of the stalker, John Hinckley Jr, who went so far as to attempt to assassinate then US President Ronald Reagan in a dodgy effort to impress the actress Jodie Foster (see page 144).

## Tea and Sympathy

You'd think that Queen Elizabeth II would have the best security in the land, but it wasn't enough to stop deranged stalker, Michael Fagan, from clambering over Buckingham Palace's 14-foot (4-metre) perimeter wall – topped with barbed wire and revolving spikes that wouldn't look out of place in a medieval dungeon – and shimmying up a drainpipe before wandering the hallways of the palace in search of the Queen. Twice he tripped alarms, but the security guards assumed that they were faulty and simply turned them off. (The Home Secretary of the time, William Whitelaw, was so embarrassed by the ensuing scandal that he offered his resignation. The Queen refused.)

At about 7.15 a.m. on 9 July 1982, Fagan strolled into the Queen's bedroom and a place in history. Reports at the time said that the 31-year-old psychiatric patient drew back the curtains around the Queen's bed and plopped himself down next to the sleeping monarch. She awoke to find a strange young man sitting beside her, dripping blood from where he had cut his hand somewhere in his entry to the palace. But in an interview with *The Independent* on 19 February 2012, the year of the Queen's Diamond Jubilee, Fagan recalled it slightly differently:

'I was scareder than I'd ever been in my life,' he says, widening his eyes theatrically as he recalls the moment he pulled back the curtains to see the Queen staring up at him. 'Then she speaks and it's like the finest glass you can imagine breaking: "Wawrt are you doing here?!"'

He insists he has 'great respect' for the Queen. Not apparently as great as the pleasure he takes in sharing the details of his moment in the royal chamber: 'It was a double bed but a single room, definitely – she was sleeping in there on her own,' he giggles. 'Her nightie was one of those Liberty prints and it was down to her knees.'

Reports at the time said that Elizabeth was initially unable to raise security, and so chatted with Fagan for 10 minutes about the details of his recent relationship troubles and his four children. A chambermaid finally entered the room to wake the monarch, saw the intruder and raised the alarm.

Fagan's own account differs again – he told *The Independent* that the Queen scampered from the room 'on her little bare feet' when she awoke to find him by her bed.

By his own account, it was his second illegal entry into the palace. On the first occasion, he had climbed a drainpipe and snuck into the royal residence through an unlocked window. He startled a housemaid, who called security, but by the time they arrived, Fagan was long gone into the labyrinth of passages, leading security to question the housemaid about what she had seen.

In the meantime, Fagan was free to wander the palace and he made the most of the opportunity, snacking on cheddar cheese and crackers he found along the way, viewing the royal portraits and even resting his weary bones on the throne for a few minutes. In searching for an exit, he somehow wandered into the post room where he found a whole lot of presents, including a bottle of white wine from Prince Charles' estate, which he swilled. He eventually found a door leading into the grounds, scaled the fence back out to freedom, and disappeared into the London night. (The details of this first intrusion rest on his word, so perhaps should be taken with a large grain of salt.)

In any event, Fagan wasn't so lucky on his second attempt – he was arrested by the Queen's security when they finally turned up, although the charges were later dropped when Fagan was committed to a psychiatric hospital for six months.

The year after his bedroom 'chat' with the Queen, Michael Fagan recorded a cover version of the Sex Pistols' song 'God Save The Queen' with British punk band the Bollock Brothers.

His later history was less illustrious. In 1984, Fagan attacked a policeman at a cafe in Wales and was given a three-month suspended jail sentence. Then, in 1987, he was found guilty of indecent exposure after he was spotted capering without trousers on waste ground in Chingford, London. In 1997, he was imprisoned for four years after he, his then wife and 20-year-old son were charged with conspiring to supply heroin.

***

You'd think after the scandal of Fagan's unauthorised entry, that security at Buckingham Palace would now be airtight, but not so. Similar incidents have happened since, including a Fathers 4 Justice protester scaling the walls in 2004 and unveiling a banner, while dressed as Batman.

All was quiet on the palace grounds until Monday, 2 September 2013, when Victor Miller, a 37-year-old, unemployed DJ, was arrested in Buckingham Palace after allegedly scaling a fence. (Note to security: perhaps it's time to do something about those fences.) The DJ was found in a part of the palace normally open to the public during the day, and no members of the royal family were present at the time.

More worryingly, on Monday, 14 October 2013, a 44-year-old mentally ill man was rugby-tackled to the ground by armed police and arrested after he jumped over a vehicle barrier at Buckingham Palace's north centre gate, watched by scores of tourists. When searched, a six-inch (15-centimetre) kitchen knife was found wrapped in a plastic bag in his jacket pocket.

In custody, David Belmar, of Haringey, north London, told the police he 'wanted to see the Queen' after his incapacity benefit was stopped. His fixation with the Queen was longstanding – in 1989, he received a caution for piffing lighted fireworks into the grounds of Buckingham Palace, and his Facebook page shows a gallery of royal portraits, including those of the Queen, Kate Middleton, Prince Charles and Princess Anne.

At Westminster Magistrates' Court the following day, he admitted trespass and possession of a bladed article. He was sentenced to 16 months' imprisonment at Southwark Crown Court on 15 January 2014.

## Princess Di's Doctor Stalker

Much has been made of Princess Di's stalking by the paparazzi, but in fact her most ardent pursuer was German-born Dr Klaus Wagner – an orthopaedic surgeon, who was struck off for writing false prescriptions to support his morphine addiction. Wagner became convinced that Queen Elizabeth II, Di's mother-in-law, was in fact a devil that had been prophesised in the Bible, in the book of Revelation – he named her 'the Elizardbeast'. He thought Diana was the true queen, and should rule in place of her ex-mother-in-law.

Here's what Wagner had to say in one public post that can still be found on the internet:

> Today I have fed some search engines with the famous true name of the so-called 'Queen' of England: Elizardbeast, which reflects the fact that she was predicted as the 'Beast 666' (nothing to do with an 'Antichrist') in the Bible, Revelation, chapter 13 as explained on my homepage ... you can see me protesting against the so-called 'Queen' with a placard last year. I did this in order to overthrow this beastly old hag to put Princess Diana in her place and I was libelled 'Diana's stalker' by the liars from the Press, when I took advantage of the enormous Press attention for Diana's public appearances in order to spread my message.

Wagner stalked Princess Diana for months, turning up wherever she was known to be appearing and holding up placards that were meant to express his devotion and to warn her of Queen Elizabeth's evil intentions. Outside Buckingham Palace, he also handed out pamphlets detailing the supposed conspiracy against her.

After one court hearing, he said that he would work ceaselessly to make people understand the truth about the Queen. He said he would not be 'deterred' by being bound over to keep the peace and that he had no intention of paying any of the fines or costs the court had awarded against him. Indeed, he said, 'I am going to continue. The more the state does against me, the more it serves my purpose.'

The 37-year-old drug user was finally sent to a psychiatric hospital in 1996 for stalking Diana – after turning up at a charity event at Harrods attended by the Princess of Wales. On Wagner's release, despite the fact that Diana had already died in that famous tunnel in Paris, he continued his quest to defeat the 'Elizardbeast' until his own death from a heart attack in 2007.

***

You don't have to be a queen or a queen-in-waiting to attract the attentions of a stalker. Like her mother and sister-in-law, Princess Anne has also had to put up with her fair share of unwanted attention, most famously from a crazed gunman named Ian Ball, who attempted to kidnap her in 1974. Ambushing Anne's car en route to Buckingham Palace, Ball shot and wounded four men, including the Princess's driver. Aged just 23 and recently married to her first husband Captain Mark Phillips, Princess Anne refused to budge from her car, saying, 'Not bloody likely!' according to reports at the time.

Ball's actions led to a major overhaul of security surrounding the royal family. The fanatical loner told police it was the 'one good thing' to come out of his crime, and confessed that he had been thinking about it for years before putting his audacious plan into action.

However, Ball was not the only man obsessed with Princess Anne. In the early 1990s, Bernard Quinn divorced his wife so he could devote his life to the pursuit of the Princess Royal. He spent the next decade bombarding her with daily love letters and poems, and was first arrested in 1996 in Liverpool after 'threatening' behaviour towards the princess. He appeared in the Liverpool Magistrates' Court charged with the offence of behaviour likely to cause a breach of the peace. The case against him was that he consistently shadowed the Princess Royal at many of her official engagements. His aim was to get as close to the princess as possible, and to breach the security cordon in order to do so. When arrested he talked to police about the sexual fantasies that he had entertained about Princess Anne. Despite this, the stipendiary magistrate decided Quinn had no case to answer and dismissed the charge on the grounds that the criminal law had not been breached.

Quinn was back in trouble the following year, when he tried to drive into the princess's Gatcombe Park estate in Gloucestershire, south-west England on Valentine's Day. He was sent to a psychiatric hospital. He was arrested again in 2000 after allegedly harassing Anne's guards. The charges were dropped due to lack of evidence that he posed a real threat, and Quinn was later admitted to another mental facility.

***

My favourite of all the royal stalkers – if it's not too weird to confess to having such a thing – is the teenage lad, Edward Jones, who was known to the London police as 'Boy Jones'. He was one of Britain's first celebrity stalkers, and went to incredible lengths to get close to the object of his affection: the newly crowned Queen Victoria.

Between 1838 and 1841, he broke into Buckingham Palace at least three times, creating a right royal fuss on each occasion, and once spending three hours hiding under her sofa while the young Victoria chatted with Prince Albert. On other occasions, he prowled through her private apartments and rummaged through her private belongings – once being caught red-handed with several pairs of the monarch's voluminous knickers. He also claimed to have sat on the throne, read books in the royal library, napped on a servant's bed, read the Queen's personal letters, eaten in the kitchen and explored the drawing room.

In *Queen Victoria's Stalker: The Strange Story of the Boy Jones* by Jan Bondeson, the author details one entry from the Queen's journal, after Boy Jones' first incursion: 'But supposing he had come into the Bedroom, how frightened I should have been.'

Authorities came down hard on the young lad each time he was caught, but his obsession showed no signs of abating. What was worse was that all the Queen's guards couldn't seem to keep him out of the palace, no matter what security measures were put in place.

He was found not guilty of theft in open court after his first break-in in December 1838, but did not get off quite so lightly the following times.

Wary of causing the monarch further embarrassment, the next time Jones was caught, the government decided that the boy should be tried in secret. He would appear in front of the Home Office and be sentenced by the privy council, in a process rarely used since Tudor times. They sentenced Jones to imprisonment twice, in December 1840 and again in March 1841, where he was forced to do hard labour.

The final time, authorities had had enough, and deported Boy Jones to Australia – not before journalists of the day had managed to interview him about his exploits. For a brief time, Jones became famous in his own right and his summary deportation drew criticism from no lesser figure than Charles Dickens.

Boy Jones initially settled in Perth, Western Australia, where he found work as a pie seller, but later moved to Melbourne to reside with his brother. He became an alcoholic and died on Boxing Day, 1893, when he fell off a bridge while drunk and landed on his head. 'Boy' was then aged in his seventies.

# Stars in Their Sights

While stalkers have doubtless been around since a disturbed caveman first stalked a cavewoman through the forest before clubbing her over the head and carrying her back to his cave, it is only relatively recently that the phenomenon has been recognised as being a serious social, psychological and now criminal problem.

It's hard to believe given how familiar the term is now, but 'stalking' really only entered popular parlance in 1989. Even then it was generally used to describe star stalkers – those who were obsessed with celebrities, and persistently followed and harassed them. The murder of Rebecca Schaeffer, in 1989, was possibly the first celebrity stalking murder, and the event that really brought this issue into the spotlight. (You can hear about the dreadful fate that befell Rebecca Schaeffer later in this chapter ...) And stalking is not alone in being a relatively new concept – think too of child sexual abuse (swept under the carpet for far too long), road rage, and also bullying ...

So if you've ever wondered what Hugh Jackman, Steven Speilberg, Leonardo DiCaprio, Sophie Monk, AFL footballer Alex Rance, Madonna and John Lennon might have in common, the answer is a stalker. (Not the same one, of course.) Even the actor who played Agro, the Australian children's TV character had a particularly persistent one.

Other public figures are common prey for stalkers too, from presidents and prime ministers to business leaders and even the Queen of England as discussed previously. Indeed, one study carried out in the Netherlands in 2002 discovered that a third of people in the public eye had been stalked.[19] TV celebrities in Germany have it even worse, with another study finding that a staggering 79 per cent of their TV personalities had been stalked at some stage, with many having *more than one* stalker at any one time.[20] It seems that a public identity attracts stalkers like pins to a magnet.

★★★

So what is the precise appeal of the celebrity or the public figure to the stalker? In their seminal book on *Stalkers and Their Victims* (Cambridge University Press, 2009), Mullen, Purcell and Pathé explain 'Public figures attract the unwanted attentions of both those who are seeking intimacy and those who are expressing resentment, as well as a mixed bag of publicity seekers, predators, and general pests.'

James McCabe, who stalked Sophie Monk for years, started out as an intimacy-seeking stalker, and swiftly moved to become resentful when she failed to respond to his overtures.

Sophie Monk was born in 1979 in England and is today an Australian-based singer, model and actress. A member of the girl group Bardot, she also released a solo album called *Calendar Girl* in 2003, and appeared in films such as *Date Movie* (2006), *Click* (2006), and *Spring Breakdown* (2009). Her Wikipaedia entry notes that she was the first Australian celebrity to have a cyberstalker charged with, and later convicted of, harassing her on social media.

McCabe, then 30, of Tasmania was arrested in December 2013 for bombarding the actress with up to 150 sexually explicit and threatening Twitter posts a day. He also spoke of 'saving' Monk during one particularly nasty sexual tweet. In many of these rambling and nonsensical messages, he claimed that he followed Satan, and instructed Monk to 'Pray, pray, pray.'

In an interview on Fox FM's Matt and Jo Show on 29 June 2011, Monk told the hosts that when she was in Australia, she was so scared that she slept with the light on. She also revealed that she had not blocked her Facebook stalker, because 'he might come and murder me'.

'I don't know what else to do, especially when you're scared like that,' she said. 'I'd rather know what's going on. Keep your enemies close rather than far away.'

She said the police would not intervene. 'I've been down to the police station because it's got really scary and the police here [in LA] don't do anything about it so instead I take it in my own hands and start speaking back to him,' she said. 'There's nothing you can do until you turn up hurt.'

The harassment intensified when she returned home to live in Australia after a period of time spent living in California. Monk finally contacted police after McCabe made death threats towards her and another family member.

Australian police charged McCabe with cyberstalking, and despite removing his phone and his massive collection of personal recordings of Monk singing, the harassment continued. In a later interview with reporters, McCabe said, 'I have followed her since *Popstars*. When I first saw her, I was a drug addict and she just stood out. I thought she was this regular girl who had turned her life around and I wanted to do the same.' He added that he had never actually met the singer/actor.

McCabe originally pleaded not guilty, but later, in the Magistrates' Court in Launceston, admitted stalking the celebrity by sending her threatening, offensive and sexually explicit messages on social media. Alan Hensley, for the defence, said that his client had schizophrenia and was under the influence of ice at the time of the offences, which occurred between January 2010 and December 2013. In May 2015, McCabe was sentenced to eight months in prison, wholly suspended for two years (which means he may not be jailed). An indefinite restraining order was also imposed, banning McCabe from contacting Monk in any way, publishing anything about her or approaching within 200 metres of anywhere she lives or works.

***

Margaret Mary Ray was another stalker who suffered from schizophrenia – as well as erotomania – which is doubtless what drove her obsession with the ageing American talk show host David Letterman. Her pursuit of the household name started in the late 1980s and lasted for 10 years, but while Letterman made use of his stalker as comic fodder on his show, the reality was far less amusing.

Ray's stalking first came to public attention in 1988 when she was caught taking Letterman's Porsche for a joyride … with her toddler son along for the trip too. The woman was caught when she refused to pay a $3 toll at the New York Lincoln Tunnel. Sprung by the attendant, she claimed that Letterman was her husband and that her son was actually *their* son. The incident hit the headlines.

What was made less public was the fact that over the next 10 years, Ray would trespass on Letterman's property time and time again, being arrested eight times in total and once even spending the night sleeping on his tennis court. She was imprisoned for nearly a year, and spent another year in a psychiatric hospital after being convicted of stalking. On her release, she swapped her obsession over to the retired astronaut Story Musgrave.

NASA had selected Musgrave, a surgeon, as a scientist astronaut in 1967. During a career that spanned more than 1281 hours in space, he logged a record 278 orbits of Earth, and flew aboard the space shuttle *Columbia* in 1996.

Ray spent four years harassing Musgrave by calling, writing and sending him packages. Then in late September 1997, she was found outside his Kissimmee home. Sheriff reports stated, 'She began banging on the front door at approximately 5.30 a.m. and then went around the house turning on all the water faucets.'

Ray was charged with stalking, a misdemeanour punishable by a jail term up to one year. The *Orlando Sentinel* reported on 26 September 1997 that in an interview with investigators at the

Osceola County Jail, Ray said, 'I love him and want to spend the rest of my life with him.' The paper reported:

> Dripping wet and dressed in six layers of clothing including various skirts and tights, Ray identified herself as a freelance journalist who travels across the country 12 months of the year, deputies said.
>
> Ray said she flew into Orlando last night and walked about 20 miles, half the distance from Orlando International Airport to Musgrave's home.
>
> 'On September 20, 1997, an article about Mr. Musgrave ran in The Orlando Sentinel,' sheriff's reports state. 'Since then, this female has called Mr. Musgrave's new residence every night, often waking him up in the early hours of the morning.'
>
> This was Ray's first visit to Kissimmee, investigators said.

In the interview, Ray claimed to have interviewed Dr Musgrave in 1994 at the Houston Space Center, and that he asked whether she would like to help him write an autobiography called *Conversations with Story Musgrave*. She said that she had initially looked for Musgrave at his Houston home before learning from a private detective that he had moved to Kissimmee. Her reason for trying to track him down? She was hoping to spend some time with him, and she was very concerned about the state of his mental and physical health. (Excellent line, coming from her ...)

Oddly enough, the phone number she gave police actually belonged to the Secret Service Uniformed Control Center at the White House in Washington. In a worrying statement, she also told police, 'My purse is in the woods by Story's house, and I will go back and get it when I get out of jail.'

Before her court appearance, a veritable alphabet soup of news organisations – CNN, ABC, NBC, AP and more – turned up at the jail to interview the stalker, whose celebrity was almost starting to mirror that of her victims. She was clearly unbalanced though, alternating between rage and flirtatiousness, and displaying intimate knowledge of details of Musgrave's life. At one point she refused to let a photographer take her picture. The *Orlando Sentinel* reported:

> 'If you looked like I am right now and had on these kinds of clothes, and you hadn't had coffee, a cigarette, or a fresh piece of fruit, would you want your photo taken?' she barked …
>
> … As to why she had drifted from Letterman, a comic, to Musgrave, a space traveler, Ray ended her long day of interviews by saying: 'Men of immeasurable intellect in this day and age are a very rare breed, and I gravitate to them naturally.'

But first there was the small matter of a trial to get through. Representing herself, she yelled wildly, screamed at the judge to 'Get it over with, Roger!', had to be restrained and was forced to wear a beekeeper's hat to prevent her from spitting on anyone. Unsurprisingly, Circuit Judge Roger McDonald sent her to a mental hospital.

Five months later she was back in court again, and was judged competent to stand trial on the charges of stalking. McDonald eventually sentenced Ray to 246 days in jail after she pleaded guilty, but had to let Ray go after giving her credit for jail time she had already served. McDonald urged her to continue taking her medication, and lamented that there was no legal way to place her under lifelong supervision for her mental illness.

She committed suicide just one year later, in 1998, by kneeling in front of a freight train in the small Colorado town of Hotchkiss. She was 46 at the time, and left five children aged in their teens and twenties.

## The Power of Media

Media figures – including radio and TV hosts like Letterman – make compelling targets for stalkers. Listeners and viewers can bring them into the intimacy of their own home, purely by turning on the radio or the TV, which can make them feel that they have a personal connection to someone they have never met – and are unlikely to meet – in real life.

But what happens when admiration and adoration turn into something more sinister? I've heard many stories from presenters and even producers who have been targeted in this way, including one TV arts presenter on Channel 31, who picked up a random nutter who became obsessed with her appearance and constantly wrote in with suggestions for more flattering colours and outfits. And displayed a worrying knowledge of where her children went to school. Meanwhile, a young male radio producer at the ABC, who was responsible for handling callers for a talkback radio program, spent months being pursued by a particularly persistent and obscene female listener.

Radio presenter and writer Helen Razer basically left her dream broadcasting role because of her own stalker. Razer was a well-known and outspoken radio broadcaster on national Australian youth station Triple J from 1990 to 1998, spending most her time there on the breakfast program with comedian Mikey Robins.

In an article, written for the website Mamamia about the bullying of Charlotte Dawson (posted online on 3 September 2012, prior to Dawson's death in 2014), Razer admitted that she (Razer) was probably 'annoying, under-informed and over-exposed' during her time at Triple J. However, she certainly didn't appreciate receiving a jar of urine through the mail, with a note telling her to 'Die Slut'. She didn't appreciate men yelling comments about her rape-ability. And she certainly didn't appreciate being stalked by a stranger for many, many months.

Suffering from the delusion that Razer was his wife, whom he had wed in a ceremony at a 'special place', the man lurked in and around her office, waiting for any opportunity to get close to her. He was committed to a psychiatric unit, but had a long history of escaping and soon enough busted out. He lied his way into Razer's studio again and physically embraced her. Whereupon Razer 'lost her shit', as she later described it.

In her 2001 autobiographical book, *Gas Smells Awful: The Mechanics of Being a Nutcase*, Razer accused the ABC of failing to protect her from the delusional male listener. Razer left the station not long afterwards. One of her regrets about the whole incident was following the oft-given advice of well-meaning individuals to just ignore it. Razer said in the Mamamia article:

> For months, acting on advice, I ignored the stalker. Thanks to my studied ignorance, two things happened: First, I wound myself into a knot of fear from which it would take years to unfurl. Second, the police were annoyed that I'd let the situation fester.

Sammy Power, co-host of Sydney's Mix 106.5 (now KIIS 106.5 FM) breakfast show back in 2005, had a similar experience with a delusional listener. It all began with letters, and then phone calls and flowers, and later even cheques to pay her bills – which were politely returned. Then the 65-year-old man began waiting outside the Australian Radio Network's studios in North Ryde as she arrived for work before dawn.

The problem escalated midyear when the man shifted his attention to a secretary at the station. In a strange twist, he then tried to take *Power* to court claiming she was harassing him and trying to block his relationship with the secretary. Both women successfully obtained court orders preventing the man from making contact for two years.

***

Award-winning radio announcer Jamie Dunn was another unlikely victim of an unlikely stalker. Best known for playing popular TV character Agro, a role for which he won several Logie Awards during the show's run between 1989 and 1997 on Channel Seven, he was also part of a breakfast show on Brisbane radio for 15 years. Like many in the public eye, particularly those on our airwaves or TV screens, Dunn fielded his fair share of hate mail, emails and Facebook trolls. Then he discovered that all the nasty messages he'd received over the previous two years were originating from the one person. He told *A Current Affair* on Channel Nine in an interview that aired on 7 October 2014:

> When someone's gone to the trouble of cutting out certain words and sticking them to a piece of paper and then jamming it in your letterbox, two or three things go through your mind. One's they've had a sharp implement, two they know exactly where you live, three they've been to where you live and they are watching now.
>
> For the first year it started as abusive and you know, sort of just name calling and occasionally quoting my children. At the end of the year – I'd kept them all on file – and the file was (that) thick.

He had no idea why the stalker was targeting him – why they could be bothered to send thousands of emails to his private address, including vicious personal comments about him and his private life. When the stalker was in full spate, Dunn was receiving up to 50 emails a day.

And then the stalker started reaching out to others too, contacting his friends, and family and work colleagues with emails accusing him of all sorts of horrors. The emails were even sent to outsiders, including a winery that was warned that Dunn was attending a concert there and that his car was likely to explode. Dunn also received a phone call from a jeweller, saying that the

$6000 engagement ring he'd ordered had now arrived. Dunn had to explain that it was a fake order. Just as he had to explain to the organisers of a charity fundraiser that no, he hadn't volunteered to make a surprise $2000 donation.

However, it was only when his children were threatened and his then 22-year-old daughter, Stella, was reduced to tears that Dunn went to the police. His stalker was identified and turned out to be Jacqueline Janine Draper, 46 at the time, a journalist and mother who had met Dunn professionally on a number of occasions.

Draper was charged with one stalking offence and 16 counts of using a carriage service to menace, harass or cause offence, before pleading guilty to two charges. She was found guilty, fined $1000 and put on a two-year good behaviour bond, with no conviction recorded. Magistrate Jennifer Batts also put Draper on a two-year restraining order, barring her from going near or contacting Dunn and his family.

Dunn was not happy with the result, telling *A Current Affair* that being stalked and threatened is like being in a natural disaster: 'You have no control over it. It's like an earthquake. If you've been through an earthquake, everything around you moves and all of a sudden you go, "I have no control over this."'

In a bizarre twist to the end of the case, just months after pleading guilty in the Caboolture Magistrates Court to the charges, Jacqueline Draper received an award for being an inspiring woman. Draper, of Neurum near Woodford, was named the 2014 Glass House Inspiring Woman by the Member for Glass House, Andrew Powell. The stalker, also sometimes known as Jackie Cochran, was given the accolade for her community work, including setting up a local newspaper and sponsoring local school awards. The award was presented to celebrate International Women's Day, with the theme being Women of Generosity. I doubt Dunn would agree.

***

It's not only radio personalities who can attract unwanted attention from their audience. Australian TV presenters Allison Langdon, Sandra Sully, Ross Symonds, Liz Hayes and Peter Luck have all had high-profile battles with stalkers.

Sully was traumatised by an incident in November 1997 when she was pistol-whipped by a hooded man in the car park of her Surry Hills apartment in inner Sydney. It was not known how long the man had been watching her, but she was arriving home after finishing a late shift at Channel 10, so basically any viewer could have followed her on an earlier occasion before lying in wait that particular night.

Her attacker, who earlier had been seen loitering near her building, wielded a silver coloured handgun and struck her twice on the head. She screamed and he ran away, dumping a black balaclava and handcuffs that were later found down the street from the scene of the attack.

And while the assumption is that it is usually young, attractive and vulnerable females who attract the attention of predators, six foot four Melbourne AFL legend and now media personality David Schwarz – also known as the Ox – spent years constantly looking over his shoulder, and feared for the safety of his family after being targeted by a serial stalker. His ordeal began in 2009, when the man – a regular caller to Schwarz's show on SEN radio – was banned for becoming enraged and threatening to kill one of the show's producers. (All 'Brad from Eltham' wanted, apparently, was the chance to air his opinion of Mark 'Bomber' Thompson.) Schwarz himself then became the target of the man's frustrations, when he did not supply free tickets to a charity golf game the stalker wanted to attend.

Now it can be disappointing to miss out on a good freebie, but this man took his frustration to extremes, sending repeated death threats via phone calls and SMS, and sending packages from a betting agency to Schwarz's home address. This was a particularly nasty stunt, given that Schwarz had overcome a gambling addiction, and the appearance of the material must have concerned his wife and family to say the very least. His car was also vandalised inside the SEN car park.

The death threats were also particularly distressing for Schwarz, whose father had been murdered after a series of what had been assumed were idle threats. David was just eight years of age at the time, and asleep in the bed next to his father. It left him distressed for years, and he told the *Herald Sun* (7 August 2012) that until the age of 17, he was always expecting someone to come through the window at night. Being targeted by a stalker must have been the fulfilment of all those childhood nightmares – no matter his size or age or achievements or celebrity.

The last straw came when the stalker – later publicly named as Steven Robert Elworthy, of Turtur Close, Mill Park – rang a rival radio station to claim that Schwarz had been seen having a punt on the football from a golf course.

Schwarz told the *Herald Sun*, 'It added stress to my wife. I had to justify myself [about the betting accusations] and it was just rubbish. It upset me and my wife to the point where we put surveillance on our house.'

A court ordered a two-year ban on Elworthy entering the premises or contacting any SEN staff and said that he must also remain a particular distance away from Schwarz and his wife. Elworthy was not present in court, but agreed by fax to the conditions of the court order. However, despite this, Elworthy, then aged 38 and a married father of one, continued to harass the Ox by mobile phone, calling him 155 times between October and June the following year. In an interview with *Today Tonight*, Schwarz said the stalker would ring every hour on the hour, starting at 10 p.m. at night – disrupting his and his family's sleep for nearly nine months. At the height of the harassment, Schwarz could receive up to 20 calls in 20 minutes.

Police charged Elworthy with criminal stalking and contravening a personal safety order. In November 2012, he was found guilty and sentenced to six months in prison. His name has not hit the headlines again, as far as I can tell, so perhaps no news is good news.

***

It is part of human nature to want to belong to a group or tribe. And this is the motivation behind gang stalking – sometimes also described as cause stalking. But while gang stalking is the stalking of an individual for any reason – he has red hair, she dissed one of our friends, we just hate you – cause stalking is more usually related to the stalker's disapproval of the victim's lifestyle, political stance or moral belief system.

Cause stalkers *can* operate as part of a gang – as in the case of the divorced fathers who join forces with another man to harass women who have had the audacity to leave or simply seek child support from 'the victim'. Cause stalkers can also operate as individuals, but either way cause stalking is generally a witch-hunt ... hopefully bar the ritual burning at the stake or deathly immersion in a local pond.

Most developed countries have laws and social mores that encourage people to accept that others may have different lifestyles, political affiliations and belief systems; however, your average cause stalker isn't so tolerant. The cause stalker believes that anyone who doesn't follow the same religion or share the same political and social beliefs is fair game. They'll go to any lengths to try to shame their victim or change their mind.

Well known examples of cause stalking include those who harass or even murder abortion doctors, those who stake out of Family Planning or Planned Parenthood Centres, those who stalk politicians who don't share the same political ideologies and also the harassment of Jews or Muslims, hippies, anti-war protesters or war enthusiasts, climate change deniers or climate change sceptics, feminists ... hell, if you believe strongly in almost anything, it seems, you could be prey for a cause stalker.

Cause stalking can be a particular problem for politicians who are, after all, generally elected on their ability to push for particular causes. But while politicians probably rate below journalists and used car salespeople on the trust scale, no one, *no one*, ever deserves a stalker.

The very existence of Hobsons Bay ex-mayor, councillor and LGBTI (lesbian, gay, bi, trans and intersex) advocate, Tony Briffa, was probably enough to set one cause stalker off. Not only was Briffa a politician, but also the world's first intersex mayor.

For 18 months, Briffa was constantly abused and threatened by email, via the council offices, and the official Facebook page. Most of the comments were vicious, homophobic, transphobic and threatening. Comments on Facebook in particular centred around Briffa's genetic intersex condition, sexual orientation and gender identity. (To make a teeny confession here, I'm finding it difficult to write about Briffa without saying 'he' or 'she', but for me that is a grammar challenge, not a challenge to whether someone has a right to exist or live without being threatened.)

Briffa, on the other hand, received calls that were so abusive that the mayor's safety both at public events and council meeting became a very real concern for both the council and Briffa. Personal protection strategies were put in place, and at the Sunshine Magistrate's Court, in the state of Victoria, two orders ended up being made against the male perpetrator. The second five-year intervention order made it illegal for the man to come within 200 metres of Briffa until midnight on 2 April 2018. The stalker was also forbidden from having any communication with Briffa, from publishing anything online or getting anyone else to do something against the councillor.

In an interview following the verdict, Briffa said, 'I am elated and relieved the Magistrates' Court issued an intervention order to protect me from a person that has been harassing and stalking me for the last 18 months.'

An ambassador for the No To Homophobia campaign, Briffa

advised anyone else who was experiencing stalking, bullying or persecution because of their sexuality to speak out and get help:

> In his calls, the accused made many homophobic and transphobic comments and threatened to 'get me'. No one should put up with that sort of inappropriate behaviour. There is no place for homophobia in society and the decision of court today shows people can do something about it.

In prepared statements, Briffa thanked officers from the Victorian Police Force for their help, giving particular accolades to the Gay and Lesbian Liaison Officers who had been very supportive throughout the process and had seen the matter through to its final resolution in court.

## Only in Hollywood

On the sliding scale of celebrity, there's no doubt that Hollywood stars and musicians are at the pinnacle – usually well ahead of radio and TV stars, politicians, other public figures and, ahem, lowly true crime authors. Celebrity stalkers may seem like harmless nut jobs on the evening news, especially when public figures such as David Letterman use their own stalkers as grist for their comedy mill. But the truth behind the canned laughter is the reality that obsessed fans can be deadly annoying at the very least, or deadly at the very worst.

It's kind of tempting to think that anyone who earns gazillions of dollars per year should be prepared for the possibility of being stalked. But all the money in the world can't necessarily provide a magical cone of protection against constant emails and phone calls or people loitering outside your house. Money also can't protect you against those with more sinister intent – who are prepared to track your every move with only one end in mind – your death.

Some of course, are not planning anything more sinister than a chat with their idol, but who can ever be truly sure? Just a quick flick around the internet shows just how many celebrities are being stalked. Just for starters, Rihanna's stalker, Robert Melanson, was sentenced to six days in jail and three years' probation (plus a year of mental health treatment) after having been found creeping round on the roof of her Los Angeles home. Melanson was ordered to stay at least 100 yards (91 metres) away from her house and/or place of business.

Meanwhile Mila Kunis was confronted by Stuart Dunn, 27, at her West Hollywood gym after he tracked her to the site on a number of occasions. Dunn had already been arrested three times by police, and had been ordered to keep his distance from Kunis after an earlier break-in at her house.

Justin Timberlake too had troubles at home, after a 48-year-old woman, Karen McNeil, was caught lurking around his Hollywood home for the third time. It was reported that the 'heavyset' stalker trespassed onto Timberlake's property, tried to gain access into his home, and bizarrely even claimed to be friends with the singer – a friendship that seems highly unlikely under the best of circumstances. She must now stay at least 100 yards away from the singer.

Religious nutters have their place in celebrity stalker land too, with Zack Sinclair being sentenced to three years in prison for stalking Mel Gibson. In court, Sinclair claimed that he had been instructed by God to pray with Gibson, and that was all he was attempting to do.

And then there are the just plain nutters, of whom Diana Napolis is possibly the most completely batshit crazy. Also found on the internet under the curious name of Karen 'Curio' Jones, Napolis started out as a therapist, but hit the big time in 2001 when she accused Steven Spielberg of running a satanic cult from his Malibu basement. Apparently he had also implanted a microchip 'soul-catcher' into her brain and now had control over her mind. On being ordered to stay away from him, she turned her attentions to Jennifer Love Hewitt, who was apparently also part of the same cult – and was also using 'psychotronic weaponry'. The two were just a tiny part of a vast satanic conspiracy designed to cover up widespread ritual abuse. Napolis said in her blog:

> There were attempts by some to impact the bioenergetic fields around the human body and interior to the body and that the utter destruction of these fields results, ultimately, in complete technological possession [...] but various cult organisations have other agendas which include unique abuses personal to their own religious persuasion such as destroying the Chakra system and the actual astral body of the target.

Napolis failed to produce any evidence of this, and the court remained unconvinced, sentencing her to probation and mental health treatment. After threatening letters and emails and several frightening confrontations on the red carpet – most notably at the Latin Grammies, where Napolis screamed out, 'Murderer! Killer! Skankhole, you are killing me!' – she was committed to a state hospital, and barred from any contact with the actress or her family for 10 years. The presiding judge warned her to stay on her medications. Yet if one views the lunatic ramblings on her blog, she did not heed the advice.

## The Pursuit of Love

Uma Thurman may have busted a few killer moves in the 2003 movie *Kill Bill*, but she probably didn't realise that this starring role would also garner her the nasty attentions of Jack Jordan, a man who was first convicted in 2008 of persistently trying to contact the actress.

In the first court case related to his stalking of Thurman, Jordan confessed to having become obsessed with her when he saw her in the 1988 movie *The Adventures of Baron Munchausen*. His feelings for her only intensified when she appeared in director Quentin Tarantino's *Kill Bill*.

After being convicted in 2008 (for stalking the actress between 2005 and 2007), Jordan was sentenced to three years' probation and instructed not to have any contact with the Hollywood star for five years. He couldn't resist though and in 2009 was rearrested after calling Uma Thurman's mobile and office, in clear violation of the restraining order against him. Indeed, when police turned up to arrest him, he was sitting in front of a computer conducting a Google search on Thurman's name.

Jack Jordan had an English degree from the University of Chicago, and had worked as both a lifeguard and pool cleaner. He also had a complicated mental health history, and had been sectioned to a mental hospital after his first trial for stalking Thurman. He said at trial that his intention for pursuing Thurman was to develop a relationship with her, a futile quest for romance he shared with Richard Brittain, a stalker whose experiences are detailed on page 230. Jordan admitted at trial that he had 'overstepped' legal boundaries.

Thurman testified that she had been completely freaked out by his behaviour, and no wonder. Jordan had sent the star many weird letters and cards – some showing menacing images such as a decapitated bride. Jordan had also showed up on the doorstep of her Manhattan home and had repeatedly called her family – telling her mother, Nena, that he had met her daughter in a previous life and they were destined to be together. He said he believed the star would only be happy if they were together, and that his hands should be on her body 'at all times'. He told Thurman's parents that if he wasn't allowed to see her he would kill himself. He also attempted to bust into her trailer on the movie set of *My Super Ex-Girlfriend*, which Thurman had been filming at the time.

\*\*\*

Others resort to more unusual strategies to win the attention of the stars they love – or are deluded into thinking they love. In 2002, Japanese citizen Masahiko Shizawa was deported from the US after stalking Britney Spears by trying to gain her affections with a steady stream of gifts – sex toys, to be precise – which he sent through the mail. He also bombarded her with love letters, emails and pictures of himself, together with messages like 'I'm chasing you'. A restraining order was issued, but Shizawa continued to stake out Britney's two houses, as well as her parents' home, trying to gain entry wherever he could. After one confrontation with Britney's bodyguards, Shizawa changed tack, deciding to sue Spears for the emotional distress her protectors had caused him by pointing a gun at him. That case was rapidly thrown out of court.

Gifts were also used as a ploy by pizza delivery boy Dante Michael Soiu, who persistently stalked Gwyneth Paltrow back in 2000. At the height of his campaign, she would receive five letters a day from the stalker, often accompanied by flowers, chocolates, pornography and pizza (free pizza may have been a perk of his job). Like many stalkers, he had also tried to get to Paltrow by going to the home of her parents. Soiu was declared legally insane at his trial and was sentenced to indefinite detention in a high-security psychiatric hospital in California.

Even more outrageous was William Lepeska, who became besotted with the tennis star Anna Kournikova. His attempt to get close to her started with him stripping naked, then swimming across Biscayne Bay to her house, climbing up onto the deck and yelling, 'Anna, save me!' The only flaw in the plan was the fact that he had the wrong deck and the wrong house. The doubtless startled owners called the police, who promptly arrested him and sent him to a psychiatric institution.

Paula Goodspeed was Paula Abdul's Number One Fan. Born Sandra May McIntyre, Goodspeed was so obsessed with the singer and choreographer that she changed her name to Paula in homage, and fashioned her modelling, singing, appearance and dress sense on her idol.

In 2005, Paula actually got to meet Paula, when stalker Paula auditioned in front of Abdul for *American Idol*. In an interview with Barbara Walters on *Barbara Live!* in December 2008, Abdul explained that Paula had been writing 'disturbing letters' to her for 17 years, restraining orders had been taken out at various times, and that she had begged producers not to let 'Paula' audition, but to no avail. In the event, the judges were less than complimentary about the aspiring singer's talent and she missed out on a spot. Three years later Paula Goodspeed took her own life by overdosing on prescription pills. She was in her car, parked outside Abdul's home. The licence plate was 'ABL LV' and a photo of Abdul was found inside the car.

★★★

Lest we forget the men, Alec Baldwin too was put under surveillance by an erstwhile colleague he'd met on the set of the 2002 film *The Adventures of Pluto Nash*. Baldwin had a small role, while Genevieve Sabourin, a French-Canadian actress, was at that stage working in the PR department.

In 2010, the two caught up for dinner, at the behest of a mutual friend, Baldwin told the court. The actor said under oath he'd never had sex with Sabourin, but had given her his phone number and email address, so she could contact him about some acting classes she planned to take.

Sabourin's story was rather different: she claimed that the two had had 'an after hours' party back in her hotel room after dinner, and when the actor later gave her the cold shoulder, she merely wanted to find out what was going on. However, Sabourin's behaviour swiftly became more *Fatal Attraction* in intent, as she began bombarding him with up to 30 voicemails a night, and hundreds of emails, hoping to develop a relationship with him.

Prosecutor Zachary Stendig read a few of the more salacious passages in open court, which were widely reported in the press. Many openly advertised her skills in the sack, and her hopes of having a 'mini-Baldwin'.

Some of Sabourin's messages:

I will be in prime of my ovulation this St. Patrick's Day and the best gift from you of all would be to conceive a mini Baldwin on this Ireland National Day ... accept my proposal and I'll take you straight to heaven. There is [sic] many things I will do to you now in order to give you all kinds of delightful pleasure. French are the best lovers in the world and I master my art.

I am less than 10 minutes away from you tonight. Say 'I do' to me.

Will you accept this simple proposal from my heart??

Let's began [sic] the best part of our life right here and today.

I know you want it, I know you need it.

Please, answer me.

It continued to get worse, a teary Baldwin testified, with the obsessed wannabe actress threatening to show up at his home, and even to join a yoga class that was being run by his now-wife, Hilaria Baldwin. Sabourin was finally arrested outside the then 55-year-old actor's home on 8 April 2012.

In November 2013, Sabourin, then aged 41, was sentenced to 210 days in prison for various charges relating to the stalking of Baldwin, as well as for contempt of court after creating a disturbance while her emails were being read out. 'Your relentless and escalating campaign of threats and in-person appearances in private spaces served at a minimum to harass, annoy and alarm Mr Baldwin,' Manhattan Criminal Court Judge Robert Mandelbaum said in court before finding her guilty on all counts, including harassment, aggravated harassment, stalking, and attempted criminal contempt, according to the *New York Daily News* (14 November 2013).

But not even prison could dampen her ardour it seems. Fresh out of jail, in an interview with the online news website *Radar* on 7 May 2014, Sabourin told the reporter she wanted to meet up with Baldwin one last time: 'I don't have his side of the story, so I feel like I don't have the full truth. I wanted to understand his side. On my quest for closure, I want to understand why he did this to me.'

She also admitted to *Radar* that her obsession had cost her dearly: 'The truth is I lost my house, my savings, my retirement plan, my job, [and] my friends. I lost everything.'

Just months after Sabourin was released from Riker's Island, it became clear that she was still hoping for that meeting, being spotted lurking outside Baldwin's Greenwich Village home, despite a no-contact order that prohibits her from going anywhere near Baldwin and his family.

## Threat Vector

Celebrity stalkers may seem harmless, but remember John Hinckley Jr, who became obsessed with then teenage actress Jodie Foster's performance in *Taxi Driver* and began stalking her? On 30 March 1981, after he had dismally failed to win her love by any other means, Hinckley shot President Ronald Reagan six times as he was leaving a Hilton Hotel in Washington, DC. In a way it was a bizarre homage to his favourite film and actress, mimicking the plot of *Taxi Driver* where the main character, Travis Bickle, tries to assassinate a presidential candidate. In a letter written to Foster, Hinckley stated, 'The reason I'm going ahead with this attempt [on the president's life] now is because I cannot wait any longer to impress you.' Whatever happened to chocolates and flowers?

Think too of Monica Seles, who in 1993 was stabbed by Gunther Parche during a match in Hamburg, Germany. Parche was a deranged fan of German star Steffi Graf and thought that he could help his favourite player by taking out her biggest rival. The 13-centimetre blade of a serrated steak knife would put the 19-year-old, No. 1-ranked Seles out of the quarterfinals of the Citizen Cup, and out of tennis completely for the next two years. (It wasn't the injuries, which consisted of a 2.5-centimetre cut to muscle tissue in her back, but missed the lungs and spinal cord, but the emotional trauma that kept her out of the game way past the physical recovery time.)

Take also, for example, the case of Dawnette Knight, a stalker obsessed with Hollywood heavyweight Michael Douglas and determined to do anything she could to get rid of her love rival, Douglas's wife, Welsh actress Catherine Zeta-Jones.

Dawnette claimed that she and Michael Douglas had pursued a secret relationship and that the Hollywood star had paid her off to keep quiet. Not quiet enough, clearly, with Knight writing 19 letters to his famous wife between 2003 and 2004, most of which included threats to kill her: 'We are going to slice her up like meat on a bone and feed her to the dogs' read one lovely missive. Knight also shared her plans to chop the Welsh beauty into pieces, just 'like Sharon Tate was'.

Zeta-Jones testified at the trial that she nearly suffered a nervous breakdown because of the threats, and read aloud a statement that said, 'Your actions will be with me the rest of my life – now I will be constantly observing, looking over my shoulder.' She also said, 'You will never be famous, you will never be infamous, you are just a criminal.' Ouch. Knight was finally sentenced to three years in prison.

***

In all these cases, the stalkers turned their rage onto an external target, a third party, but in other instances, when stalkers are rejected – either intentionally or not – they may end up directly threatening the object of their obsessional love. Even Jerry Lewis, the beloved American comedian who also became a cult hero in France, had a stalker. Gary Randolph Benson was imprisoned after showing up at Lewis's Las Vegas home armed with a pistol. In 2000, he had sent the star a letter reading, 'Dear Jerry. Your [sic] Dead. Your friend, Gary Benson.' Benson had already served six years for stalking Lewis, and had been released from prison just months before sending the death threat.

But Benson was to escape further sentencing. His trial was delayed when a judge ordered a psychiatric evaluation of the diagnosed schizophrenic. Before it could take place, however, the 57-year-old man died in his sleep in the early hours of the morning at the Clark County Detention Center.

Mental illness is a common theme among stalkers, particularly celebrity stalkers it seems, as is shown by the case of British man, Bassey Essien, who convinced himself that the real Beyonce had been killed by an imposter, who was now living the megastar's life. Essien began sending threatening letters to the singer, calling her out for being 'a fraud'. Beyonce was first targeted by the man when he met her at a function in London back in 2009 where he tried to give her a book of notes he had made about religion. She eventually won a restraining order against the fan in 2013.

***

It's hard to resist the temptation to drop a 'pubic nuisance' or 'pubic enemy number one' pun into this story, but Hugh Jackman's stalker, who threw a razor filled with her pubic hair at the actor, was rather more serious in her intentions.

On 13 April 2013, 46-year-old Katherine Thurston accosted the *X-Men* star at Gotham Gym, which he was visiting. She ran past the front desk at the gym, before assaulting the actor, screaming that she loved him and then pulling an electric razor filled with pubic hair from her waistband and flinging it at Hugh Jackman. (Jackman reportedly assumed that the woman had been going for a weapon rather than a pube-filled electric razor.) A trainer and security staff intervened and Thurston fled, only to be arrested a few streets away. The address she gave to the arresting officers was a homeless shelter in Harlem for people with mental illness.

She was transferred to Rikers Island in lieu of $7500 bail, and ordered to undergo psychiatric evaluation. Jackman gave a statement to the press, saying, 'Here's a woman who obviously needs help so I just hope she gets the help she needs.'

Kind words from a man who had been stalked by Thurston in the past – he had even seen the woman outside his then seven-year-old daughter's primary school in Manhattan and also outside his home in the West Village, where he lives with his wife, Deborra-Lee Furness. (Some press reports also claimed that Thurston had told Furness that she was going to 'marry your husband'.)

Thurston was initially found not fit to proceed to trial by Manhattan Supreme Court Justice Maxwell Wiley, and spent six months in a psychiatric institution before facing court. She was eventually sentenced to six months' time served and five years of probation. During this time, Katherine Thurston must stay away from Jackman and his family and must continue mental health treatment. The press reported that she was going to fly to California to stay with her daughter.

## Marriage on Their Minds

In 2010, Jennifer Aniston was granted a three-year restraining order against a delusional stalker who carved 'I LOVE YOU JENNIFER ANISTON' into the bonnet and side of his car and drove from Pennsylvania to Los Angeles on his quest to marry her. Jason R Peyton's father found a worrying note after he left, and alerted police that his son was on his way to try and meet the star, best known for her role in the hit TV comedy *Friends*.

Police picked Peyton up after he had spent eight days trying to find the *Friends* star on Sunset Boulevard. When he was taken into custody, he was carrying a sharp object, duct tape and love notes addressed to Aniston.

A temporary order was immediately put into place with court documents at the time stating Peyton was 'an obsessed, mentally ill and delusional stalker, with a history of violence and criminal stalking, who drove cross-country in his delusional "mission" to locate and marry [Aniston], with whom he believes he is in a relationship'.

Later, a more permanent restraining order (three years) was put in place by the court, ordering Peyton to stay 100 yards away from the star's home, places of work and vehicles. He was also barred from contact with any of Aniston's employers, agents, managers or other representatives. Neither Peyton nor Aniston appeared in court. Peyton was on involuntary psychiatric hold, and Aniston sent a prepared statement:

> Mr Peyton has aggressively sought to have personal contact with me and integrate himself into my life. Due to Mr Peyton's delusional compulsion and increasingly harassing, stalking and threatening conduct, I have been subjected to a course of conduct which has and is seriously alarming, annoying and harassing me.
>
> Mr Peyton's ongoing, ever-increasing, aggressive and harassing conduct are extremely distressing. I fear for my personal safety and that of those around me.

***

Back in 1996, Madonna too, was in fear for her life, thanks to a deluded Romeo who had plans either to marry her or 'slash her throat from ear to ear'. Robert Dewey Hoskins had been obsessed with the 'Material Girl' for years, and was known to be both violent and persistent – not traits anyone would welcome in a suitor. He

A Facebook stalker, hiding behind a false identity, lured teenager Nona Belomesoff into a death trap, tempting her with the promise of a job with the animals she loved

Lisa Harnum was planning her escape when she died at the hands of her fiancé, Simon Gittany

Simon Gittany hurled his fiancée, Lisa Harnum, to her death from the balcony of their apartment, which had been bugged to monitor her every move
*AP Image/Damian Shaw*

*Left:* Michael Fagan famously clambered over the walls of Buckingham Palace for a night-time visit with Her Majesty
*PA via AAP*

*Right:* A royal title is enough to attract stalkers – by the hundreds in the case of Princess Kate. Young Prince George already has his own, and Princess Charlotte is likely to receive the same unwanted attentions
*AP Photo/Lefteris Pitarakis*

*Left:* Before her death in 1997 in a tunnel in Paris, Princess Diana was hounded by paparazzi, but also by German-born surgeon and stalker Dr Klaus Wagner
*John Stilwell/PA Photo*

*Right:* Klaus Wagner was determined to protect Princess Diana against a satanic conspiracy supposedly being waged against her by Queen Elizabeth II, 'the Elizardbeast' as he dubbed her
*PA via AAP*

Australian TV and radio personality Jamie Dunn – seen here with much-loved puppet Agro – was relentlessly stalked by a local woman over a two-year period
*AAP Image/Brigitte Riffis*

*Left:* Thurman's starring role in *The Adventures of Baron Munchausen* first attracted the attentions of stalker Jack Jordan. His feelings for her only intensified when she appeared in director Quentin Tarantino's *Kill Bill*
*AP Photo/Louis Lanzano*

*Right:* Hollywood actress Uma Thurman
*AP Photo/Louis Lanzano*

Hollywood star Alec Baldwin was bombarded with dozens of phone calls and hundreds of emails every day in a relentless and escalating campaign of harassment
*AP Photo/Seth Wenig*

Genevieve Sabourin, an obsessed wannabe actress and erstwhile colleague of Alec Baldwin, claimed to have had an affair with the actor
*Topshots/AFP Photo/Stan Honda*

*Above:* Hollywood royalty
Catherine Zeta Jones
and her husband Michael
Douglas
*PA via AAP*

*Right:* Dawnette Knight,
a stalker obsessed with
Hollywood heavyweight
Michael Douglas,
threatened to slice her
love rival 'like meat on a
bone and feed her to the
dogs'
*AP Photo/Ric Francis*

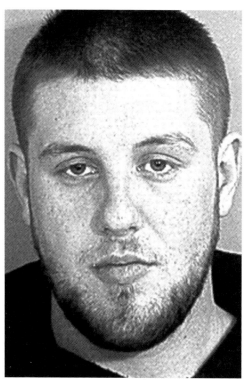

*Above:* Erstwhile pin-up boy and newfound bad boy Justin Bieber is a magnet for stalkers
*Doug Peters/EMPICS Entertainment*

*Left, top:* Prisoner 'Dana Martin', aged 45, tattooed a picture of Bieber on his leg and wrote numerous fan letters. When he received no response, he masterminded a plot to kill the young singer

*Left, centre:* Dana Martin's ex-cellmate, Mark Staake, agreed to kidnap Bieber, cut off his testicles, kill him, and then post Bieber's testicles to Martin as 'trophies'

*Left, bottom:* Naive or plain greedy, Tanner Ruane was convicted for going along with his uncle Mark Staake and stalker Martin in the plot to kill Justin Bieber

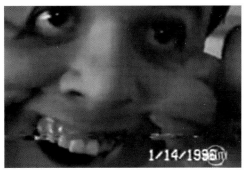

*Left:* Icelandic singer and musician Björk had a lucky escape in 1996 when police intercepted a letter bomb sent by her stalker
*AAP/ABACA*

*Right:* 'I am a monster,' Ricardo López told the camera early on in the 22 hours of video diary he shot. After mailing a bomb to his victim, Björk, he returned home and committed suicide

*Left:* John Lennon: Beatles singer and songwriter, and two-time member of the Rock and Roll Hall of Fame. Born 1940, murdered by a stalker in 1980
*PA WIRE*

*Right:* Mark Chapman, who infamously killed Beatles legend John Lennon, is a classic case of a resentful stalker. He thought Lennon had sold out on his idealistic views

*Above:* Robert Bardo's stalking and murder of Rebecca Schaeffer prompted groundbreaking legislation against stalking worldwide
*AP Photo/Kevork Pjansezian*

*Left:* Rebecca Schaeffer was the young star of the hit TV series *My Sister Sam* when she was gunned down by her stalker
*AP Photo*

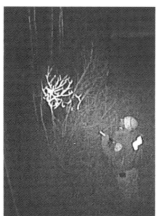

*Left:* Twenty-year-old Morgan Ingram was stalked for four months, and on 2 December 2011, was found dead in her bed at home. Her death was initially described as natural, then an overdose, but her family remain convinced that the stalker was to blame
*Courtesy Toni Ingram*

*Centre:* The sheriff checking Morgan Ingram's windows after responding to another stalking incident just days before she was murdered
*Courtesy Toni Ingram*

*Right:* Smart but troubled: Richard Brittain pleaded guilty to stalking a fellow student at university. His blog, book and planned kidnap attempt hit the international headlines

was finally arrested for his pursuit of Madonna in 1995.

At his trial the following year, Madonna – born Madonna Louise Ciccone – gave testimony that Hoskins had repeatedly scaled the fence of her Hollywood home and that she found it difficult to sleep at night because of nightmares, the press reported at the time. On one occasion, Madonna's bodyguards had been forced to shoot Hoskins when he once again had clambered over the perimeter in a vain attempt to either marry or slaughter Madonna.

Hoskins was sentenced to 10 years in prison, but the nightmare was not over yet for Madonna. In 2012, Hoskins escaped the mental institution where he had been committed – the Metropolitan State Hospital in the Los Angeles suburb of Norwalk, where he was receiving treatment to prepare him for release back into society. Los Angeles police issued a warning to the public saying Hoskins 'is highly psychotic when not taking his medication and has very violent tendencies'. He was apprehended by police eight days after escaping, and returned to the hospital, where he was doubtless put under stricter supervision.

***

I, for one, completely fail to see the appeal of pinup boy and so-called singer Justin Bieber. Maybe that is because I left my teenage years behind me too many years ago to count. But there is also the small matter of those weird faces he pulls whenever I've been unlucky enough to see him in action (on TV and not in concert, I should point out). Not to mention his evolution from boy next door to bad boy – noted for his hard partying lifestyle and being arrested a number of times for drink driving, assault, and egging his neighbours' houses and garages. And there was also the issue of the monkey he abandoned in Germany. (Monkeys, like puppies, are not just for Christmas, Justin.) But to add to his long list of issues, the Biebmiester also has a stalker.

It would be easy to assume that the stalker is probably aged under 18, female, given to screaming and a true 'Bieleber', but in actual fact, Bieber's stalker is a 45-year-old man who goes by the name of Dana Martin. Martin started out by getting a tattoo of the pop star on his leg and writing fan letters to his young Romeo, but when he received no response, he took offence. And then he took action.

At the time, Martin was in prison for unrelated offences (he is currently serving two consecutive life sentences in a Las Cruces prison for raping and killing a 15-year-old girl). Where better for a spurned fan to find someone to carry out a murder for cash?

One inmate, Mark Staake, signed up for the mission – which was to include kidnapping Bieber, cutting off his goolies and then killing him, plus his bodyguard and two other people. Bieber's testicles were supposed to be sent to Martin as 'trophies'.

On his release, the hitman recruited his nephew, a hulking bouncer called Tanner Ruane, and the two set off in pursuit of their prey. However, their map-reading skills were not as sharp as the implements they were carrying, and when pulled over by police at a border crossing – they had ended up in Canada rather than their planned destination of Vermont – the plot was uncovered. I'll never look at garden shears in the same way again.

Martin himself was interviewed for the American magazine *Details* (1 April 2013), and possibly the most chilling part of the story is the harm Martin claimed he would inflict upon Bieber if he weren't currently locked up: 'If I was free, here's what I'd want to do – put Bieber in a cage, rape him repeatedly, and put it on YouTube.'

***

Singer/actress Selena Gomez (and Justin Bieber's ex at the time of writing) was possibly luckier. Her *own stalker* was the one who told her to take out a restraining order against him. Thomas Brodnicki said in a statement that:

> I believe that a restraining order should be issued against me to prevent me from trying to contact Selena Gomez. I do not wish to object to the restraining order against me because I know it is the only thing that will make me stay away from Selena.

Apparently, Brodnicki had been having over 50 conversations with God – *each day* – about killing Ms Gomez, and naturally enough knew that something wasn't quite right about what was going on inside his head. A three-year restraining order against Brodnicki was promptly handed out in January 2012. This was probably as a result of Brodnicki's prior form as a stalker as much as the judge's concern for Gomez. Brodnicki had stalking arrests and convictions in Illinois and Iowa and had already served a three-prison sentence for stalking a waitress in Chicago. Based on court documents reported at the time, Brodnicki harassed the waitress for more than eight years.

During Brodnicki's psychiatric evaluation for stalking Gomez, he told the doctor he had made many visits to her workplace and had been thinking of ways to hurt or kill her.

## The Stalking of Björk

Ironically, Ricardo López was a pest control officer. He was also a serial pest for the Icelandic singer Björk, and ended up attempting to kill her in 1996 after becoming enraged at hearing she had entered into a relationship with the British musician and actor, Goldie.

Goldie is noted for being a British electronic music artist, DJ, graffiti artist and actor, with appearances in the 1999 James Bond film *The World Is Not Enough*, Guy Ritchie's *Snatch* (2000) and the classic British soap opera *East Enders*. He also directed the critically acclaimed *Sherlock Holmes* (2009) and its sequel *Sherlock Holmes: A Game of Shadows* (2011). But Goldie's achievements, let alone his mixed race background, did not qualify him for a relationship with Björk according to López's twisted thinking.

López was born in Uruguay and moved to Georgia in the United States as a child. He was smart but also a socially awkward loner. He never had a girlfriend, and dropped out of high school at an early age to work as a pest controller at his brother's business. He had big ambitions of becoming an artist, but his eventual notoriety was to come from other personal interests. Namely Björk.

López's family warned him about his obsession, and his brother even told him to get a real woman. But no one thought he was capable of violence. Even the psychiatrist who was treating López said that he was not dangerous even if he was suffering from 'schizoid personality disorder with passive aggressive features'.

His obsession with Björk was spiralling out of control though, and in a written diary, López talked of creating a time machine so he could travel back to the 1970s and befriend her. The diary eventually totalled EIGHT HUNDRED AND THREE PAGES, much of which was about the singer (408 references), but also touched on other celebrities (52 references), his problems with his weight, and his embarrassment at having gynaecomastia – a common hormonal disorder in which there is a benign enlargement of breast tissue in males. Oh yes, and he also mentioned suicide (34 times) and murder (14 times). He noted that he had never been liked or loved by any girl – in all, classic 'incompetent suitor' material.

By this stage, López was living alone in an apartment and getting weirder by the day. Then he read the article that mentioned Björk was in a relationship with fellow musician Goldie. He noted in his diary, 'I wasted eight months and she has a fucking lover!' Furious at this 'betrayal', López began plotting her murder, documenting his thoughts in the form of a video diary. He began filming these on 14 January 1996 – his 21st birthday. In his own words, the purpose was to document 'my life, my art and my plans'. On the first tape, he continues immediately: '... Do you want to see something funny. I am going to show you who I am ... I am a monster.' Then he steps forward to the camera and pulls a face. (It is one of the most chilling sequences I have ever seen on the internet.)

Twenty-two hours of video diary would be shot over the next nine months. (The FBI later released them to the press, and they were then leaked to the internet, where they can still be found today. I watched snippets from a few of them at home alone on one dark and stormy Saturday night and, believe me, it was NOT a good idea. My overwhelming feelings were of horror, revulsion and – oddly enough – pity. It is discomforting at the very least to watch a man unravelling in front of one's eyes.)

In these lengthy films, he shared his (low) opinion of the singer, her choice of lover, and a few other select topics. Through much of the footage, he was ranting and raving, and in various states of undress (yes, he really did have breasts). He also meticulously documented his plans for disfiguring or killing the singer, saying, 'I'm just going to have to kill her. I'm going to send a package. I'm going to be sending her to hell.'

One plan was to send her a bomb filled with tiny needles containing HIV-infected blood. He was apparently planning to collect this from a prostitute – whether willing or not, was not detailed. Another idea was for an exploding cassette, which would contain a message from him and then detonate at its conclusion. In the end, he settled for a letter bomb, disguised as a book, which would explode on opening and also shower the recipient with sulphuric acid. He constructed the bomb on 12 September 1996 – again he documented this on a video tape, carefully labelling it: 'Last Day – Ricardo López'. He then filmed himself preparing to leave for the post office to send the bomb to the singer's London home (disguised as coming from her record label, Elektra Records).

On his return from the post office, López turned on the camera again (I have not watched this part, but take my information from Wikipaedia, where some obsessive has obviously been prepared to sit through the chilling ending to the video diary):

As Björk's music plays in the background, a nude López shaves his head then paints it with red and green greasepaint. He then colors his lips with black greasepaint. López then spends some time looking at himself in a mirror and tells the camera that he is 'a little nervous now. I'm definitely not drunk. I am not depressed. I know exactly what I am doing. It [the gun] is cocked back. It's ready to roll.' As Björk's song 'I Remember You' begins to play, López says, 'This is for you.' and shoots himself in the mouth with a .38 caliber pistol. López groans and his body falls forward, out of the camera's range. The camera continued to record as López lay dead out of camera range. A hand painted sign bearing the handwritten words 'The best of me. Sept. 12' hung on the wall. Police theorized that López intended on covering the sign with his blood and brain matter as a result of the gunshot. That plan failed as the small caliber bullet did not exit López's head and his body fell away from the sign.

Four days later, a maintenance worker noticed a foul stench and streams of blood seeping through the ceiling of the apartment directly below López's. Police were called and on discovering the body – and the ample evidence documenting López's plan (including a message written on the wall in foot-high black letters: 'The 8MM Tapes Are A Documentation Of A Crime. Terrorist Material. They Are For the F.B.I.') swiftly alerted Scotland Yard, who were able to intercept and detonate the parcel without any problems.

In a final twist, López had not realised that Björk and Goldie had ended their relationship just a few days before he mailed the bomb and killed himself.

## Kill Your Darling

Most of us envy the rich and famous to a certain extent – the seats at the pointy end of the plane, the power, the money, the luxury and everything that goes along with that. But consider the *everything* part for one short minute. Sometimes *everything* comes at a cost. The next two celebrity case studies prove the point all too well.

---

## Too Much Information

John Lennon notably commented that the Beatles had become 'more popular than Jesus'. However, with great celebrity comes great risk, as Lennon discovered when Mark David Chapman, an avid fan, decided that Lennon had sold out to the dark side.

Chapman was depressed and drinking too much, and, in 1980, had already compiled a hit list of celebrities that he was planning to kill: Johnny Carson, Elizabeth Taylor, Jacqueline Kennedy Onassis and Walter Cronkite ... and also John Lennon. But Lennon was promoted to the top of the list after Chapman became disillusioned with his former idol. Once a hero of the counter-culture movement and famous for his bed-ins for peace and concerts for peace, Lennon had crossed to the dark side, according to Chapman.

The publication of a biography of John Lennon *One Day at a Time* by Anthony Fawcett was one factor in his disillusionment. In a later interview, Chapman said that the biography made it clear that Lennon's fight for peace was essentially a 'put-on'. The other publication that essentially signed Lennon's death warrant was a newspaper article about the taping of Lennon's latest album. This identified Lennon's home address as the Dakota building in New York. All Chapman had to do was stake out the luxurious apartment block on Manhattan's Upper West Side until their paths crossed. On 8 December 1980, Chapman achieved his goal when the singer returned from a recording session with his wife, Yoko

Ono. Chapman shot Lennon five times, which lead to his death. Lennon was just 40 years of age.

Chapman was sentenced to 20 years in prison after pleading guilty to second-degree murder.

At his eighth parole board hearing in August 2014, Chapman outlined the meticulous planning that had gone into the killing of Lennon. Indeed, he had stalked the music legend for months before the shooting, splashing out on plane tickets to and from his home in Hawaii, where he lived with his completely oblivious wife, who thought Chapman was travelling to New York to write a children's book. (He funded his travel from the proceeds of the sale of a Norman Rockwell painting, which were meant to go to his father-in-law.)

Chapman bought the gun in Hawaii, but had picked up the bullets in Atlanta – ironically from an old friend who happened to be a policeman. (He would not have been allowed to buy bullets in New York, according to the local laws.)

The hearing heard that Chapman had actually made contact with Lennon earlier in the day of the shooting, and that the singer had signed an album for his 'fan'.

Records from the hearing state:

Q. He was kind to you. I believe he signed an album for you?

A. Yes, he did. He was very kind.

Q. What were you looking to get? What was the real purpose? You say you wanted to get out of your doldrums. Why kill someone?

A. I had extremely selfish motives for my own self-glory. That's about the best way I can say it …


When asked why he decided to target Lennon, Chapman said he couldn't resist the fame that would come with the crime. 'That

**Protect Your Privacy**

In this age of over-sharing and instant access to information via Twitter and the internet, celebrities in particular should be very, very careful about what information they divulge in public forums. Sharing information about their home is a particular red flag, according to research carried out by Gavin de Becker and published in *The Gift of Fear: Survival Signs That Protect Us From Violence* (Bloomsbury, 1997). This can lead to a false sense of intimacy with the celebrity, and also give the impression that their home is public property. Oh yes, and it may also provide the stalker with the exact address, as was the case with Lennon and Chapman. At the very least, a 'Hello' style spread of a star's home can unwittingly provide an obsessed fan with hints as to security systems, fences, doors, floor plan layouts and much more.

Likewise, celebrities would be wise to refrain from sharing details of their favourite local restaurant, children's school or footy club, or even where they plan on going on holiday.

I would suggest that lesser mortals think twice too about what is shared on social media sites such as Facebook.

bright light of fame, of infamy, notoriety was there,' he said. 'I couldn't resist it. My self-esteem was shot, and I was looking for an easy way out. It was a bad way out, but it was the way I chose and it was horrible.'

The parole board determined that Chapman should remain imprisoned because there was a 'reasonable probability that [Chapman] would not live and remain at liberty without again violating the law. He will be eligible again for parole in two years.' Chapman remains in involuntary protective custody, being considered a key target within prison for Beatles fans and those intent on getting *their* names in the paper.

## The Young One

Robert John Bardo had early form (and a pretty rough childhood from all accounts, growing up in a large family and subjected to much emotional and physical abuse). Without making excuses, this may explain why, aged just 13, he stalked the child peace activist, Samantha Smith, who had achieved fame as a 10-year-old in December 1982 for writing to then Soviet leader Yuri Andropov to ask if he was going to wage a nuclear war against the US. The following July she toured the USSR at Andropov's invitation and as a result, became known as America's youngest goodwill ambassador. In 1985, she was cast in TV series *Lime Street*, with actor Robert Wagner.

Bardo had caught a bus from Tucson, Arizona to Maine to make contact with the young star, but was returned home when authorities found him wandering the streets. Samantha Smith died shortly after in 1985 in a plane crash while returning from London.

Thwarted by the unexpected death of his first target, Bardo turned his attentions to the star of *My Sister Sam*, Rebecca Schaeffer. He was then aged 16, and working as a cleaner in a fast food restaurant. He built a shrine to the young actress in his bedroom, and began writing letters to her – as teenage fans are wont to do.

She replied to one of these, saying that his letter was 'the most beautiful' that she had ever received, signing it 'With love from Rebecca', and drawing a heart and a peace symbol. Bardo noted the momentous occasion with an entry in his diary: 'When I think of her, I would like to become famous to impress her.'

In June 1987, Bardo turned up at the Burbank Studio gates where *My Sister Sam* was filmed, carrying gifts for Rebecca; however, the guard refused him entry. Bardo returned a month later armed with a knife rather than gifts, but didn't gain entrance then, either. In his diary, he wrote, 'I don't lose. Period.'

What had tipped the young man over from fan to fanatic was seeing Schaeffer in a sex scene in the film *Scenes From the Class*

*Struggle in Beverly Hills*. He decided that she was just another of those 'Hollywood bitches' and would pay for her betrayal of him.

On 17 July 1989, Bardo contacted Schaeffer's agent's office and tried to discover where she lived. Refused this information – unsurprisingly – he then paid a private investigator $250 to find her. In turn, the smart investigator paid $1 to retrieve this information from California's Department of Motor Vehicles.

Now armed with her home address – and unaware that he'd just paid $249 too much for the information – Bardo showed up at her apartment, rang the doorbell and shot Schaeffer in the chest when she opened the door. According to Bardo's testimony to police, the last thing Rebecca screamed out before she died was 'Why?'

Bardo was seen fleeing the scene, dressed in a yellow shirt, jeans and sandals. Rebecca Schaeffer was rushed to Cedars-Sinai Medical Center. She died 30 minutes later.

On hearing the news, Bardo's sister contacted police to say that she had recently had a worrying communication from Bardo – a rambling letter in which he implied that if he could not have the actress, no one could. The *LA Times* also reported, on 21 July 1989, that he'd rung his sister on the day of the murder to say that he was just a block and a half away from Schaeffer's home.

Bardo was coincidentally picked up by police shortly afterwards back in his home town of Tucson, staggering disorientated on a busy freeway, in an apparent suicide-by-car attempt. He promptly confessed to Schaeffer's murder, and witnesses in Los Angeles confirmed that he was indeed the man who had been seen running from the scene. Acting on information he told investigators, police later recovered a yellow shirt, a gun holster and a paperback copy of the novel *The Catcher in the Rye* just a few streets over from the Fairfax District apartment where Rebecca Schaeffer had been murdered. (For the tabloid hacks of the day, the discovery of the book proved eerily reminiscent of the 1981 shooting in New York City of John Lennon by Mark David Chapman, who was carrying the same novel.)

Bardo later gave an interview in which he told the reporter that he was a fan who had 'carried it too far'. He also expressed remorse for Schaeffer's death, and said that he was not a monster.

Bardo was tried and convicted by prosecutor Marcia Clark, who would later go on to make headlines for prosecuting OJ Simpson for the murder of Nicole Brown Simpson. Convicted of capital murder in a non-jury courtroom, Bardo was sentenced to life without parole by Superior Court Judge Dino Fulgoni on 20 December 1991.

The only good thing to come out of Bardo's murderous rampage was that the case provoked then State Governor George Deukmejian to pass a law that prohibited the state Department of Motor Vehicles from releasing addresses to members of the public. Community outcry about Schaeffer's death also prompted the passing of the world's first ever anti-stalking statute in California.

# The Stranger in the Shadows

It's a sad fact that many victims of crime are often called liars, have their sanity called into question, or are accused of being responsible for *inviting* the acts that have been committed against them – like anyone wants to be harassed, followed, raped, attacked, swindled, abused or killed. And the same holds true for victims of stalking.

I was lucky in the police officers at my local station who handled my complaint, and there were several that I needed to deal with over the weeks I was being harassed. Yes, it was frustrating to have to cover the same ground each time a new officer happened to be on duty, but at least no one accused me of making it up, or having done something to draw down the wrath of the foul-mouthed pensioner pervert.

I am doubtless lucky to be living in an age where phone messages can be recorded on voicemail and emails can be saved. I still feel disgusted at the content of the messages that were left for me, and while my instinct was to delete them immediately – rather than knowing they were festering somewhere in the bowels of my iPhone – I knew that by saving them, I would have evidence to show the police.

I was also lucky that this guy had form – the police knew exactly who he was, and what he had done to others before (not that they shared the details with me). I was also undoubtedly lucky that he was too thick or too pissed to realise that his late-night texts or emails or voicemails would be read or heard by a friendly police officer just as soon as I could pack my son off to school and get to the cop shop.

As shown in the case of Antoinette (detailed further on in this chapter) – who was stalked for a period of years in the 1960s – it can be hard to prove that you are being stalked without physical evidence, and it can be even harder to prove that you're not just some hysterical attention seeker.

In the separate case of Morgan Ingram (which you can also read about later in this chapter), even her *death* wasn't enough to quell her critics and unbelievers. Should her parents ever choose to Google their daughter's name or delve into the numerous blogs written by strangers who believe they know Morgan's life better than anyone else, they could read any number of theories that supposedly account for how their daughter died. Suicide, drug overdose, Munchausen's by proxy ... the list goes on.

Like Antoinette 45 years before, the Ingrams had little physical evidence to prove that their daughter was being stalked. Yet somehow she ended up dead. Her parents have to live with the knowledge that many people think 'it must have been something she did'. Or – even worse and even more horrible for any parent – 'something that *they* did'.

## Victim Blaming

Despite lessons learned in the notorious case of Lindy Chamberlain – who was raked over the coals in the press and around barbecues across Australia for not 'showing enough emotion' over the disappearance of her infant daughter at Uluru – it seems that not much has changed for victims of crime. Attitudes certainly hadn't changed much by 2001 when Englishwoman Joanne Lees was suspected of the murder of her boyfriend, Peter Falconio, purely because she too did not react in the emotional way the press expected. (An Australian man Bradley John Murdoch was later convicted for the crime.) It is obvious that it remains all too easy for those on the outskirts of a tragedy to question, ridicule or even point the finger at victims. It must have been their fault, the critics cry.

In my hometown of Melbourne, two recent incidents immediately spring to mind. First, the Catholic priest who told parishioners that if murdered ABC employee and Irish national Jill Meagher's faith been stronger, she would have been 'home in bed' and not walking down a street late on the night she was savagely raped and murdered by Adrian Bayley in 2012. (Bayley, a convicted rapist and murderer, was later sentenced to life in prison with a minimum term of 43 years.) Yep, it was clearly Jill's fault that Bayley made the fatal decision to rape and then murder her.

The priest's original audience – the congregation – numbered around one hundred individuals, but news of the priest's remark swiftly spread and an apology was later made by church officials, as heard on a report on radio station 3AW:

> The reference to Jill Meagher in particular was offensive and inappropriate and the people of Victoria and Ireland mourn her sad and tragic death.
>
> We do not share the sentiment of the homily this morning and we certainly apologise for the hurt that this homily may have caused today.

The priest's comments came a mere week after police had blundered by suggesting that women should not walk alone in parks. This was after a teenager from Doncaster, Melbourne – Masa Vukotic – was killed on 17 March 2015 while taking a break from study around 6.30 p.m. and out walking near her home. She was 17 years old, she was wearing headphones, it was still daylight, and she *invited* her death?

Again there was public outcry, not just because Masa was only 17 and should have been looking forward to a full life, but because it was a brutal reminder that women have been, and continue to be, unsafe in our world. We're told that we are responsible for our own safety – we need to carry keys laced in our fingers when walking down the street, let our friends know where we're going.

We shouldn't be out after dark and we should always be vigilant. But what happens if even your home isn't safe? What happens if your home is not the refuge you assume it will always be?

## The Haunted House

It was tough becoming a divorcee back in the 1960s. First there was the stigma. And then there was the divorce process itself. This was often protracted, brutal and bitter, mainly because in the years before 'no fault' divorce laws were passed, it was essential for someone to be cast in the role of the villain. This proof could take many forms – desertion, adultery or cruelty – but the law demanded to know *some* reason why the marriage could no longer continue.

And there was clearly plenty of *Mad Men* style behaviour going on in the sixties in Australia – almost half of the divorces in 1962 cited desertion as the reason, and more than 20 per cent cited adultery. A huge number also cited drunkenness.

For Antoinette, the decision was easy – well, as easy as these things ever get. In true Don Draper style, her husband had been out on the town having numerous affairs while she was at home looking after their three young children.

Getting shot of her husband was a no-brainer, but there were certainly many other things to consider. Like how she was going to keep a roof over their heads and food on the table. After all, no laws existed to ensure that a woman would get support for either herself or her children – there were no formal property settlements or custody agreements in those days. Antoinette did get some money from her ex, but it was barely enough for the young family's survival.

Few women were in the workforce and mothers were also much younger back then, with most women popping out babies in their early twenties, if not before – a far cry from today, when it's not unusual for women to have their first children in their mid-thirties. (I discovered to my horror when I became pregnant in *my* mid-thirties that the medical profession even have a delightful term for this – elderly primigravida, which describes a woman who gets pregnant for the first time after the age of 34. Elderly, indeed.)

Antoinette was in her mid-twenties when she found herself a single parent to three children not yet at school, working part-time as an antiques dealer, and living in an old Edwardian house in the leafy suburb of Canterbury – just over the back fence from what is now regarded as one of Australia's most expensive streets, Monomeath Avenue. (Canterbury consistently ranks in the top three suburbs for average house prices in Melbourne.)

Noted for its wide green boulevards and opulent historic residences, today Canterbury is known as one of Melbourne's most exclusive suburbs, particularly the 'Golden Mile' – a term for the stretch of Mont Albert Road that runs towards the CBD from Balwyn Road, but that also encompasses the avenues branching off it. These streets are lined by ancient and spreading oak trees and grand mansions, and have been called home by many diplomats, politicians (Andrew Peacock, Sir Rupert Hamer to name but two), leaders of business and industry, world-renowned scientists (such as Macfarlane Burnett) – and the parents of Kylie and Danni Minogue.

Back in the 1960s, Canterbury was also home to Antoinette and her children, their dog – and possibly her stalker. It was a campaign of terror that was to last not weeks, but years.

'I can't remember exactly when it began,' says Antoinette today. 'In those days, no one bothered locking their back doors, at least not in a *nice* suburb like Canterbury. It was definitely after my husband had left though, so I was on my own with the children. I think the first thing I noticed was that items were constantly moving around the house. I'd be sure I'd put something down in one place, and then it would turn up in another. I thought I was going mad.'

The suburb may have looked nice, but Antoinette had often felt that there was something weird about the perfectly maintained fences, manicured lawns, perfect homes and the perfect families who lived there. There was also a somewhat disturbing history to her house: she and her husband had bought it after the previous owner, an old man, had died. It turned out that his wife had been in the mental asylum for decades – she was still alive at the time of his death, but hopelessly insane. He had only been to visit her once, but when she tried to kill him, had never returned.

And Antoinette thinks she may suspect the reason. After they'd taken possession of the house, they had found a carved wooden stick, much like a walking stick, carefully hidden in the rafters of the attic. One end was intricately carved into the shape of a massive penis. 'It was seriously creepy. I never found out anything else about the couple who had lived there before us, but it was an unhappy, dark house, right from the first moment we moved in. In some ways, I believe it attracted evil.'

After her husband left, Antoinette would have happily moved, but the finances didn't stack up at that stage. 'I didn't have much of an income, and the mortgage was big, so I couldn't afford to leave. I was stuck.'

'My neighbour on one side was a complete cow – I think it was because I didn't mow my lawns often enough to suit her view of what a perfect Canterbury lawn should look like.' On the other side of Antoinette lived a family – mother, father and their two sons Oliver* and Craig*, both of whom were in their late teenage years.

Already unsettled by the way objects moved around the house, and doors seemingly opened and closed at will, Antoinette was further disturbed by odd noises in the middle of the night. This was definitely manmade. 'Whoever it was used to get a stick and run it down the side of the house, or tap on the windows, or call out my name. It was obviously someone who knew me.'

'Sometimes, it would get really intense and then it would all go away for a while. I'd just be starting to relax, and then he would start up again. Maybe he'd been away somewhere, or maybe he was just prowling around quietly. He obviously hadn't forgotten us.' By this stage, Antoinette had called the police numerous times, but they had not discovered any evidence of an intruder, and could only say that she should pray it stopped soon. 'One of them even suggested that I must have been doing something to get his attention – getting changed in front of an open window or something,' Antoinette says.

And then she caught her first sight of the stalker. 'We had a driveway that led up the side of the house, and the dining table looked out over this. One night at dusk, we were sitting there having dinner and we spotted a head moving past the window, which then disappeared down the driveway towards our back garden.'

Antoinette went out to check out who it might be, but the mysterious figure had disappeared. 'Our garden was very deep, and the gardens of some of the surrounding properties were almost like being in the country, they were so huge – full of big trees and rhododendrons. He must have jumped over one of the fences and escaped into one of the gardens.'

It was not to be a one-off occurrence. Over the next months, Antoinette would often get the feeling that she was being watched, and look up to see a figure moving away from the windows. 'Most of the time, I was home on my own with the children so I certainly wasn't going to go out there and hunt him down.'

But friends and visitors also saw the shadowy figure, and eventually Antoinette decided to advertise for a lodger – to have another adult permanently on the property, as much as anything. Her dog had so far proved useless – not barking or alerting the family when the intruder was around – a sign that the stalker was known to the family, Antoinette believes, or that the unknown man had taken the time to befriend and bribe the dog with treats.

Soon after her decision to advertise a room for rent, 18-year-old David*, a lad from the country, moved into the bungalow out the back. Like Antoinette, he was also soon suffering from broken sleep, with the stalker delighting in banging on the walls of the bungalow at odd hours of the night.

One night, David and Antoinette were alerted by a rustling noise and went outside to found someone – possibly the intruder – perched high in a huge old bay laurel. Hidden by the leaves, he shook the branches at them 'much like a menacing gorilla', as Antoinette describes it. They couldn't see his face, and they certainly weren't going to climb up after him, but they could call the police – and did. However, by the time the police arrived, the intruder was gone. The city certainly must have seemed a strange and menacing place for a kid from the bush, where the worst thing you can stumble upon is a snake that's probably more scared of you than you are of it.

Another night, Antoinette and her lodger were so freaked out by a spate of broken nights of relentless tapping that they decided to share a bed – fully clothed – just for solidarity. And that really, really seemed to annoy the stalker. 'My bedhead was against the outside wall of the house, and the stalker was standing on the driveway banging on the wall and yelling things like – "Toni, don't! Toni, don't!"… it was just so creepy.'

Then one morning David told her something even more disturbing. 'He used to get up at 6 o'clock to get ready for work, and would come into the house to make a cuppa. That morning he'd noticed that the kettle had already been boiled. I was still asleep in bed, so it was obvious that someone had come into our kitchen and turned on the kettle.'

Not even locking the doors was enough to stop the stalker, it seemed. Objects kept turning up in unexpected places. Doors that had been firmly closed before the family left for the day were later found open. 'I can only think that the stalker had taken copies of the keys before I wised up, so still had access when we were out of the way,' Antoinette says, and she regrets that she was not in a position to change all the locks. By now, the windows too were permanently closed – even in the middle of summer – because

Antoinette was so scared by the tapping and whispering. It did not do much for the rising damp, but at least Antoinette had the illusion of safety.

Antoinette was not comfortable arriving home alone after dark, and arranged for her lodger to be there if she had gone out for any reason. They organised a system where she would pull into the driveway, then call for David to open the front door. Then one night Antoinette ducked out for groceries. On arriving back, she called out for David but there was no response. 'I was yelling his name, and it took about five minutes for him to come to the front door.' It seemed that just as her car had turned into the property, David had been called to the back door. 'It was a man yelling "David, David ..." in a high-pitched voice.' David responded, not realising that Antoinette was stranded at the front of the house. Who knows what the stalker was planning, or perhaps it was just done for the sheer nuisance value.

The stalker clearly had it in for David too. 'One night, my lodger chased the prowler down into our very dark back garden and came back with his head punched in,' says Antoinette. Sadly, David hadn't been able to get a good look at his assailant.

In the end, the constant strain was all too much for her lodger. He gave his notice and left, leaving Antoinette and the three children in the haunted house.

Antoinette hadn't told her son or two younger daughters about what was going on, wanting to protect them from the fact that a stranger was lurking around the house. But she was terrified to hear one of her daughters say one morning that she'd woken up in the middle of the night to feel someone holding her hand. The person ran out of the room when she woke up. 'I told my daughter that she should have yelled or called out to me, but she thought she had dreamed it all.'

But Antoinette was sure that her daughter had not been dreaming, having had a very similar experience herself. 'The scariest moment for me was one really hot summer night when I'd gone to bed naked and just had the sheet over me. The sheet had become tangled under my leg during the night, and I woke up in the pitch darkness to feel someone very gently tugging the sheet free. I froze. My brain was awake, but my body hadn't registered and I couldn't scream or move or do anything. Then I felt his hand move under the sheet, and it was at that point that I was finally able to move, and he fled the room.'

After that night, Antoinette slept with the dog on her bed. 'And when that dog died, the next one slept on the bed too. In fact, it took me 20 years to be able to sleep by myself, without a dog to protect me,' Antoinette explains today.

★★★

To this day, Antoinette remains convinced that the culprit was the neighbour's younger son, Craig. Antoinette wasn't on particularly friendly terms with her neighbours, but they would nod hello or stop for a chat if they met on the street. She describes the parents as 'not her style, but decent people, hardworking and quite simple'. There was nothing to suggest anything weird about them.

Their two boys were about 15 and 16 when Antoinette and her family moved into the house – both still at secondary school. Over the years, they grew up and got jobs, but they still lived at home. And this is one of the reasons Antoinette believes that at least one of them was involved. The stalking continued for the whole time she lived next door.

Her money is on Craig. Aged about 15 when the stalking first began, he was an odd boy and socially inept, beyond the usual teenage shyness around adults. 'The older boy, Oliver, wasn't bad looking, but Craig was just a bit of a blob with pimples. Oliver had a bit of a hope in life, but the younger one really didn't have much going for him. He'd just stare at the ground if we crossed paths in the neighbourhood. He wasn't retarded, but he was definitely a bit odd.'

The police also thought that it may have been Craig, despite Antoinette never having been able to get a good look at the face peering in the window over the years. 'The police used to come around to the house after anything really odd had happened, like the time the stalker was up the tree and shaking branches at us. One time, they actually booby-trapped the yard with trip wires to try and catch him, but nothing happened. It was like he knew what we were planning, which he may well have done if he had been watching from his house next door or listening into our conversation out in the back yard.'

Who knows, maybe the arrival next door of an attractive, slightly older, single woman did tip a troubled, socially awkward teen over the edge? Antoinette certainly believes so. 'It would have been so easy for him to pop out of his house at night and into our yard. And after he'd banged on our windows or yelled out my name, he could have easily just jumped the fence and gone in through the side door of his house before anyone noticed he was missing. It could also explain why I felt like I was being watched all the time, and why he seemed to know what I was planning to do. He was probably close enough to listen if he wanted to.'

It certainly may also explain how Craig knew that Antoinette was late at work one Friday night and the children were home alone. Despite Antoinette having given her son strict instructions not to leave the two younger girls alone, he did what many young boys would do: ducked out for half an hour to play with his mates in the dusk. By the time he returned, the girls were nowhere to be seen. And by the time Antoinette returned at 9 p.m., he was beside himself with fright and worry. 'They're gone, Mum. The girls have gone,' he told his mother.

It was not for another couple of hours that the girls were located – next door at Craig's house. Later, Antoinette heard from her daughters that as soon as their brother had left them alone, someone began rapping on the windows and scraping something down the side of the house. They'd bolted out the front door, and had run straight into their neighbour, Craig, who was standing on the footpath out the front. He asked the girls what was wrong.

The girls explained that someone had been tapping on the windows, so Craig told them to go into his house with him, where they would be safe. 'Eventually we worked out that the kids were in there – I don't think he would have done anything to hurt them, but I think he did want to freak me out.'

Antoinette admits that one evening, after years of being stalked, she did finally attempt some payback. 'I'd had a gutful one evening, so I hopped over the fence and let down all the tyres on his car. In the morning, he had to get the RACV out, because he obviously couldn't go anywhere. Nothing was ever said, and I don't know whether he knew it was me, but I felt better. It was like I had finally let him know that I knew it had been him, all those years.'

The police had pretty much given up on the case by then. It had been years, and there was still no hard evidence linking the young neighbour – or indeed anyone else – with the endless rapping, and tapping and odd events. 'In the end, the cops came round and said that the only way I was likely to stop it would be to sell the house and not tell anyone where I was going to move,' says Antoinette. And the moment she could afford to do so, she did.

Forty-five years after she finally escaped her stalker, Antoinette still remembers the feeling of freedom a new start offered. 'The new house radiated light, and it was a joy being able to have the windows and doors open again, and to go to sleep without wondering whether he was lurking outside.' Her daughter, however, still remembers the sensation of a man holding her hand in the middle of the night.

Antoinette has no idea what happened to her former neighbour – if indeed he was the stalker – but thinks that he is probably married with kids and a so-called pillar of society. Probably living in Canterbury.

## Designed to Scare

Lesley, now aged 51, was haunted by an unknown stalker for almost a year back in the late 1980s. A designer by trade, she ran her own studio and would often work late, alone. This didn't fuss her; it was what she kept finding the morning after that was more disturbing – obscene messages from a male caller on her answer machine. It was always the same message. 'He'd moan and groan and talk about me unbuttoning his shirt or whatever, and it was clear that he was getting off on the other end of the line, which was just disgusting,' says Lesley today.

'I actually wasn't very worried by the calls at first. I just thought it was weird and a joke, but after the second, then the third and fourth time I started to become more concerned and disturbed.'

The odd thing was that the calls never came through when Lesley was in the studio, despite her erratic hours. Somehow the man knew when she was there, and avoided ringing at that time. 'I wasn't frightened in the same way I would have been if he'd been ringing my home rather than work – it was more like, "What the hell?!"' says Lesley. Sometimes weeks would go by without a message and she'd almost believe that he'd given up, then another call would come. After the umpteenth call, Lesley contacted police – having wisely saved all the messages she had received.

Police were sympathetic, but said there was little they could do but place a trace on the phone. Some weeks went by, and Lesley was hopeful that her ordeal was over. Then one day she was working out in the back of the studio. The phone rang and Lesley answered it, only to hear her stalker – the first time they had actually talked.

'He actually seemed surprised that I was there. He said, "Oh you're there ... just say 'fuck'." And I said, "I'd appreciate it if you would stop leaving obscene messages on my answer machine,"' says Lesley. And then she remembered the trace. 'I knew I had to keep him talking for three minutes so they could trace the call, but I couldn't bear to listen to him so I put the phone down on the desk as quietly as possible. But I think he heard the click, realised what was happening and immediately hung up. There was no way for the police to trace the call; as it turned out, the trace had been turned off a few days earlier.'

Lesley says that the police didn't tell her that the trace would only be active for a month. If she had known, she says she definitely would have asked them to reactivate it after that time, given the sporadic nature of the calls. 'I thought the trace was still active and I remember thinking at the time, "Bloody fantastic! I've got you now, you prick. Now I'll be able to find out who you are and embarrass the pants off you!"'

But that pleasure was not to be hers. 'I was really pissed off at the police for the fact they had not informed me that the trace would only be active for one month and I would need to renew it each month,' Lesley says.

However, she recognises that the idea of any police involvement was probably enough to put the wind up her stalker. There were no more calls. But then one day Lesley was appointed to an industry board and in her first meeting, she heard a very familiar voice addressing the room. It was a fellow director.

'I wasn't looking at the man at the time,' she says. 'I just heard his voice – the same voice I'd heard so many times on the answer machine – and the hairs on the back of my neck stood up. I think it was even more potent because I wasn't looking at him at the time. It was just his voice in isolation, the way it had been.'

But Lesley didn't have any hard evidence to back up her conviction. 'I just made sure I never sat anywhere near him, or engaged with him beyond the necessary.' But she did do some digging and was not surprised to find that his office was directly across the road from her studio, and on the same floor. 'I think he had been watching me from his office, and when I left the studio, he'd leave his nasty messages. He only got caught out the one time when I was working at the back of the studio where he couldn't see me.'

## Then the Snow Came

Carbondale is a tiny and picturesque town in Colorado, with a population of around 6500. Once a rich agricultural area, then a booming heart of the silver and coal mining industries, it is now a dormitory town for workers in the nearby skiing mecca of Aspen and increasingly a centre for arts, recreation and tourism in its own right. The town is the epitome of a quiet and family-friendly place to live.

However, all may not be as it seems. In 2011, 20-year-old Morgan Ingram was stalked for four months, and on 2 December 2011, she was found dead in her bed early in the morning.

This case is the most haunting example of the shadow stalker I encountered in my research for this book. Morgan's death notice gives some idea of her gloriously normal young life, but sadly it is for the manner of her death that her name has become known.

Her death notice in the *Aspen Times* on 5 December 2011 read simply:

Morgan passed away suddenly at her home in Carbondale on Friday, December 2, 2011. She was 20 years old. Her life in the mountains and snow were an inspiration to her, she had been waiting for it to snow, and her snow came that night. She was born at Valley View Hospital in Glenwood Springs on August 16, 1991.

Morgan was a student at Colorado Mountain College, with a love of philosophy, a passion for dance, and a constant appreciation for all forms of art. She was an extremely gifted artist and a loving person, and she saw and gave beauty to others through her photographs. Forever in tune with nature, she loved animals, music, playing piano, and singing.

Always smiling and always caring, she was an amazing person who touched absolutely everybody in her life. Morgan had the unique ability to bring a smile to all people lucky enough to have met her. She left our lives too soon and will be deeply missed by many. This amazing, creative, vibrant, and loving girl was an inspiration to all.

She was the bright light shining in the hearts of her parents Steve and Toni, sister Kristin, brother Ryan, niece Joni-Ann, nephews Odin and Jarred, her cat Mogwai, her puppy Wylah, and her horse TC.

There will be a celebration of Morgan's life on Tuesday, December 6, 2011, at 6 PM, held at Christ Community Church, 20351 Highway 82, Basalt, Colorado.

The death of any young woman is tragic, but what makes Morgan's death even more distressing is the questions that will forever haunt her family and friends. Why was Morgan stalked for four months before her death? Who was the mysterious stalker and why couldn't the police manage to catch him (or her) despite being called out to the Ingram household 50 times in just four months? Why was her death initially ruled natural causes, and only later changed to suicide? And given all this, why is a healthy young girl dead? Why does the case remain closed?

By all rights, Morgan should still be alive to enjoy the delights of Carbondale today, or to appreciate returning to her hometown after heading for greener, wider pastures. By all rights, her parents should be still living in Carbondale in the home they enjoyed with their family for so many years, celebrating their daughter's graduation, a new romance or marriage for her, a new job, perhaps a new grandchild.

Instead, Morgan is dead, Toni and Steve are living elsewhere – forced to leave town after essentially being harassed themselves for accusing a local boy and girl of being involved in stalking and murdering Morgan. (At one point, the Ingrams themselves were subjected to a temporary restraining order relating to the accusations they had made.) I explored quite a few of the websites and posts discussing the stalking of Morgan before interviewing Morgan's mother, Toni, and I can't help but feel distressed on the family's behalf. Imagine losing your daughter only to be accused of everything from smothering her with motherly love to murdering her.

Morgan's extended family still attends grief counselling sessions ... 'every Friday for the past three years,' Toni says. Today, she and Steve are still fighting for justice for Morgan, maintaining a regular blog that can receive thousands of hits each day, and petitioning for her case to be reopened. They are convinced that they know who the stalker was and want their daughter's death to be recognised as murder, not suicide or natural causes.

They simply want the stalker to face the consequences of his and/or her actions.

***

In the Ingrams' blog, Toni describes the day that the stalking of Morgan began:

> We had just returned to our beautiful valley in Colorado from vacationing with Morgan. On our drive back we had picked up her new puppy Wylah May. Morgan had never had a puppy of her own and she was so excited about her little Australian Shepard [sic]. She treated her as though she were her own baby, spent every dime she earned on special food, toys, everything for this little puppy. She brought her down to the river this afternoon (one of her favorite spots to meditate), and little Wylah May seemed to love everything about the outdoors. This evening Morgan drove into Carbondale to show her friends her new puppy – when she arrived home later that evening, she went directly into her room, started to undress in her bathroom in order to take a shower, and then heard tapping on her bathroom window. Morgan's bathroom window was made

of obscured glass so you could not see in, but someone outside could see the light go on, and possibly some shadows. Morgan jumped, but then thought it must be a branch or a bird tapping the glass so she disregarded the noise ... this was the start.

It was 2 August 2011, a couple of weeks before Morgan's 20th birthday. Someone had fixated on Morgan and was about to turn her life – and her family's life – into a living hell. At first the Ingrams weren't too concerned, thinking that the noises probably had a natural explanation. But the noises didn't go away – for the next few days, about 15 minutes after Morgan arrived home and went to her room, she'd complain to her parents about the tapping noises. A few days later, Morgan reminded them to check on her window, and that's when Toni and Steve's suspicions were first raised. There was no nearby branch or other object that could have caused the disturbance. Indeed, there were no branches within 15 feet (4.5 metres) of her window. If anything had been tapping on the window, it had to have been human – or at least controlled by a human.

Again, from Toni and Steve's blog:

In the morning during breakfast Morgan reminded us to check the windows outside her room to see if anything could be rubbing up against them. The three of us all went to go look outside and to our surprise realize nothing, not a branch or anything, could be tapping on the windows, so now we are all very concerned ... Morgan said she will let us know if it happens again. She was pretty upset and decides to go hang out with friends until later around 10.00 p.m.

This same evening tapping occurred again after Morgan returned in the evening within 15 minutes of her coming home and going to bed. Her dad and I go running outside trying to catch this person, but we saw nothing. We must be getting slow or there are just too many trees, bushes and shadows to hide in. We start to brainstorm to try and come up with a plan that will work in order to catch this person.

Weeks went by, and the disturbances continued. Morgan began to suspect that she was being followed when driving her car, and that someone was watching her while she was walking her dog. The sound of tapping at her window continued too, and on many nights she chose to escape and sleep in her parents' walk-in wardrobe (with her beloved puppy) instead of in her own room. After a few weeks, she chose to return to her bedroom, but she was still haunted by the night-time tapping. Seven weeks after the stalking began, the local sheriff opened a felony stalking investigation.

Toni explains that they were told to keep it quiet: 'I knew nothing about stalking when all this began, so when I was told to keep what was happening quiet, I did. I regret that today, knowing what I now know.'

Like most parents who have lost a child under any circumstances, Toni torments herself with what she could have done differently – the 'what if' syndrome. Police advised Toni and Steve that it was best to keep the stalking quiet – that they'd have a much better chance of catching the intruder if the whole neighbourhood was not on alert. Today, she believes that letting the neighbours know what was going on might have made a difference – the more eyes on the lookout for something suspicious, the better.

Perhaps a neighbour might have spotted someone acting furtively near the Ingrams' house and reported it to police. Or perhaps they could have provided definitive identification of the mysterious shadow. (The police believed that the stalker had to be a local, given that he always seemed to know whenever Morgan arrived home, and would often be tapping on the window within minutes of her entering the house.) In the end, Toni only let her neighbours and others know about what was happening to Morgan when the man across the road directly questioned her about why police cars had been seen so often at her house.

Police attended the Ingram family home more than 50 times over the course of four months. But it was to no avail. The family would call the local station after each incident and officers would turn up perhaps half an hour later – when the stalker was long gone. Toni says, 'You could imagine [the stalker] just thumbing his nose and thinking, "Yeah, come and get me." The police eventually gave us a direct contact with a card and a number to ring, but before that, we had to explain ourselves from scratch every time, which obviously delayed their response.'

Eventually Toni and Steve took matters into their own hands, installing a wildlife camera (activated by movement) above the front porch. More cameras followed, and the family rotated where these were positioned to maximise the chances of catching the intruder on tape.

'The first night we put the camera up, we caught his image on the camera. I told my husband, "Oh my god, there he is!"' But Toni adds that the camera flashes a little red light immediately before it takes pictures, and the man they suspect was stalking Morgan was a hunter. 'He would have seen the flashing light, known what we were using, and then took care to avoid being caught on camera again.'

That image of the man – by the shape it clearly looks like a male – can be found on the internet today, but the online community varies in their response to what they are actually seeing. Is it a bloke wandering up the driveway in search of an address, a passer-by, or even a photoshopped image? The internet conspiracy theorists have had a field day with Morgan's death, but few seem to consider that this is not a whodunit but a personal tragedy – both for Morgan herself, obviously, and also her friends and family.

★★★

Morgan's life had changed dramatically in just the space of a few months. From being a happy-go-lucky girl with plans to continue on to law school, now she was living in virtual lockdown. She broke out in a stress rash on her face and chest, and Toni would never leave her alone in the house, in case the stalker should come calling.

In her blog, Toni describes some of the precautions the family took:

> Morgan always sends me a text or calls to tell me when she will be driving up the driveway ... I always meet her in the driveway carrying pepper spray when she drives up. This always happens up until, and including the night Morgan died.

The whole family was terrified – and not only because there was so little evidence on which to go on. Some grainy footage from the surveillance camera of a stranger leaning on Steve's truck *watching the police drive away*, some more of a man walking down the street past Morgan's bedroom, a few footprints in the garden bed outside Morgan's window, and – of course – the relentless tapping and knocking noises. The keypad lock on the front door would also often sound at odd times of the night – perhaps the stalker trying to crack the code, Toni and Steve think. Morgan also believed that she'd been followed in her car on several occasions, but one can also perhaps consider that the ongoing campaign of harassment had made her hyper-vigilant – a common symptom experienced by victims of stalking.

A little harder to explain is the cracked guttering above Morgan's bedroom window – the sort of cracking that was not found elsewhere around the house or on any of the 16 neighbouring houses and was not the result of weathering or age. Was it caused by someone repeatedly lying on the roof, leaning over the gutter and tapping some kind of object on Morgan's window?

The family took further measures: a panic button was installed so that Morgan could press it at any time of the day or night and an alarm would sound in her parents' room, some distance away. She always kept her phone within reach too.

Friends and family provided crucial support during this time, although Toni admits that everyone treated what was happening in completely different ways:

> Some were almost dismissive – like, oh, it's just someone fooling with you. Others were more concerned. Morgan's ex-boyfriend – they were still on really good terms – came over and even slept out in the garden one night trying to catch the guy. Of course, the stalker didn't show that night. Others really wanted to be proactive and help, but what can people do?

One friend of Morgan's, a guy who'd known her for years, became very concerned when he found out how serious the stalking had become:

> So a few times [Morgan would go to] see her friends, trying to have some kind of normal life, and he would follow her and just stay in his car and keep an eye out while she was visiting. Then he'd follow her home. But one day she spotted him and was furious with him because he hadn't let her know what he was doing.

On the morning of 2 December 2011, Morgan Ingram was found dead in her bed at her family's home in the Aspen Equestrian Estates subdivision, east of Carbondale. There were no signs of assault, according to police.

On an episode of the *Dr. Phil* show, aired in July 2013, Toni and Steve told Dr Phil what happened on that morning:

> TONI: We were in constant fear of what was going to happen to Morgan. One morning I went and I knocked on her door, and she didn't answer and I shook her shoulder and she didn't respond.

STEVE: I just knew something was wrong. I thought – I knew something was – I knew something was really wrong.

[Steve then commenced CPR.]

TONI: He's saying, 'Morgan, take the breath out of me, please, breathe,' and he couldn't get her to breathe.

STEVE: I knew that she was dead. I knew she wasn't going to come back, and my thought was what do I tell Toni? How do I tell Toni that Morgan's dead?

TONI: It was a parent's worst nightmare.

From the start, Toni told investigators that something didn't add up about the way her daughter was found. 'She was lying on the wrong side of the bed, facing in the wrong direction. I told them that I knew my daughter and she never slept like that. She always slept on one side of the bed, and curled up under the covers with her panic button close at hand on her nightstand.'

Toni pointed out to investigators that the panic button had been ripped off and thrown across the room. Likewise, the phone Morgan always kept nearby was found under the bathroom door.

And then there were Morgan's pets: her dog Wylah May and a cat, which were found 'together in Morgan's bathroom – she would never have put them in there, let alone together,' says Toni. 'And when I opened the door up, they were looking at me like "What happened?" The dog and cat were scared of each other and would never be together voluntarily. Everything was wrong with the picture I was seeing.'

Morgan's parents had the dreadful task of telling family and friends that Morgan had died. The entire grieving clan gathered at a nearby house – the Ingrams' own house having been declared a crime scene. Toni wrote:

The detective finally showed up and he wanted to start talking to everyone about what they knew ... while he was there, he overheard my son Ryan raging against ... the guy we thought was doing the stalking. So what did the police do? The sheriff called me in and warned me that Ryan would be taken into custody for making threats.

Give me a break – who wouldn't mouth off if their sister was found dead? In the end, they left a police car sitting outside Ryan's house for one frigging week to monitor him and make sure he didn't do something stupid. That alone infuriated me. If only they had bothered to do something similar for us while Morgan was still alive. And now they were prepared to protect [the alleged killer] from US?

Not long after Morgan's death, Ryan moved away from the neighbourhood and his parents – the once close-knit family destroyed by the malicious actions of Morgan's stalker.

***

Toni says the way the stalking was handled by authorities 'was not an efficient process – in fact, it was really *bad* process, not just for Morgan, but for all of us. And it didn't improve after Morgan's death.'

Toni and Steve firmly believed that their daughter had been murdered by her stalker. However, the original autopsy report, dated 19 December 2011, stated that Morgan had died of natural causes, namely 'marked pulmonary oedema' (fluid in the lungs) and 'acute intermittent porphyria' (a metabolic disorder that can cause crippling stomach pains).

On 28 July 2012, however, a revised post mortem report was issued stating that Morgan had died from an overdose of the prescription drug amitriptyline, used to treat symptoms of depression and pain associated with migraines and nerves (for example, nerve pain after shingles). Morgan had taken a low dose of this drug in the past as a preventative measure for her migraines and stomach pains, and still had some in her possession – but not enough for the 'twice the fatal dose' that was found in her blood, Toni says. And there were no signs of Morgan having ingested any tablets – no pills or granular residues were found to be present. Toni is convinced Morgan was either injected with a lethal concoction or forced to drink it in a liquid form. She is equally convinced that Morgan was not suicidal – if she had been, there were sleeping pills on hand that she could have taken – and that the drug evidence simply doesn't stack up.

While Toni freely admits that Morgan had once had a permit for medical marijuana – to help with the gastric problem she had had – she says that the problem had resolved and for 18 months before her death Morgan had not been taking anything stronger than supplements from her naturopath, organic products and fresh juices. 'My daughter did not poison her body at all.'

No answer has been found to *how* the suspected stalker gained access to the house either. There were no signs of a forced entry and the parents had heard nothing.

The sheriff was quoted by press at the time as saying that he was sorry for the Ingrams' loss and though he understood they were clearly struggling to deal with the death of their daughter, he stood by the autopsy and pathologist's report.

***

So who was Morgan's stalker? Toni and Steve firmly believe it was a young local man, the ex-boyfriend of an acquaintance of Morgan's.

Later on, much later, Toni found out that this man had been living just three houses away from the Ingram family home and would have been perfectly positioned to keep an eye on Morgan's movements. Steve Ingram said that he was told by three separate people that the female acquaintance of Morgan's had said, 'That bitch is going to get it someday.'

Toni says that Morgan told the sheriff about her concerns regarding this male and that he could be involved in the stalking, but they didn't find anything on him at that time. He was questioned following Morgan's death, but the police concluded he was not involved.

***

On losing a child, most parents are destroyed by grief. Some never recover; some seek solace in revenge; some seek answers; some do their best to forget. So how do Toni and Steve Ingram and Morgan's siblings cope? Toni insists that they are not brave in their quest for justice for Morgan: 'We are just parents. At times, we feel like we can't continue – that we are frozen [in time on the day that Morgan was killed], but we have so much support from friends and family that somehow we keep going.'

It would be easy too, for Morgan's parents to have lost contact with her friends after her death. However, Toni says that in fact the opposite has happened: 'Morgan's friends have been amazing. Right now, she would have been 23 years old. Her friends who themselves are now that age are still so caring. They talk to us, they visit us ... they call us. They really want to support and help us. That is a huge source of strength our family.'

At the time of writing this, the Ingrams were running a petition on Change.org to get the state governor to re-open the inquiry into Morgan's stalking and death, despite Garfield County Sheriff Lou Vallario telling television station CBS4 that his department spent a lot of time working on the case, and that it will remain closed.

He told reporters, 'We investigate every death we come across as a homicide and then again we let the facts and the evidence to take us where it's going to take us. We have no reasonable suspicion, let alone probable cause that we have any suspect.'

The Ingrams' campaign has inspired an outpouring of powerful comments supporting the family. 'Since I started the blog in 2012, I've had people commenting from 115 different countries – many of them from Australia,' says Toni. They have also been blindsided by a barrage of insults from online haters – 'The Others', as Toni calls them – who believe that the Ingrams are stirring up trouble in their quest for answers.

In the first year after Morgan's death – and after the launch of her blog – Toni was drawn to reading the online comments off and on, but found it hard not to react to those she knew were completely wrong.

'After our appearance on the *Dr Phil* show, a lot of new supporters found the blog, but then some other people came on and started attacking. I just tried to ignore it, but the hard thing was that it got so nasty that I had to start blocking them,' Toni says.

'I could not accept what they were saying about my daughter. This is the girl who was always the designated driver – the first girl people would ask to drive them home when they were wasted. People who didn't even know Morgan were painting a picture that was the exact opposite of our daughter.'

Toni and Steve have now blocked The Others from their lives. 'I don't engage with them, I don't worry about what they say about Morgan or us. We just focus on what we need to get done.' Toni spends time talking to victim support groups and victims themselves – some as far away as India. She hopes that what she has to say will help other victims, but knows that nothing will help bring Morgan back. All she and Steve can hope for is that one day they will be able to see Morgan receive justice.

'The thing to remember is that it's never about what the victim does or who they are,' says Toni. 'Anyone, absolutely anyone, can become a victim.'

# Love Gone Wrong

The end of a relationship is never much fun, but as this chapter shows, some people simply can't let go of the past. Rather than taking it on the chin and moving on to another fish in the sea, they decide to do whatever they can to win their ex back. The problem is, repeatedly calling, emailing, visiting or following someone is not only dead cert guaranteed to drive the loved one even further away, it's also called stalking and it is illegal.

Rejected suitors are the most common type of stalker. Predominantly, they are men stalking women with whom they have once been intimate (although women can and do stalk men who have rejected them). The stalking is often a combination of wanting to punish the person for leaving them, as well as – bizarrely – trying to win them back. It all comes down to a sense of entitlement: 'How dare she reject *me*! I'll teach her a lesson! I want her back and I *will* get her back!' The victim's feelings are given no consideration at all.

Unfortunately, rejected suitors such as these are the most persistent of all stalkers. Recent research also shows that while stalking by partners is a risk factor for serious violence, including sexual violence and homicide, it is often not taken seriously, with police and many in the community perceiving partner stalking as less serious than stranger stalking.[21]

It's a bit like the way we in Australia view terrorism. Case in point: we're prepared to spend billions of dollars a year on attempting to protect Australians against terrorism – a threat that has killed precisely zero people on our shores. At the same time, funding for domestic violence services are being slashed – and this at a time when women are dying at the hands of their partners and ex partners at a rate of *more than one a week*. This is a statistic that confounds both humanity and commonsense. Don't get me started.

If asked to describe a typical stalker, most people plump for a stranger targeting a random victim – your classic Hollywood horror film. But the truth is far more prosaic. Your ordinary, everyday stalker is far more likely to be someone with whom you have been intimate. This may also explain why intimate partner stalking has significant effects on the mental health of victims, even years after the stalking has ended. The very person you once loved to bits now may want *you* in bits.

Stalking has been linked to increased risks of homicide, with one study finding that 68 per cent of women had been stalked in the 12 months leading up to an attempt on their life, or their eventual murder by an ex.[22] In this research the most frequent types of stalking included following or spying on the woman, unwanted phone calls, and surveillance by the perpetrator.

## Crazy Love

The 22-year-old girl (unnamed in court documents) was frightened. Some nights, she awoke to the sensation that someone was standing at the threshold of her bedroom. Other times, she could swear that she had felt the weight and warmth of a body lying next to her in the bed, or perched on the edge. So she turned to her former boyfriend – Jonathan McAlister, 23 – for help.

The pair had first come into contact at St Stephen's Presbyterian Church in Ipswich, Queensland, and their later breakup had been amicable. Perhaps McAlister could help her. And perhaps McAlister could: he installed a chain lock and a deadlock on her door. Perhaps he also could have STOPPED SNEAKING INTO HIS EX-GIRLFRIEND'S BEDROOM IN THE MIDDLE OF THE NIGHT.

What she didn't realise was that the one man she had turned to for protection was the one man that she should have been trying to keep out.

It seems that McAlister had not felt so sanguine about their separation after all. He began drinking heavily, and couldn't resist the temptation to see what his ex was up to in her new life. So he hacked into her Facebook account to check on her – using combinations of words and numbers that he knew she had used before – and then he took screenshots of any Facebook conversations she had with any men and saved them in a folder called 'cheating'. And he didn't stop there.

With access to information about her social life – where she might be going and who she might be seeing – McAlister stepped up his plan to see off any competitors and win her back. Any male who visited 'his girl' would return to his car to find that all the tyres had been let down. But when McAlister decided that 'his girl' was seriously dating someone else, he ramped his campaign up a notch. First, he poured petrol over the back steps of the Auchenflower, Brisbane home of a man he believed his ex was dating. The people inside put out the fire out with a garden hose and a bucket of water. Foiled by chance, McAlister then constructed and threw three Molotov cocktails at the house – only to have the wind blow out the flames before they exploded. At the court case, McAlister's lawyer claimed there had never been any intent to hurt, only to scare.

The judge was having none of it, according to the *Queensland Times* (17 September 2012), and said that the woman had been fooled once as to McAlister's real character, and been doubly fooled into thinking he could offer her any kind of protection thereafter. His obsession with the young woman was a sign of his immaturity, and also his need for psychiatric help. His actions were described as 'serious and alarming'.

McAlister was sentenced in September 2012 to two years in prison, but was immediately released on parole as he had already served more than 200 days in custody. McAlister's name pops up in later press reports when he appealed against a Blue Card cancellation order – given because of his history as a stalker, arsonist and computer hacker. McAlister wanted to volunteer at a Christian program for boys, the aptly named Boy's Brigade, but the Commissioner for Children and Young People feared he would be 'an inappropriate role model for children'.

McAlister's appeal was upheld, with QCAT member Ron Joachim saying, 'I accept that Jonathan works well with children and has always behaved responsibly around children … I am satisfied the applicant poses no real risk to children.'

No mention of the risk to any future girlfriends.

***

Rejected suitor stalking doesn't just happen to heterosexual people, as AFL player Alex Rance found out to his cost. Scott Raymond Thomas, 35 at the time, was sentenced to jail for one year (later reduced on appeal) and fined $3000 in the Melbourne Magistrates' Court in 2013 after pleading guilty to 27 charges, including stalking the then 23-year-old Richmond defender, harassing Rance's sister Alianne and scamming $50 000 after posing as a doctor and setting up a fake medical clinic in South Yarra to sell human growth hormones. If that wasn't bad enough, he'd also pretended to be a musician – a musical medico, no less – claiming to have performed at different licensed venues in a bid to fleece royalty payments from the Australasian Performing Rights Association.

Thomas created a fake Facebook profile and befriended Rance through this means in 2011. He lured in the football star with promises of an audition for a role on a non-existent sports-based reality television show on MTV. The pair later met up to discuss the program, Thomas using the pseudonym 'Scott Raymond'. The friendship lasted for four months in 2011, during which the pair went shopping together, ate out, saw movies together and texted constantly. And Thomas/Raymond was rapidly developing romantic feelings for Rance, telling him that he loved him and that he looked like a Greek god.

When Rance cooled on their friendship and began dodging further contact with him, Thomas did not take it well. He started sending Rance highly critical SMS messages and also hacked into Rance's online accounts, going so far as to message Rance's now-wife Georgia that Rance was 'living a lie and was in fact homosexual'.

In one message to Rance's sister, he wrote:

Wakey, wakey. Rise and shine. You know what your brother has to do within three hours or something bad will happen.

Another to Rance himself read:

This is the key words of wat I'm tryin to help u with -- Richmond fc, alex rance, off season testing, ur contract, sanctions, suspensions, media. U best get a heads up so call me.

However, possibly the weirdest thing that Thomas did was to organise a gay orgy at Rance's parents' house. Rance's sister and grandmother were home at the time when a parade of suspicious looking characters rocked up to the front door. Thomas also sent messages to members of the Richmond Football Club questioning Rance's integrity. The prosecutor told the court that Thomas's crimes had involved significant planning and intelligence and his hacking was extremely concerning for anyone in the community who uses the internet.

Thomas, from Newcastle in New South Wales, already had a significant criminal history in NSW and the US where he had been jailed for deception offences. His lawyer explained that he was mentally ill although that fact was little consolation for Rance and his family, who in their victim impact statements described how Thomas's behaviour had jeopardised their sense of personal and family safety.

## The Not-so-Casual Hook-up

I put out a call on social media for people who might be willing to talk to me about their experiences of being stalked by an ex. Fiona* was not only willing to talk, but also wrote her experience down for me. It shows that even the briefest, most casual of relationships can hold its dangers ...

My story starts at a particularly low point in my life. I'd just gone through a wreck of a breakup that lasted for several months and had left me emotionally destroyed, and him in a mental hospital.

I decided to put my feelers out for potential new interests, and I thought I hit gold. I found a rather attractive man via the internet (the same place I'd met my ex), and I'd agreed to meet him. Looking back, I probably should've known something was up when he kept adjusting our meeting plans closer to his place, and eventually to his place. But, my guard was down, and I agreed.

For now, let's just call him 'Larry'.

In full rebound mode and convinced I'd never find a lover again, I had sex with Larry, still unaware of anything odd until about two days later when he started talking about moving in together! I really didn't know what to think, other than that there was no way I was moving in with someone so quickly ... let alone with someone I had no interest in beyond physical comfort. So I started thinking of ways of letting him down nicely (since he clearly had thought we'd been in a relationship since Day 1). In the meantime, I continued to enjoy the comfort of a warm body next to me again.

One night, I stupidly agreed to smoke pot with him, which I'm quite convinced he had laced with heroin – especially now that I know he's a heroin addict. That night was terrifying. I could barely move, and I just remember drowsy, rough, uncomfortable sex that left me bruised, and not in a way that I enjoy. I was so incredibly subdued by whatever was in the pot that I couldn't bring myself to do anything but lie there.

He'd taken a pair of my knickers, which he, by admission, creepily obsessed over when I wasn't there.

Anyway, I continued with my decision to 'let him down easily'. I planned to do it on December 26th, because, for some reason, I thought he wouldn't freak out as much if it weren't on Christmas Day. I spent Christmas with a friend and her family, and I told her that if she didn't hear from me by 10 the next morning, to come or send someone to his address. So, obviously, while I still didn't know how bad things were, I knew something was very wrong.

I got up early, wrote a long letter, left it, and left.

Then the calls started.

At first it was whiny, crying calls, and I answered some.

Then they started coming in the middle of the night. I'd block his number, and he would call from another.

New Year's Eve was the point when I really knew it wasn't okay. My best friend was in town, visiting. Larry started calling early in the evening, and I ignored the calls. My friend knew something was up but wasn't sure what. By midnight, I had at least 20 missed calls, and they didn't stop when we got home. She threatened to call the police, wanted to talk to him, and begged me to go to the police the next day.

I woke up to a 'Happy New Year' post from him on my Facebook wall, calling me a loose slut, for my whole world, including my family, to see. I hadn't previously worried about Facebook because he never used it, as far as I could tell. I deleted his post and blocked him. So he created a new account to message me from. Blocked again.

I don't know why I didn't go to the police at this point. I think a lot of my reasoning, stupidly, was embarrassment. It's odd because the few friends who knew (I wouldn't even tell my therapist) were willing to go with me. I also really didn't think I had enough evidence for an order of protection. Now, I'm aware that there were already several orders against him.

Over the next couple of months, the calls continued. I kept my door locked 24/7 and never answered knocks. I refused to go out, for fear that he would turn up wherever I went.

Then I got an email from someone, asking if a particular craigslist post was about me. Larry had posted pictures of me and written terrifying things, saying I had herpes and was a whore. Fortunately, I got the person to take a screenshot of the post, because it had been deleted by the time I looked. So then I was able to print my first bit of actual evidence that he was doing something. [But] even that, I was sure, wouldn't have been enough to get any help from the police.

He would occasionally get through via the random numbers from which he called me. Usually, there were threats about destroying my future job opportunities because he knew people where I was interning/wanted to work. I was just waiting for the day that my supervisor would take me aside to talk about some creepy email or phone call about me. Luckily, that never happened.

Several months later, I'd posted an ad of my own on craigslist. I got a few responses, and then one from a guy who included some pictures, but something didn't seem quite right about it. After I responded once, I got a terrifying reply – from Larry, of course – all about what a terrible human being I was for this, that and the other thing.

I think what disturbs me the most is that I *barely knew* this person. We interacted (by choice) for maybe two weeks of my life. I never could have imagined years of terror resulting from that.

***

By summer, I was dating one of my friends. Together we went to karaoke. I'd previously refused going to karaoke events with friends for months before because I knew Larry was a regular. But this was at a gay bar: I didn't imagine he'd be going here, so I figured it was safe.

At this point in time, I'd threatened him that I would call the police if he contacted me again, as I really couldn't deal with what was now more than six months of threats and harassment.

He was there. Not only was he there, but he had the balls to walk up to my then boyfriend and ask to use his pen, clearly to see if he could unnerve me. I asked if we could leave.

Over the next year, I still received periodic calls from him in the middle of the night from random numbers. The threats stopped, although I'd get an occasional email from him from a new email address or a social networking site.

By the next summer, even these had mostly stopped. I still get a call or an email once in a blue moon, but they are sporadic enough that I can try to slough it off to a wrong number or a coincidence in name. Recently, I've gotten a bunch of texts from a random number – from a person who appears to know a bit about me. While I can hope that it's one of my friends messing around, I still have some concern that it may be Larry rearing his head.

About a year ago, I decided to finally join a particular alt-lifestyle website that friends had recommended to me for years. Who was the first face to pop up? Larry! I immediately blocked him. Then, I started looking into events and I learned that Larry had been going to them. Not surprisingly, though, I learned through another individual that he was banned from future gatherings due to his behaviour and drug use, so my fears were assuaged again.

Today, I occasionally see him roaming around on his bike, which sends me driving off in the opposite direction. While I have bought a new car since I 'knew' him, I still feel like he has some weird spidey sense and would see me instantly.

I still lock my doors all the time. I still often don't answer when someone knocks. My friends are very aware that I don't appreciate calls/texts past a certain time of night, due to it triggering memories. I still get nightmares that he's broken into my house and killed my cat. I am still afraid that he'll remember me and start up stalking me full-force again. I still regret ever talking to him in the first place. But, I'm incredibly glad and lucky that it wasn't any worse.

---

## I Don't Want to Be the Person I Am

Unlike Larry – and I am making a massive assumption here – some stalkers *do* realise that what they are doing is wrong; they are just unsure how to break the obsession they have developed. In one post I found on the internet, a stalker shares his struggle for freedom from his ex. I've edited it for clarity and grammatical sense, but otherwise it's in his own anonymous words. I hope for his sake and that of his ex, that he finds a solution.

Hey, really don't know where to go from here. It's horrible to admit, but I am a stalker and it feels so degrading. Basically, I broke up with my ex a few months ago. Since then I haven't been able to go a week without making any contact with her. I email her, I text her and I WhatsApp her. But she has now blocked me on Facebook, as well as WhatsApp. I've texted her up to 15 times a day and although she writes back most of the time, I still continue with the texting and harassment whenever she stops [responding].

I've been begging to meet up with her. I just can't take no for an answer. I've texted her up to 20 times today and I've found out she has had sex with another guy – she told me so.

Now I've been pestering her trying to find out who it is. It's torture not knowing who this person is, but I just can't help myself. She has now threatened to call the cops on me and I've never felt this low. I don't know what's wrong with me. I'm an attractive young guy, I get attention from girls pretty much every night I'm out, but I just can't seem to move on. I think about this girl quite literally every minute of the day and it's ruining my life. I'm no longer happy and this is destroying me.

When we first broke up, I went to see a counsellor and was prescribed anti-depressants, but months on, I still have not moved on from square one. Can anyone offer any help or words of advice as I can no longer see any light at the end of the tunnel? I wish I was normal. I wish I could deal with this break-up but I can't. I would do anything just to have her memory erased.

***

## Below the Glossy Surface

Simon* and Andrea* appeared to be the perfect Sydney couple. Both were highly successful businesspeople, fit, good looking, A-listers on the social scene, and loaded to boot. But underneath the designer clothes, the beautiful homes, the well-tended bodies and the luxury cars, a rotten secret was hiding. Andrea was mentally unstable. Even at its best, their relationship was volatile.

'It was like nothing I'd ever experienced before,' says Simon. 'I've been in love twice, and married once. Twenty-five years and three kids later, my wife and I divorced. That was tough at the time, but the eventual outcome has been good.' Simon dated a couple of women briefly after his divorce and then he met Andrea. 'She was gorgeous, exciting, energetic, and so vibrant. She was just great to be around.'

However, it didn't take long for the cracks in Andrea's perfect edifice to appear. 'At the start it was like 100 per cent happiness and zero per cent neurosis – then she changed.' In the blink of an eye, Andrea could veer from being sweet and loving to hopelessly neurotic, accusing Simon of infidelity, selfishness and worse. She'd insist he give her his phone and then scroll through his messages and emails, demanding to know exactly who each person was, and why he was in contact with them. 'It was like she was on a witch hunt, but there was nothing there for her to find. I don't multi-task,' says Simon. 'It was incredibly hard to cope with. It was like a seesaw, but over time I experienced a lot more of the neurosis and very little of the happiness.'

And it wasn't just him who noticed. After just a few dates, a friend of Simon's told him that he suspected Andrea was either anorexic or bulimic. 'His wife had seen Andrea throwing up after a dinner, and he'd laboured over whether to tell me or not.' In the circles in which he moved, Simon knew plenty of women who were razor thin and dined on lettuce leaves, but in the first flush of love, he figured that he would be able to cope with whatever problems Andrea had. 'I'd signed up for the whole package.' Andrea was five feet nine (175 centimetres) and lucky to weigh 48 kilos, Simon reckons.

The smallest things could set her off – like not being able to find a parking space outside his house. 'I'd be cooking dinner for her, and she'd flip me a text saying that she would be there in 10 minutes. Then she would ring and scream down the phone: I can't get a park, and someone abused me, and rah, rah, rah. And then she'd hang up on me.'

That time Simon rang back, 'I said, "Number one: do not hang up on me. Number two: I went to the market this morning. Dinner is almost ready, the candles are lit, the music is going, the heating is on. What is your problem? If you'd taken the time to actually listen to me, I would have told you to park across the neighbours' driveway as their garage is full of crap and their own cars are parked on the street." I told her to pull up out the front of my house and I would park the car for her.'

Describing the meal that night as a tense affair, Simon adds, 'I told her, "I am fairly accommodating. One hand washes the other, and a relationship has to be about give and take. So if I am cooking for you, at least be respectful."' Simon is not the type of person to take crap from anyone anywhere else, as his business record would suggest, so when Andrea started purring and suggesting that they retired upstairs, he pushed back. 'I couldn't switch off from what had happened before. It was like "Oh, and now you want me to *perform*? You're in my head in all the wrong ways, and that is NOT going happen."' After incidents like these – and there were many – Simon would usually withdraw for a few days.

In all the years they were together, Andrea never apologised for her behaviour. She told Simon that any problems they were having were his shit, not hers. 'Sorry,' he explains, 'is not a word she uses. If, just once, she'd walked back in and said, "That was a terrible outburst and I'm sorry," I would have given her a hug and asked what had been bothering her and what could I do. But it never happened.'

Having been slapped down time and time again, Simon decided it was time to take a stand. Whenever Andrea behaved badly, she was banished. 'There were times when she'd only been in the house five minutes when I told her to get out. I told her not to speak to me in that way, because I was already raw.'

Simon never raises his voice at work or at home, and because of his own family background is adamant that he would never hit a woman or child. If she'd been a man, he says it would have been a different matter. Instead, he decided they should seek help. The pair saw a couple of psychologists, who basically, as Simon describes it, told him to cut his losses. The words they used were 'borderline personality disorder'.

Simon wasn't convinced: 'I've spent my whole life fixing things. I do a lot of self-analysis and I'm supersensitive. I recognise that this is both my biggest strength and my biggest weakness. Her behaviour was hurtful, but I thought I could fix it. After all, I've never argued with my children. I've never had a single argument with my best friend. I looked at all that and thought: what's going on here when the rest of my life is perfectly calm?'

Because Simon and Andrea were well known, questions were being asked – in their social and business circles – about whether the couple was indeed still a couple. It was undoubtedly a difficult time for both. Simon thinks that the fact that Andrea's ex-husband had re-partnered and then fathered another child was a definite factor in her downward spiral. 'Her behaviour just escalated. She would say it didn't bother her, and I would encourage her to "just fucking admit that it bothers you! Have a good cry and let's talk about it."' But Andrea was more concerned about appearing fabulous than working on her emotional issues. Simon kept fighting for change. 'I kept saying, "You're already beautiful – forget about how you look. Work on your soul, you know. Mediate. Go to yoga. Walk. Get some help."'

The end came in January 2012 when Simon went to meet Andrea overseas, where she was doing some business. 'Her behaviour was so awful that I checked out of the room and hotel we'd been in. I can safely say it was the worst holiday of my life.' Andrea did not take it well. She started stalking him.

***

On the Tuesday before I interviewed Simon, he'd spotted Andrea crouched behind a Porsche outside his house. I carefully parked some houses away, having already heard some of his story and wondering whether she might target the car of any female visiting 'her man'. (Hefty insurance claims and insurance premiums matter to writers, let me tell you.) And it would not have been the first time Andrea had targeted a car connected to Simon.

The pair had swapped house keys – as you do in a relationship –

but when theirs had ended, Simon had had the locks changed, after his cleaner had found Andrea casually strolling around the house while Simon was at work. 'I'd already asked for them back and she had returned them, but she'd obviously copied them first.'

One time, Simon had been travelling overseas when Andrea sent him a photo of a woman that she'd heard he had been seeing. 'I thought, "For fuck's sake – what is this about?" Then she sends me a picture of my unmade bed. Then she goes through my bathroom cupboard and finds two packets of condoms – both unopened, I might say – and she opens them up and spreads them over the floor and photographs them and sends me a picture. I don't know what the hell you'd call that, other than obsessional.' (At least Andrea hadn't actually turned up at his overseas destination – she'd been known to do that too.)

Another time, Simon had parked his car outside his local pub only to find it gone when he returned. Initially he thought it may have been towed or stolen. 'It is worth a bit of money, just quietly, which probably makes me sound like a wanker, but I was concerned. I knew where I had parked it and thought I was going mad. I'd forgotten that six months earlier I had given her the spare key in case I ever had a problem. But the guy I'd been drinking with knew Andrea and he suggested that she'd taken it. Which she had. It was outside the front of my house.'

Despite having since had the locks changed, what he *hadn't* considered was that the key to his car also opened the door to his garage, which then gave Andrea direct access to his house. She had not only been inside his house, but she had stolen his iPad and from the comfort of her own home had then checked out his emails. Simon – now single – had asked another woman, Anna*, out on a date to a business function, but although there had been a fair bit of cheeky email banter backwards and forwards, Anna's child had been sick and she hadn't been able to go after all. Andrea was furious: she had the back of the iPad engraved with the words 'Traitor, liar, stalker', and then posted it back through Simon's letterbox.

Simon says with some chagrin, 'So now I had to ring this girl, Anna, and say, "I'm really sorry but my ex has just stolen my car, entered my house and stolen my iPad and read our emails and, um, you might get a call from her." Anna said that she had already had a nightmarish husband, didn't need the hassle and for me not to call her again.'

Another night, another date at home, and again the garage door went up. In marched Andrea, demanding to know who the woman was. It was definitely time to get a new key programmed …

***

Despite this, over the course of the next two years, Andrea and Simon probably reconciled – and then broke up – another 20 times. 'I felt torn – I'm still torn, if I'm honest. I feel sorry for her, because there is a beautiful woman trapped inside a little box trying to get out.' He says he has had a lot of trouble letting go too, but … 'I don't go to her house. I don't follow her. I don't chase her in my car. I don't feel the need to stalk her.'

Andrea has certainly done all of the above – one time going so far as to wait outside Simon's house all night for him to emerge, then when he did – 'She leapt out of the car and started running towards me. I'm backing out of the garage and she's trying to hit the side mirror, and I ended up slapping the left hand side of the car into the bloody house – three grand's worth of damage. I roared off and she chased me down the street in her car.' But Simon is a keen car racer, so swiftly – if perhaps illegally – managed to lose her in the space of a few turns.

Simon blocked Andrea on his personal social media, but she still sent emails to him at work and commented on his company's social media feeds. His PA had the task of deleting them.

Sometimes Andrea would insist to him that it was all over, that she just wanted to be friends and that he could date whoever he wanted, but when he acted upon this, by actually asking someone out on a date, 'Andrea would start in on me, as if we were still in a relationship and I was cheating on her. She even threatened me recently that if she had a gun she'd use it. I can't call her on bullshit like this because it is completely futile.'

One of his first dates with another woman – four months after Simon and Andrea had once again parted ways – ended with Simon and his date returning to his house, only to find Andrea was hiding behind a sports car in the street outside. There was a very awkward moment, where Simon was forced to introduce his stalker ex to the girl with whom he was hoping to get lucky. Simon sent Andrea packing, but the next day Andrea contacted him angrily to say that she had 'seen me rolling around on the floor with the girl'.

Andrea's stalking was doing nothing for Simon's putative attempts to have a love life. 'I invited one girl, Lauren*, around for dinner and the whole time Andrea was sitting out the front in her car. In normal circumstances, Lauren probably would have gone home about 10.30 p.m., but she was so terrified that it wasn't until Andrea finally got out of the car at 2.30 a.m. and went for a walk around the block, that Lauren was able to make a run for it. The whole time she was saying, "You can't send me out there in front of your neurotic ex-girlfriend!"'

Another woman Simon briefly dated also refused to leave his house until he had made sure the coast was clear. For the six weeks they were dating, she refused point blank to sleep over.

***

No longer having access to Simon's house, Andrea took desperate measures. Simon was lying in his upper-storey bedroom one night when suddenly a large bang on the roof above his head woke him up. ' "Fuck, that's a big possum," I thought to myself. "That's a polar bear possum!" ' He put on a robe and took a look out on the balcony, only to find Andrea standing there. She was 'full of valium and alcohol', Simon says, and claimed she just wanted to talk. He escorted her out and as he watched from the doorway, he saw her remove a small stepladder from the wall and stow it in her car. She'd somehow managed to gain enough height to scale the wall of the building and crawl across the roof to access the balcony.

While furious at this invasion of privacy, Simon is still concerned for Andrea's safety – heights and a head full of alcohol being no great combination at the best of times. 'I worry about her falling off, I worry about what I might find on the ground outside when I go outside every morning. She could be injured or even worse. The newspapers would have a field day with it.' Sleep is not so easy to come by these days he admits, always aware that she could be preparing to make another high-level foray.

His sons are concerned at how the stalking has affected their father, taking note of each new security precaution – the new keys and garage remote, and even the reinforced steel flap over the letterbox. That last addition was made after Andrea admitted watching him through the gap while he was entertaining a group of friends. 'She actually gave me a blow-by-blow description of what went on that night, right down to the number of times I went to the bathroom and when I changed my top.' Andrea also claimed to have employed a private investigator to film his movements, but it seems that she could not stop herself from carrying out her own surveillance.

A neighbour rang Simon at work one day to complain that he'd found her crouched down behind his rubbish bins, keeping an eye on Simon's front door. Simon himself often sees her doing drive-bys. 'And I've come home at 2 a.m. in the morning to find her standing outside the front of my house. I confronted her. I asked her what she thought she was doing. I said, "Are you happy now? As you can see I'm coming home alone. I'm pretty much fucked. I can't go on with my life because you're stalking me. And I can't go back to you because you're so fucked up. And I'm miserable because I'm stuck in a void."'

The police were finally called in when Simon arrived home one day to find an upstairs window had been broken, and her footprints nearby – distinctive shoeprints with a crisscross pattern like a cooked steak, he notes. The blinds had been down, and Simon thinks she got angry or frustrated at not being able to see in – or perhaps she was just cross that he was not home. They visited her at home, and Andrea then texted Simon to say, 'Best we don't communicate any more.'

Even though their paths do occasionally cross in social and business circles, 'people know that if they invite me, they really can't invite Andrea, and vice versa. I'm fine with that. I just want my life back.'

Simon hopes that the police warning will stop her stalking him. But he does care about what happens to her. 'Intuitively, I'm the kind of person who will nurture someone who's helpless. I always wonder when I'll get a phone call to say that something has happened to her – whether drink driving or drugs or something else. I dread that day.'

---

## Never Let Go

Research from the US and elsewhere shows that domestic violence perpetrators are far more likely to stalk their exes than ordinary folk. And it makes sense if you think about it – a violent and controlling man is the last person to meekly step aside and wish his wife or girlfriend all the best for a new life without him in it. This was certainly the case for Jenni*, who survived years of domestic violence before finally escaping – only to find that she hadn't really escaped at all. Her enraged ex, Stefan*, was never going to let her go.

Jenni's daughter, Mia*, says that she has few happy memories of her teenage years. 'There was a lot of violence at home while I was growing up. I wasn't really aware of it as a younger child, but as my sister and I hit our teenage years, things became steadily worse.'

Stefan was working away from home at that time, and would only return on weekends. 'On Friday afternoons, we'd basically just shit ourselves. Then he would arrive home and on some pretext, he'd start a heated argument, which would be followed by violence. My sister and I would be thrown out of the house and we'd head around the corner to the park to wait until our mother could come and pick us up.'

Mia and her sister used to try and intervene when their mother was being bashed or bullied, and that only led to Stefan turning his fists on the two girls. He'd also use violence if they didn't behave exactly as he wanted. 'He was very cunning. He'd be very careful to hit us in areas where the bruising wouldn't show. We'd get punched in the stomach – stuff like that. He was also very good at emotional manipulation.'

Today Mia thinks that her father's own childhood may have had something to do with his attitude. 'Apparently my grandfather was quite violent too – there were stories of my father being scrubbed with a wire brush, beaten with a cast iron frying pan and stabbed in the chest with a fork when my grandfather was "emphasising a point". My grandfather wasn't like that to me at all ... he was wonderful, but I know he behaved badly towards my father.'

But the girls refused to be cowed by their father. 'There was no way we were going to go down meekly and mildly.' The police were no help. 'Dad was a coward – when things got out of control at home, he would ring the police and they would come around to the house and tell us off! Police don't think that perpetrators make phone calls to the police – they assumed it was us causing all the trouble. They thought we were delinquent girls and he was a nice man trying to raise his daughters the right way.'

The two girls avoided bringing friends home to such a toxic environment, and Mia says there was little support to be found elsewhere. 'I acted up in high school, but no one ever bothered to find out why. People just don't understand domestic violence.'

Mia remembers one of her bosses once saying that she didn't get why kids don't disclose about domestic violence. 'And I just looked at her and said, "They don't know that there is anything wrong – that there is something they *should* disclose. It's all they know. That's normal life for them – it's the way things are, and have always been. They think everybody's life is like that."'

Mia acknowledges that her sister probably bore the brunt of her father's aggression. She was assaulted regularly, ended up leaving school at 15 and was thrown out of home by her father not very long after. She then had a series of abusive relationships and became dependent on drugs. 'I thought she was lucky because she was able to escape and get out of the house.'

There had been a brief respite when Mia was aged 13, and her mother found the courage to leave Stefan. The three ended up living in a caravan, and Jenni worked hard to keep their heads above water financially. But Stefan wasn't going to give up that easily. 'He stalked her and he stole her car. He also tried bribing us back by buying gifts for her and for us, and when that didn't work he escalated the stalking.'

Statistics show that a whopping 85 per cent of women who leave an abusive relationship will return, with financial dependence on the perpetrator and not wanting their children to experience a decline in living standards being significant factors in that decision. In particular, having at least one dependent child, not being employed outside of the home, possessing no property that is solely theirs, and lacking access to cash or bank and credit accounts are common reasons for going back into such a dangerous environment.

Jenni was in regular work so had some financial resources, but Mia knows the situation was much more complicated. Stefan's family had no idea about his behaviour and Mia's mum was isolated from family support too, as they lived in a different state. Both families had opposed Jenni and Stefan's relationship from the very beginning.

209

Mia adds, 'People saw my dad very differently to how he actually was. He was a quiet, unassuming, diminutive man.'

Jenni finally gave into Stefan's threats and returned to the family home. Mia admits she was resentful and found it difficult at the time to understand why her mother would put them back into that environment again. 'We knew he'd stolen the car, and that he'd bought us gifts, because we saw them. But we didn't know the whole story. Mum was like most mothers who've suffered domestic violence – no one really knew what was happening because she didn't tell anyone, and she was also trying to minimise the impact on us kids.

'In a warped kind of way, I think she went back for us. It must have been hard trying to pick the lesser of two evils. As an adult, I understand that life is difficult and things are more complex than they first appear. So I can't make any judgement of my mother – she did what she thought was best at the time.'

Mia got her own chance to escape aged 19. And shortly afterwards so did her mother. Again, Stefan was relentless in his pursuit of his ex. Mia wasn't aware of the full extent of what was going on – being caught up in her studies and her new life – but her dad did his best to get her on side. 'He'd turn up at my place at all hours of the day and night to tell his side of the story. He was pretending to be a concerned husband who was simply worried about what was going to happen to his wife if they got divorced. He claimed she would spend all her time at the pokies spending all his money. He was pretty relentless with other members of the family as well. He tried to convince the world he was right … but he was a power freak and simply couldn't handle rejection. I think he had a fantasy of his family in his head that didn't relate to reality at all. There was no way he was ever going to back off.'

Mia admits she found it difficult dealing with her mother during that time too. 'It must have been tough on mum. I understood why she had left him and didn't blame her, but I hated the consequences: Dad constantly phoning and turning up at my place to whine, and all this at a time when I was going through my own family difficulties. And the fact that he was stalking her was hard to deal with too … When someone has been stalked for a long time, you tend to not take them seriously. You think that maybe they are exaggerating what is happening. I know that sounds *horrible* for me to say that, but that's how I felt at the time. I was aware of what Dad was doing, but not the full extent of it.'

What her father was doing was yet to become a criminal offence in Australia – but essentially it involved endless phone calls, turning up at the house at all hours, turning up at Jenni's friends' houses at all hours, following Jenni's car and bugging her house. On a number of occasions police found him in the back lane outside Jenni's house and also hiding in her garden. Then in February of that year, Stefan cracked and assaulted Jenni with a lump of wood. He was charged with malicious wounding and a trial date was set, but before that day rolled around, he went one step further again. Jenni was murdered.

It was in the days before mobile phones and Mia was away on holiday and out of contact, but one day she rang her ex who was looking after her children while she was travelling. 'He asked me how quickly I could get home. He wouldn't tell me why and I thought it was something to do with the children, so I became hysterical. Finally he had to tell me that my mother had died – that she had been murdered.' It was the return trip from hell, with her motorbike breaking down, a friend picking her up in a car and then putting her on a train, and the police picking her up at the other end to take her down to the police station. Throughout it all, Mia says she felt out of touch with reality. The one thing she was sure of was that it was her father who had done it.

Today Mia says she has difficulty remembering the date of her mother's murder – 'It was either April 23 or 25. I always confuse the date with the number of stab wounds that my mother had.' Unbelievably, given the ferocity of the attack, Jenni was able to dial triple zero, give her address and name her killer before collapsing.

She was also able to name her ex-husband to an ambulance officer at the scene, and also her attending doctor when she reached hospital. Then she died – at least four of the stabbing wounds to her jugular and liver and spleen had been lethal, not to mention the impact of so many cuts, including defensive wounds to her hands and arms.

Stefan was charged with murder and held in remand pending trial.

★★★

'I never once thought he was innocent. There was no doubt in any of our minds that Dad was guilty. But he was still my father. You want to hate that person with all your heart – and you do – but you also love them. It's complicated,' says Mia with admirable understatement.

While Stefan was in prison awaiting his trial for the murder of his wife, Mia received many phone calls from him. It was a bizarre situation. 'I don't think there are too many other people who have to deal with the stalker and murderer of their mother ringing them from jail. The corrections officer would ask if I was prepared to take the call, and I just couldn't say no. He was still my father. So I would have to sit there and listen to him proclaiming his innocence.'

The court case finally took place two years after Jenni's death, and many of the revelations were to prove shocking. To avoid identifying Jenni, I'm not going to share too many here, but suffice it to say that not one friend or family member or even neighbour stood up for Stefan, who claimed to have been fast asleep in bed at the time of the murder. Several acquaintances instead told of the pleasure Stefan had said he'd experienced in seeing fear in Jenni's eyes when he assaulted her. Another said that Stefan had told him that he would cut Jenni's throat rather than provide a divorce settlement.

There were allegations of contracts that had been taken out on lives: hitmen, and private investigators, and bugging and surveillance. There was evidence given that the front door had been forced on the night Jenni died. No knife had been found, but investigating officers did find a stun gun in the bedroom where Jenni was attacked, along with a tyre iron and .357 Magnum revolver.

Stefan's defence team countered with accusations of mental instability (Jenni's not Stefan's), and promiscuity – neither of which claims Mia believes held a single grain of truth. They blamed Jenni's death on a hitman, and provided details of a likely character who may have done the job, but no trace of him could be found.

Mia and her sister took the stand and gave clear and compelling evidence against their father. Both the judge and jury were convinced: Stefan was convicted of murder, and he immediately lodged an appeal.

Stunningly, at the second trial, Stefan was found NOT guilty – and this despite the fact that Jenni had clearly identified him as her attacker before her death. This is known as a dying declaration, and as the law would have it:

> The principle on which this species of evidence is admitted is, that they are declarations made in extremity, when the party is at the point of death, and when every hope of this world is gone; when every motive to falsehood is silenced, and the mind is induced by the most powerful considerations to speak the truth; a situation so solemn and so awful is considered by law as creating an obligation equal to that which is imposed by a positive oath administered in a court of justice.[23]

In essence, the second judge in all his wisdom decided that even though Jenni said on her deathbed that her estranged husband was the one who attacked her, she was wrong. In fact, *because he had been stalking her* in the previous months, the judge said she simply assumed that her assailant was her husband. Stefan was free to resume his life.

'He got away with it,' Mia says.

***

But it was not over for Mia or her sister. The day her father got out of jail, Mia received a phone call, telling her to 'Die slut.' Mia immediately rang the detectives who'd investigated her mother's murder and was told to get out of the house straight away and go to the local police station. The local coppers were less understanding. 'They had the attitude: "Oh, I don't think your father would do that, darling,"' says Mia. There were no more death threats, but plenty of hang-up calls over the next while – each time, terrified for her life, Mia would flee the house and stay with friends. Eventually, Mia made the difficult decision to take her children, leave the stable home she'd created for them and even change all their names. She knew exactly what her father was capable of, and had no intention of letting him find her.

Thirty years later, Mia is not even sure whether her father is alive. She did contact her grandmother – her father's mother – on one brief trip back to Australia, but was less than impressed when she tried to convince Mia to contact Stefan and forgive him if she ever wanted to get her inheritance. The family has also warned her that Stefan has said he'll leave the money to the RSPCA if none of his children will talk to him. 'Like I care about that!' says Mia. 'I've forgiven him – I don't hold hatred in my heart – but I can't absolve him from what he has done. I just don't want to have anything to do with him.'

If Mia sounds remarkably calm about the violent incidents that shaped her past, it is a hard won sense of peace she enjoys today. For a very long time, she was frightened and hyper-vigilant about the safety of her children. She found it difficult to trust new people, and went through what she describes as 'mental and emotional agonies'. One counsellor had said to her that emotionally she was like a champagne bottle that had been shaken up, that she should take care to take the cork out slowly or the bottle would not be able to handle the pressure any more and would explode. In 2004, at a low point in her personal life, that's exactly what happened. 'It was totally debilitating. I couldn't stop crying, and I'd never been a crier in my life. I was a total wreck: I couldn't work, I couldn't do anything.' She credits some skilful counsellors and the support of some amazing friends for helping her move past the grief and anger. 'It's going to sound very strange, but my mother's death turned out to be an incredible growth experience. When faced with such a terrible, horrible thing, you can either let it destroy you or you can grow from it.'

# Through the Eyes of a Stalker

It's not easy finding someone who is prepared to admit that they are a stalker. So hats off to Lea\*, from Los Angeles – a friend of a friend – who responded to an email callout for people to share their experiences. Lea was still a high school student when she first became obsessed with Jenner\*, and her experience – in her own words – shows just how damaging obsession can become for all concerned.

What drives someone to stalk someone else is a question I will leave for the psychologists. But hearing Lea's story, I could empathise with her desire for closure at the end of a youthful relationship that meant a lot to her. And I can definitely empathise with Jenner, the young man Lea has pursued for 11 years.

It's a little like one of those perception puzzles: is it a witch or a beautiful young girl? On first sight, this seems like a clear-cut case of unrequited teenage love. On closer examination, however, Lea's lack of insight into her own behaviour and her insistence on 'just happening' to run into Jenner make it clear that she's still a long way from letting go. Without victim blaming, it's also clear that Jenner has played his own part in her obsession – perhaps out of a misguided idea of being kind to an ex-girlfriend. On the one hand, he calls her a stalker. On the other, he strings her along with fake promises – 'I'll call you.' One wonders what might have happened if he had emphatically told her, 'Leave me alone' or sought help from the authorities when it became clear that she was not going to leave him alone. It is never the victim's fault, but the victim's response to a stalker can affect the outcome.

## The High School Crush

I first met Jenner in my freshman year of high school. We had an English class together and one day we made eye contact while passing back graded papers, and it was all over for me. I had a big crush on him, and it was obvious he was keen too, but nothing was said at that stage. Originally he wouldn't talk to me, and just followed me in the hall, when I was walking to class or my locker or even to the bike rack. He kept a fair amount of distance between us – I'd wave at him when I saw him following me, but he never came close enough to say hello.

After about two weeks of this, I wanted more, so on the way to my bike one day, I quickly dodged behind a door so when he came out, I was behind *him*. The disappointed look on his face when he couldn't see me was priceless. I gave him a nice surprise when I stepped next to him and said, 'You waiting for someone special?' His reaction confirmed both our feelings.

Being young, we started off lamely passing notes during the class we shared. Unfortunately, being young *and* stupid, it was about this time that I started experimenting with drugs – mostly prescription drugs such as muscle relaxants and Xanax. Occasionally I had also a bit of weed and alcohol with my friend, Karen, and some of her girlfriends (although I was never particularly close to them). I became famous for bringing the snacks, usually homemade brownies and cookies I'd made from scratch.

One day at school I was sitting on the floor by my desk with a big headache and struggling to stay awake when I found a long note from Jenner. It was two pages from front to back and in it he described how he'd liked me from the first day he saw me, but was too nervous to tell me (hence him following me around). He explained how he was having trouble functioning as he was planning what to say to me to ask me out, but didn't have the courage. He'd then copied out the song lyrics from The Ramones' 'I Want to Be Your Boyfriend' – that's how he first asked me out.

We would have lunch together, hold hands, make small talk, and *that was it for months!* I wanted more, so at one point I told him, 'I'm gonna do something crazy, just go with it ...' and I pushed him into a wall and kissed him hard. He was less than into it – like he was just going along with the kiss just to humour me – and I noticed and felt that spark just twinkle away. I apologised and told him to forget about it. I even gave him a bag of apology gifts. I'm an idiot.

Summer holidays were approaching and we had gone back to 'baby steps', but I could still sense tension. And despite the fact that Jenner and I were pretty well established as girlfriend and boyfriend, we'd never actually been out on a date. At the time, that really pissed me off. So did the fact he didn't want to move forward with anything more physical – my teenage hormones were raging.

I confided in my friend Karen about it and regrettably we got so stoned that I did some things I now wish I hadn't – starting off with Karen and me calling him at home. His mother answered and said that no, he wasn't there and no, she didn't know he had a girlfriend. I said I'd call back later, but given our drug-addled state of mind, we didn't even wait an hour. I think we probably rang her three times that day. I'm an idiot.

It wasn't pleasant to admit or experience, but I realised that my emerging drug problem was helping to ruin things between Jenner and me, so I quit. Withdrawal was hard – not shivering in a corner kind of hard – but I was moody, sweaty and was constantly fighting temptation. The lack of physical action with Jenner was difficult too. One day he asked me how my morning had been and I jokingly replied that 'I'd some good vibrations on my bike on the way to school – so that was nice.' The look on his face showed me that perhaps that might have been the wrong thing to say.

Later on, one of the girls in my class told me that Jenner went to her church and his parents had been 'kinda strict' with him lately because he'd been acting out. He never told me any of his background although it would have explained a lot – why he didn't show affection, why his mom didn't know we were together and probably even why we never went out on a date. I felt bad not knowing any of that. I feel that if he'd shared this information, it may have changed the course of our entire relationship. Thinking back, at one point I even asked him if he'd like to take my virginity in the janitor's closet to which offer I distinctly remember him responding, 'I'm really interested, but no.' I'M SUCH AN IDIOT!

Summer break came along and this was probably when things really went downhill and crashed and burned ... and if that wasn't bad enough, I then reset the fire and added more wood.

Okay, I'll admit that I became pretty stalker-ish over that time. School was over, I wanted to hang out with Jenner, and how else was I going to see him? I called him multiple times. Sometimes we would have conversations for hours on end about what we wanted out of life and what next year was going to be like, but we never met up. Then eventually my phone calls started to be answered by other people who'd tell me that Jenner wasn't home and they didn't know when he would be back. This went on for almost a month. At one point I said to myself, 'Forget this; it's not worth my time. If he can't make time for me and put in some effort this isn't gonna work.'

I thought we should meet up in person because breaking up with someone over the phone is rude and the coward's way out, and I'm someone who likes clarity. I called him every day three times a day for two weeks, wanting to explain this. It was getting ridiculous hearing the same thing every time I rang: he's not home. It was pretty obvious that I was not only wasting my time, but also giving a horrible impression of myself. I'm an idiot.

I decided to leave things as they were and never picked up the phone again. Why waste my time, right? I even went out on a few ACTUAL dates with a guy who had just graduated from high school and been accepted into university. That didn't last long as he ended up getting back with his ex (this didn't bother me as he was a little too old for me at the time). I also went out on another date with my neighbour's son – who was visiting for the weekend – but we didn't click. Not a big deal; I was content.

And this is when I really lost it.

Exactly one week before school started up again, I returned from a friend's house and my mom told me I'd had a phone call. I assumed I'd left something behind at my friend's house, but no. It was Jenner. I don't recall the exact conversation, but it went something like this:

ME: 'Hey, what's up?'

JENNER: 'There's something i need to tell you ...'

ME: 'Okaaaay?'

JENNER: 'We need to break up. I'm sorry. This just isn't working out.'

ME (stunned because I totally thought we already had broken up): 'Uh ... okay?'

JENNER: 'Bye.'

Click. Jenner hangs up.

That son of a bitch! There I was thinking that he's an asshole who can go fuck himself for ditching out on me and ignoring me to death. But after I'd already moved on, after the wounds had healed and I was back on the dating merry-go-round, and then he pulls a stunt like this?

***

The new school year started and I thought it was best to stay away from him at all costs – if only to avoid an awkward confrontation. Then, in the first class of the day, it turned out that he had been assigned the seat right next to me. (Coincidentally, my best friend Karen was assigned to sit in front of me.) Talk about an awkward situation; she was no help as she thought it was funny that I was embarrassed to be sitting next to him. She even asked me directly about how things had gone with Jenner over the summer when he could clearly hear everything as he was sitting RIGHT THERE! She also asked about the college guy I dated. I assume she meant well – to show Jenner just how over him I was and what he was missing out on, but I only realise that now. At the time, I was just embarrassed.

At the end of this very awkward day, I stopped on the way home to get a slushie at 7-11 and guess who happened to be there with his friends? Yep, Jenner. All his friends yelled out, 'Hey, here's Jenner's ex!' and he looked at me like I had intentionally followed him there. He gave me a wave and that was it. I hopped on my bike to ride home when my chain broke and my day became even worse. At that point, I decided to take the bus rather than walk home, but when I got on, who was sitting there but Jenner. We both tried not to make eye contact the whole time we were on the bus together.

I seriously don't know if I was unconsciously doing this, but these coincidences went on for MONTHS. I'd go food shopping with my mom, and there he was. I'd go with my friends to an amusement park, and there he would be. We'd run into each other in the hallway and even at the family picture day at Sears. WTF was going on here? I know he wasn't following *me*, because he always there first. I knew he wouldn't say anything to me, and talking had never really worked for us before, so I handled things the best way I knew: I wrote him a note.

In the note, I described how I felt when he'd rung to break things off with me, and how I'd thought we'd already broken up and that I'd already moved on. I also explained how I felt anxious about his friends taunting me as 'Jenner's ex' even though we never officially went out in the first place. Then I questioned why the universe kept putting us in the same place way too many times and asking if he was actually really good at running into me or if I was right and it was just a coincidence. It was actually making me furious not knowing why this was happening.

When I went to give the note to Jenner, he wouldn't take it – he called me a stalker and actually backed away from me. I insisted that he take it, which he eventually did, but I never got an answer. He probably never read it.

Thankfully, later that year I moved to another city, never to be tortured with this crap again ... or so I thought. I ended up doing really badly at school, frequently truanting at one point. I'm afraid to say that one day I took a trip to my old school to surprise my friend Karen and get her to ditch with me, and guess who I ran into first ... Jenner. He made eye contact then kept walking as if I didn't exist. I never went back again.

Some years down the line, I quit school entirely, got married and had two kids, then separated and moved back in with my mom. I signed up for a school that teaches massage therapy, and was at last feeling great about myself. My crappy marriage was over and I was gaining some independence. Then all of a sudden, it started again.

I was riding the bus home from class, exhausted and still in my scrubs, when a bearded guy across the way caught my eye. 'You wouldn't happen to be Jenner, would you?' I asked, and with a sigh, he responded, 'I guess that makes you Lea.' I'll admit I got a little excited – I asked him about what he'd been up to the last few years and told him about my kids and marriage. He said that he was on his way to work and that he was in and out of different bands and living on his friend's couch because he couldn't stay with his family anymore. I felt good knowing I was better off than he was – smug even. I was so wrapped up in feeling awesome, that I excused myself with a big smile on my face only to find that I had hopped off the bus at the wrong stop. I'm an idiot.

★★★

One day, my mother and I went to a sandwich shop – my first ever visit to that particular shop. I was a bit taken aback when the guy serving greeted me with a 'Hey, Lea.' Of course, it was Jenner. And of course, my mother decided that this sandwich shop was her new favourite. After only three more visits from us, Jenner quit his job there. One of his co-workers told me that he was now working at a hot dog place up the street.

One day I was dropping the kids off with my babysitter and they started whining about being hungry, so I ran to a nearby restaurant to grab them some food. Why didn't I just get McDonalds? Instead, I stopped at a hole-in-the wall place called Buldogis, and I hadn't even gone through the door before I heard a familiar voice: 'Hey, Lea.' It was Jenner, and this was the hotdog place where he now worked. I'm an idiot.

It took all my energy to try to keep it casual. I ordered my food and he started talking to me while he was cooking – in fact, he was super nice and even gave me a business card for his new band (which I didn't even look at, and later lost). Everything would have been great, if I hadn't blushed so much and if my hands hadn't been shaking like crazy. What was wrong with me? My adrenaline levels were going through the roof.

★★★

I started dating a guy and for our first date we went to a pub to play pool. I noticed that his shirt said 'Rent Ratz*' and I asked if that was his band because I knew he was a singer, but didn't remember the name of the band. He explained that it was his friend's band and that he was going to play a show with them that weekend and that I should go.

The day of the show came around and my boyfriend introduced me to his band and then to the members of Rent Ratz, and it turns out the bass player is ... FUCKING JENNER! What kind of world would allow this? My boyfriend noticed the look of shock and embarrassment on my face and he said, 'You know each other?' to which Jenner replies, 'Yes, she's my stalker and she's very good at it.' That was the most awkward night I had had in years.

Being with someone who is in a local band you notice two things: 1. All their music sucks, which is why they have never made it big; and 2. Local bands frequently play together. Trying to support my boyfriend, I sucked it up every time his and Jenner's bands did a show together, but the adrenaline rush I experienced whenever I saw Jenner was getting out of hand. I hate to say it, but I wanted more. One night we went to a lame after party, and as Jenner's ride didn't want to go, I offered him a lift. I drove like a maniac that night to the point it was almost embarrassing. At the party, there was a pool and weed and booze and we played drinking games and just chilled. I was hoping that if I made a good impression, Jenner and I could at least be friends instead of awkward acquaintances. But it didn't work out that way.

Not long after, my boyfriend's band kicked him out and he got all depressed and asinine so I moved out. Two months later, he ended up running away to California and marrying his high school girlfriend after only reconnecting for one week. They now have a kid and he still owes me around $1100 for the apartment fines he left.

I honestly thought that was the last time I was ever going to see Jenner because I had no reason to go to the shows anymore or to use the babysitter near his restaurant. But I couldn't help myself – I frequented it a lot – more than a lot actually – at least once a week. Jenner doesn't have a Facebook account but his band does, so I also kept up with all his shows and updates and even brought my friend Karen to a few of them so it looked like we were hanging out. Sometimes he would approach to say hi and those moments drove me crazy, but that's all that ever came of it.

***

Unfortunately, my need for more hit a brick wall one day so I stopped at the restaurant and gave Jenner my phone number. He said he'd love to hang out sometime, which was enough to make me regress. The last time I went to the restaurant, I asked him out to a show and he said, 'Probably not, but I still have your number. I'll call you.' He never did and I have never gone back. His other band members frequently invite me to their shows and I'll admit I still want to go but I don't want to seem like I'm an obsessive running joke that won't go away. Like I can't take a hint or that he was just being polite all this time. I'm an idiot.

To this day, I still drive by his house and hope to get a glance, or look on Facebook to see if a new photo of him has been posted. I still hope one day to get that call from him. I wonder how long it will be before I run into him again. Sometimes I also talk to his friends on Facebook and hope they'll bring up his name in conversation so I sound less like a freak. As I think I've said, I am an idiot.

## The Power Aphrodisiac

I have to admit that the Police song 'Every Breath You Take' inspired the title for this book. Even as a teenager, I found the lyrics pretty, well, stalkery. Every move you make, I'll be watching you, indeed. It could well be the stalker theme song of the century.

And there is definitely something about Sting and stalkers. The other song of his that really freaked me out as a young lass was 'Don't Stand So Close to Me'. The idea of a teacher lusting after a student kind of turned my stomach, if I'm frank. (Or maybe it was just the male teachers at my school. Maybe I would have felt differently if Sting had been standing at the front of my classroom and not the dreaded Mr Weelin.)

But the idea of having a relationship with an authority figure – whether a celebrity, politician, boss or teacher – is the stuff of fantasy for many. It's when fantasy tips over into reality that the real trouble can start, as the following post from a young student on an anonymous forum shows.

It's easy to dismiss this as a schoolgirl crush – much like Lea's – but I am sure the teacher in question would feel less than comfortable about the level of interest in his personal life she has shown, and also what she has been able to uncover so easily. It's a lesson for all of us about the importance of maintaining strict cybersecurity, and how easily techno-savvy teens can exploit loopholes that older users simply don't know exist.

HELP ME

I can't believe that my life has come to this point. It's really scary when I think about it. It started in Year 8, and he was my teacher. His insight, intellect, and sense of humour is what drew me to him initially. I would talk to all of my friends about him and they would call me crazy and tease me. They didn't understand how much he actually meant to me. I was head over heels with him, but he was as old as my brother (who is about 15 years older than me).

After that year, I kind of forgot about him, but when I moved up to Senior School, he was there too and I was flooded with a familiar sense of want. Some of my friends had classes with him so I would go into their classes and hang out with them until the bell rang. Again, my friends called me pathetic, but I didn't care. They didn't understand.

It got worse over the course of the year. My locker was right near his classroom, and it just about drove me nuts. I would go out of my way to have a CHANCE to see him standing by his classroom, and I was always almost tardy to the last period of the day because of that. He started to take over my mind. He was all I thought about and every action revolved around the possibility of seeing him. I started to visit him after school, and would make up some excuse just to speak with him. But I was running out of excuses. So I used the lovely site of Facebook. Of course his profile was set to private, so I did a search of the old fashioned phonebook and figured out who his parents were and where they lived. Then I tracked them down on Facebook.

It felt creepy looking at his family, but I couldn't help myself. I found pictures of him and lots of posts about him. They made me giggle and feel happy. I had already known how old he was because he had told our class in Year 8. Now I found out he was born in August. Raised in a small town. One of his parents is also a teacher. He has one sister who is younger and married. He isn't married and has a 'partner'. I know what his house looks like because pictures of it have been posted. I know exactly where he lives. I know his 'partner's' name. I know way more about him than I should. But I can't help it; I just get lost in it.

What is making me so scared is the fact that a month or so ago I found out which car in the teachers' car park is his, and I've memorised his license plate number. Now I am so scared because I think my interest in him has gotten out of hand. He might be my teacher next year and he and I are fairly close. But

I don't want to **** that up by being his stalker instead of his friend. Do I need help? Do I need to tell someone about this? It all started so innocently but now it's gone far enough to where I am afraid I will hurt him (not physically). Help.

***

Aside from teachers and others in a position of authority, doctors and others in the medical profession seem particularly prone to attract stalkers. Perhaps it is the nature of their work – caring for others – that can lead an ill, lonely or mentally disturbed patient to mistake their doctor's professional concern as a romantic interest. In any case, research shows that healthcare professionals – particularly those working in mental health – are frequently over-represented amongst stalking victims.[24]

One friend of mine, a psychiatrist, was haunted for months by late night phone calls to her mobile from a (female) patient. Lisa* handled this with sensitivity, but when her young son was diagnosed with kidney failure and placed on the organ donation priority list, those obsessive phone calls almost drove her to breaking point. The mobile would buzz at 1 a.m. and Lisa would leap for it, hoping each time that a life-saving kidney had become available. Hearing her patient's voice on the other end of the line was a crushing blow, and no amount of reason could get her patient to desist from ringing 'for a chat'. (Lisa's son has since received a new kidney, and Lisa is very thankful indeed to be able to turn off her mobile at night.)

Cecily* is another woman obsessed with her psychiatrist, a man. She began seeing him five years ago when Cecily and her husband were having marital difficulties, and her interest in him was at first purely professional.

She says, 'I Googled him after our second session out of sheer curiosity (looking up his background) and came across his name in relation to a real estate transaction that had been covered in the local paper. It mentioned his and a woman's name. I forgot about it for a while, but as I began to go through more turmoil in my home life, I became attracted to him and more needy. I thought of him like a guru. And my husband disliked him.'

Cecily and her husband had been to one session together and had been counselled about therapy options. Her husband believed that the psychiatrist was biased towards Cecily, which she thinks was probably true, but it made her feel vindicated. She continued to see him by herself after she and her husband agreed to separate.

After some months, the psychiatrist suggested Cecily should try online dating, as she seemed emotionally ready. 'A month later, who does the site pair me up with but him!' Cecily says. 'Now that I knew for sure that he was divorced – I already suspected it from some of the things that he'd said – this made things even harder for me.'

In any event, Cecily reunited with her husband and dropped off the site – at least for a while.

'I poked around one insomnia-fuelled night and found out that he was still online. Before I knew it, I had created a new online dating profile. I never initiated contact, but the profile was attractive and he contacted "me". Soon we exchanged emails ... he initiated all contact, but I'll admit that I baited him. It was exciting to have this small amount of personal contact with him that the real me could never have. I felt too guilty to pry too much, and he is smart enough to keep his guard up somewhat, so I didn't have any earth-shattering discoveries. But he shared enough personal information that I have insight into his personality and that makes the obsession worse yet again!'

Cecily did have enough of a filter to limit herself, and in fact went so far as to make her online personality slightly obnoxious so that he would stop contact. He did, but Cecily discovered that she 'missed the rush' from finding his messages in her fake inbox so lured him back into contact again. She says that she never tried to take their relationship offline, and she has never tried to find out where he lives or any other personal details, but she suspects that one day the temptation will prove too much.

'I want to come clean so he can help me through this,' she says, 'but am aware it's impossible to predict how he will respond. It could be a positive or VERY negative experience. When I see him in person, I am flustered but do go to sessions prepared with questions and completely avoid any friendly chitchat. I am not at all provocative with him, and he is always very friendly and nice, offering whatever help I need. I doubt he suspects that I have been stalking him online.'

Cecily regrets that she didn't mention spotting him on the dating site when it first happened. 'It was one of those awkward situations where I just didn't know how he'd react. I guess I shouldn't worry so much about that and think more about how it is affecting my behaviour. But I'm afraid of losing him as a doctor, so I avoid the topic.'

A female clinician would probably be a better idea, Cecily admits, but then in the next breath she says that she thinks that he would be most helpful, given that she has severe social anxiety with men. To this day, she is torn between her need to protect her own mental health and her desire to continue clandestine contact with a man who has no idea that he is being stalked. 'If he has no idea of the extent of my problems, he can't really help me. I hide so much in our sessions together and really want to ask him for his help, yet know that this is probably not going to happen if he finds out what I have been up to,' Cecily says.

## The One

'Feel free to use my real name,' Richard Brittain told me when I asked if he'd rather travel under a pseudonym within this book, 'My story is all over the internet in any case.' And it's true. Even without Googling the name 'Richard Brittain', the moment you put the words 'benevolent' and 'stalker' together, you'll find pages and pages of vitriol about this young Englishman, the author of a blog post entitled 'The Benevolent Stalker'. (Note: if inspired to do this at home, please don't get Richard Brittain, the benevolent stalker and former UK *Countdown* champion, confused with Richard Brittain, the Scottish professional footballer.)

Our Richard Brittain's musings about his obsession with a fellow university student were first picked up by the online community, and then rapidly went viral via opinion pieces on sites and in papers such as *Jezebel*, the *New York Daily News* and the *International Business Times* amongst a host of others.

One of the online responses to his post describes it as 'one of the most chilling, creepy depictions of stalking I've ever read'. Another says, 'Fuck this creepy, violent motherfucker. I desperately and sincerely hope he ends up spending a lot of time in a Scottish prison and is taken off the streets before he can hurt anyone else.'

A friend had sent me a link to Richard's blog, and I then emailed him directly. I didn't think for an instant that he'd reply to an author and complete stranger on the other side of the world given all the trolling that he'd – rightfully or wrongfully – received. But I was keen to know the story behind the headlines. It's one thing reading about stalkers in the papers, but what about in real life. What is it like to be a stalker? What made him do what he did, and also – *what happened next?*

The following section doesn't condone Richard Brittain's behaviour, but it does attempt to explain what was going through his mind at the time he was stalking a victim. More than anything, interviewing Richard brought home to me that it is easy to judge someone for their behaviour as seen through the prism of the press or the internet. It's less easy to be judgmental when you have actually spoken to someone and heard them articulate their feelings at the time of the offence, and also how they are continuing to battle the mental health demons that trashed their reputation, their career and possibly their future. I wish Richard the very best – not only for his sake, but also for those who may suffer should he not receive the help and understanding that he needs, Mental health issues are not so dissimilar to any other health issues. It's how they are viewed and approached and treated that makes all the difference.

***

But first, here's the start of Richard's post – the post that started the internet shit storm, reprinted here with full permission:

> It was her smile that enchanted me, which may sound clichéd, but it is the truth. Her smile stimulated the deepest feelings of wonderment inside my being. Some people offer fake smiles, but a smile should never be forced. There is something incredible, infinite and indefinably good about a genuine smile. She was pretty, too. We did a quiz together, and I kissed her cheek when I left.
>
> I invited her onto the BBC University Challenge team that I was putting together. 'I don't know if I'm brainy enough Rich,' she said.
>
> 'We need beauty as well as brains,' I replied.
>
> She agreed to be on our team. 'Don't worry honey, I'll get these forms filled out for you,' she said when I provided her with the paperwork, as though it was a privilege to have her on our team, which it was. She let me choose a picture of her to use on the form, since she was busy.

That evening, I went through her many Facebook pictures. 'Maybe this one?' I asked in a chat message.

'It's not opening,' she said. 'What photo is it?'

'You're wearing a low-cut black lace-trimmed top. On your pink lips, a mischievous smile is playing,' I described.

'Ermm, if you think I look smart enough,' she replied.

'Well, I can't see any of you in your glasses,' I quipped.

'I hate wearing them!' she said. 'There's like 3 in existence.'

'You look pretty in them,' I said.

Determined to impress her and get our team onto TV, I intensively revised my general knowledge. I also frequented the student bar where she worked. I figured out what hours she did each day and went at those times.

A couple of weeks before our University Challenge audition, she unfriended me on Facebook. I was a little shocked and asked her why.

'You're kinda freaking me out,' she explained. 'You're a good guy but you're being far too forward.'

'Are you still doing University Challenge with us?' I asked.

'Only as a friend, but nothing more,' she replied.

For some reason, I then decided to tell her how I really felt; that I had become infatuated with her, and that I was in love with her. With hindsight, of course I wouldn't have done that. In fact, I would have done almost everything differently but, at the time, I felt compelled to do what I did.

She pulled out of the team. We found a replacement and failed the audition anyway (I doubt that her inclusion would have made a difference). My dream of winning University Challenge and impressing the maiden was shattered.

Richard admits – among many other things – that he had become obsessed with Ella*. (This isn't his victim's real name, but it is the name he gave the heroine of the book that he later self-published as a tribute to her.)

'I can understand now that I behaved inappropriately. It's only now I realise that she didn't really have a choice about seeing me at the student bar because that was where she worked. She couldn't do anything about it if I turned up at the hours when I knew she would be working; I didn't consider that at the time,' he says.

When Ella unfriended Richard on Facebook and severed all personal contact with him, he was confused and distressed rather than angry: 'I felt that she had been giving off signals that she was interested, although I understand now that she clearly wasn't. I thought she was putting on an act – she does do a lot of acting. In fact, her degree was politics and drama. I found her quite a difficult person to read.'

Richard convinced himself that Ella was playing a game: 'I thought she was trying to get me to prove how much I loved her.' And just like the epic romantic heroes of old, Richard determined that he would overcome all obstacles that were between him and the hand of the fair maiden he desired – even obstacles like her going to the police to get him to desist in his attentions.

Instead, Richard took heart in every smile he glimpsed from her in the bar, and every Tweet that he thought had been directed at him. 'I was delusional,' he now admits. 'I'd send her a message on Twitter saying something like "I just wanted to wish you a happy Christmas" and later she would Tweet "I just wanted to say that I loved you". I thought it was a coded message for me. It could have been to anyone.' (It probably didn't help that Ella was a keen Twitter user, so Richard had plenty of material to misconstrue …)

Even before he became obsessed with Ella, Richard had had little experience of romantic relationships. 'I had never had a girlfriend – I was always a bit too geeky.' He developed very strong feelings for Ella, very quickly.

In conversation, he's clearly very, very smart, and comes across as sweet, but also a bit naive and not particularly socially attuned. (Or maybe it's just that he didn't laugh at any of my attempts at humour.)

235

For that reason, I can understand why he may have been subject to the 'He's A Nice Guy But ...' syndrome. Everyone – male or female – faces this particular challenge at one time or another. But while some might shrug, chalk it up to experience and move on, others react differently.

Richard says he understands now that mental health issues had been affecting him for a long time. Even before he met Ella, he recognises that he had had troubles with impulsive behaviour– gambling away money he didn't have, drinking too much ... 'I've always had quite poor impulse control. Some people write emails and decide not to send them – I'm the kind of person who just hits SEND.'

Ella contacted their university and made a complaint about his attentions. Richard was called in for a 'chat' with his tutor, and was warned that Ella wanted no further contact with him. 'There were a number of rules I had to comply with – when I went into the student bar I was not allowed to talk to her or approach her, and had to wait to be served by someone else.'

The university organised a couple of sessions with a counsellor for Richard, and he says it was helpful to talk everything through with her after having been locked in with his increasingly obsessive thoughts for so long. But the mental health support he received was not nearly enough.

Richard became very angry at the rules laid down by the university. He started drinking heavily and became alienated from his flatmates – one of whom was a friend of Ella's. 'I became quite unpopular when they got wind of the fact that I was stalking Ella. The whole thing affected me hugely – I went kind of mental. I would drink two bottles of wine, jump over fences to get into nightclubs, and often get into fights and be thrown out ...' Richard was also banned from his student union, which meant that he could no longer go to the bar where she worked – something that Ella, at least, may have welcomed.

The university hadn't thought to ban Richard from *writing* to

Ella though, so Richard composed and sent a few love letters – about one a month, he reckons, and complete with drawings and poetry. 'Occasionally, I also left messages on her phone. I asked if there was any chance of her changing her mind and explained how I really felt about her.'

In June 2013, Ella called the police. A policewoman rang Richard and warned him that he had to cease *all* contact with Ella. Again, Richard was angry with what he perceived as their interference. 'I didn't feel like what I was doing constituted stalking – I'd associated stalking with the sort of thing you see in movies, with a creepy guy watching some woman through binoculars. I didn't think what I was doing was that bad – all it amounted to were a few love letters and a few phone calls.

'I told the policewoman that I was pretty sure that most girls wouldn't go to the police [over behaviour] like that. Nonetheless, I was told that I would be arrested if I made further contact.'

The warning worked to scare Richard off – for a while at least. 'I knew it was serious if the police were involved. And my friends were all saying to me, "Just stop. After all the complaints that have been made against you … now she's contacted the police, you have to stop." None of them were on my side, as I saw it. They all told me to give it up.'

Richard says that he hadn't really explained the situation fully to his friends, as he didn't think that they would understand. 'Ella was on my mind constantly – every minute of every day. She still is to a certain extent. It's more difficult than you can imagine to eradicate those feelings. But today, I just don't act on them,' he says.

In the event, Richard managed to keep out of trouble and away from Ella for six months, but mid-November 2013 rolled around and he knew that she would be back in town for her graduation ceremony, having graduated in July of that year. At the time, Ella was living in Somerset and Richard was working in London, so he saw it as an ideal opportunity to see her once more. He was there on his own, and soon enough he espied Ella surrounded by her family and friends.

'The ceremony was being held in a big open space with pillars to one side,' he says. 'I went and stood beside them, and watched from there. When she spotted me, she kind of freaked out. She was talking quickly to her family and pointing at me. When I saw that she was concerned, I realised it was a bit weird that I was there so I walked away. That day I realised I still had really passionate feelings for her and that was when I picked up [the stalking] again.'

Richard waited a couple of weeks and then sent Ella some text messages declaring his love for her. And he wrote her a couple of cards – one for Christmas and one for Valentine's Day 2014. As Richard explained in his 'Benevolent Stalker' blog post, that card contained an 'elaborate drawing of a wild scene. In it, she became the character Ella Tundra, and that is how [I began writing] my book *The World Rose.*'

*The World Rose* was Richard's paean to the object of his obsession. It consumed him for the nine months it took him to write; he self-published the book in September 2014. 'It basically took over my life. I could think of nothing else but Ella and the book. It consumed my whole thinking. It was very obsessive. I did nothing but write the whole time, and I felt better for it.' And then he came up with an ill-advised idea to gain readers and some vital publicity. He decided to stage a fake kidnapping of Ella.

He discovered that Ella was now living in Glasgow, and decided to make the trek up north – armed with camping equipment and other supplies – and ask her to hide out with him for a few days. His idea was to spur a hunt for her, and gain the attention of the national press. Then the two would appear – they would both be famous, she would understand how dedicated he was, and their story would become known as one of the great love stories. As an added kicker, when *The World Rose* was turned into a film, Ella could play the title role – the role that had been written just for her.

It was delusional thinking, but Richard was blissfully unaware.

Somehow he thought that if he simply asked Ella to go off into the wilds with him as part of a publicity stunt, she would agree. As he says, 'I thought she might change her mind when she discovered that I had written a book about her.'

He didn't think about how she might have felt about him. How she had reported him – firstly to the university, then to the police. He didn't think that it might be considered odd behaviour for a stalker *to ask his victim to run away with him.*

Then again, Richard didn't consider himself a stalker, but more of an admirer. The post that set the internet alight (and that was posted not long after his life completely ran off the tracks) read:

But what does stalking really mean? It seems to mean that you truly love someone who does not love you back.

Every great romance is about two partners who are utterly obsessed with each other. Romeo, Juliet, Tristan and Isolde are people who are so passionately and powerfully in love that nothing else matters to them. But what if that feeling was felt on only one side? What if Juliet had rejected Romeo? Would he become a stalker?

It seems that modern society drools over depictions of this intense, obsessional love, but only when it is mutual. When it comes from just one side, it is suddenly deemed a terrible thing.

When I was listening to The Beatles, I realised that a lot of their early music suited my mood. Much of it is about being utterly obsessed with a particular woman [such as 'I'll Get You'] . . .

Are the Beatles creepy stalkers? Of course not. How about Sting [with his 'Every Breath You Take']?

These songs are about obsessional love, which is both natural and beautiful. Benevolent stalking is different to malevolent stalking. The latter is intended to cause harm or induce fear, but the former is purely an expression of affection.

Actually, I'd take issue with Richard's views in this post – both of these songs send unpleasant shivers down my spine. However, I do understand his confusion about societal expectations of romance. Just as the sexualised images with which we are bombarded affect our own sex lives and even how we view our bodies, so too do the stories we are told about love affect how we behave in our romantic relationships. When you add mental illness into the equation, it can be an explosive combination, as Richard himself now admits.

Richard never got the chance to tell Ella of his grandiose plans: 'I saw her in the street and called out her name. She freaked out and said something like "How? How are you here?" She took photos of me on her phone, and then hurried away. People were staring so I didn't pursue her. I never got the chance to tell her of my idea, or even about the book. I thought that if she doesn't want me now, this is definitely the end. But she contacted the police, and because I had already had a warning, I was arrested.'

***

When I spoke to Richard he was out on bail, having been charged with stalking. His solicitor entered no plea – which means there will be no court case – and he is still awaiting the verdict in terms of his sentence. He suspects it will probably be a restraining order. Going to court was both a salutary and an unsavoury experience, as he recalls it: 'Glasgow Sherriff's court is the busiest court in Europe. Before the hearing, I was held in custody for three days – locked in a cell with seven other criminals. One was in on an attempted murder charge, and there were a couple in for domestic violence. I wasn't expecting to be put in a holding cell with people like that – it was a scary experience.'

On the plus side, Richard says that it did give him valuable time to think about how far his life had changed since his days as a quiz king on the British TV show *Countdown*. 'That experience changed me,' he says. 'I was happy to do those three days, to mull over what I had done and how I needed to change my ways or face the prospect of ending up in a prison cell long term. I could no longer flagrantly disregard what people had been telling me. I was deluded.'

Richard was released on bail, but there was no mental health support and things rapidly spiralled even further down. Again, it was related to his stalking of Ella, and his book about her, *The World Rose*. During the writing of the book, he'd become part of an active community of online writers, but his attitude to criticism of the extracts he'd released – and some of the comments he'd made in return – had been taken badly: 'They threatened me that when I did publish the book, then they would only give it a one star review. I had no contact with them for a month before the book came out and had basically forgotten about it, then I saw they had indeed given it one star. They called it appalling, awful ... every adjective in the dictionary. And I got incredibly angry.'

What happened next was 'pure stupidity on my part'. What happened next was that Richard tracked down the reviewer who'd given him the one star, travelled north to Scotland again, and assaulted her in a supermarket. He is facing charges for this too, and again will not contest them. 'She didn't deserve to be physically assaulted for writing a review. I accept I was completely in the wrong.'

★★★

One might think that, okay, it's relatively easy to do the wrong thing and then apologise for it, but one also needs to consider the issue of mental illness and how that affects every aspect of life. When I spoke to Richard, his psychiatrist had put him on quite strong anti-psychotic medication. From swooping between manic highs and devastating lows, Richard was feeling substantially better. Talking therapy is helping too. 'It's only now that I understand that Ella didn't want me at all. That's what I'm talking to my psychiatrist about now – how I managed to maintain that level of delusion. Whether I am bipolar or schizophrenic or psychotic, whatever my particular problem might be, the medication is helping.' So too is the support from his family and friends – people who'd been worried about him for years, but whose opinions and help he had previously been too stubborn to accept.

The question now is: How does one recover from making headlines around the world – not for one's general knowledge or academic achievements – but for stalking a fellow student and attempting to brain a book reviewer? In the age of the internet, these things are likely to follow Richard for the rest of his life. How forgiving is the world?

Richard today is finally getting the help that he needs and while it's not doing much for his job prospects – how many employers would welcome a worker taking two days off each week to see a psychiatrist – it is certainly helping him come to grips with what he has done and who he is. And what he needs to do to stay well.

Part of it, for Richard, has been apologising to the women he has both harmed and scared. This was not an action ordered by the courts, but something that he felt had to be done:

I have re-evaluated my stance on many things. My blog post entitled 'The Benevolent Stalker' made international news and was roundly condemned. For every supportive comment I received, I had about a hundred negative ones. This level of response was helpful because 99% of people cannot be wrong. At the time, I didn't realise just how terrible my behaviour was. I did have benevolent intentions but I now realise that there was nothing remotely benevolent about what I was doing. Stalking in any form is horrible and it is unacceptable to attempt to justify it.

... Romance is generally cast in a positive light in movies and literature, but when I thought about it, I realised that most of those stories are written by men. We're not seeing things from the female perspective. What I also realise now is that if you act the way that those characters do, in real life, you may end up in jail.

# The Victim Impact

One of main revelations I had when researching this book was how everyday actions could suddenly take on horrific meaning. The tap of a branch on a window. The ping of an email in an inbox. Someone walking past your house. A footprint in a garden bed. A phone call from an unknown number. A phone call from a *known* number.

Until you have been personally targeted by a stalker, it's almost impossible to imagine the impact of such ordinary events on your life, and your mental health. For those who are targeted for vast stretches of time, the impact can be immeasurable. Anxiety, depression, the list goes on ...

How society views victims also has an impact. Some of the people in this book were actually put under the spotlight for crimes *committed by their stalker* – like the poor folk in Queensland whose digital identities were used to carry out a number of fake bomb and hostage hoaxes. And who also had to put up with the arrival of hundreds of unwanted (or at least un-ordered) pizzas (see page 100). Being targeted like this truly must be hard to swallow – on the one hand, you are a victim; on the other, people think you are actually the perpetrator. Not only by the pissed-off pizza delivery folk in this case, but also by the police and security forces.

## The Victim Profile

It's clear from the case studies in this book that practically anyone can become a victim of stalking. Public figures and medical professionals seem to be most at risk, but no one can claim immunity – age, sex, religion, socioeconomic status, job or cultural background are pretty much irrelevant in a stalker's eyes.

That said, women are more likely to be stalked than men according to research, both in Australia and internationally. A whopping 75 per cent of victims are female.

In one Australian survey, one in every five women said that that they had been stalked at some point in their lives (after the age of 15). That figure startled me when I first started looking into this topic, but a straw poll of my own friends and acquaintances gave similar results. Everyone knew someone who had been stalked – along a sliding scale of severity – although some did not classify it as stalking, but rather as bullying or even 'loser behaviour' or a 'nuisance' rather than as a criminal offence.

The perpetrators are overwhelmingly male, although female–female and female–male stalking does also occur, as the cases of Dawnette Knight–Catherine Zeta Jones (page 145) and also Andrea–Simon (page 199) show.

Over the years, researchers and shrinks and psychologists have had a field day deciding how to classify victims of stalking. Various categories have been suggested, from the simple 'Known to Victim' and 'Unknown to Victim', to the more complex, where 'Known to Victim' could include everything from Personal (Prior Sexual Intimate, Serious Date or Casual Date), Professional, Employment, Media and Acquaintance. It's enough to make your brain hurt.

For that reason alone, I quite like the categories outlined by Mullen, Pathé and Purcell in *Stalkers and Their Victims,* which seems to cover everything. Their categories include:

- Prior intimates – the most common category (e.g. former spouses or girlfriends or boyfriends).
- Estranged family and friends – for example, a parent or child or ex-bestie, who holds a grudge or wants to exert control over the victim.

- Casual acquaintances – such as a neighbour (or some loser with whom you strike up a conversation at a local cafe, in my case).
- Professional contacts – teachers, doctors and lawyers seem to head this hit list. The stalker does not work with their victim, but may hold a grudge for some reason – a child's bad school report, a psychologist who ceases treatment, a lawyer who loses a case …
- Workplace contacts – I work from home, alone, so luckily the chances of this happening are pretty remote, unless you count my chances of being stalked to and from the fridge by the ever-hungry cats and dog. But for those in more conventional workplaces, the dangers of office politics pale in comparison to the dangers posed by an employer, employee, co-worker, supplier or customer who decides that you are 'The One'.
- Strangers – someone with whom you have never had prior contact, but who has now made themselves known to you.
- Public figures – celebrities, politicians or others with a high profile in the community.
- Unknowns – unlike being stalked by a stranger, when you're being stalked by an 'unknown', it means you don't know who it is that is targeting you. This was the case for Morgan Ingram (page 175), who was stalked by a person whose identity is still unknown (unproven, her parents would say). Morgan's stalker could have been someone she knew, or could have been a complete stranger – the point is, no one knows for sure who it was.
- Secondary victims – it's not only the victim who suffers when a stalker is in operation. Family members, friends, work colleagues, acquaintances and housemates of the victim may also come to the stalker's attention. And not in a good way. Direct or indirect threats or action may disrupt their lives to devastating effect. Think, for example, of a domestic violence victim who moves to a new home with a new flatmate – only

for *both* to be on the end of countless late night phone calls, and attempted intrusions. Or a young girl who sees her mother disintegrating as she tries to provide a normal, happy childhood for her daughter, while also handling the constant stress of a stalker's attention.

The last category Mullen, Pathé and Purcell describe is that of the 'unusual victim'. In my earlier book *Love Behind Bars*, one of my interviewees described his bewilderment and disgust at receiving adoring letters from women on the outside, drawn to him purely for his notoriety as one of Australia's most wanted men for a while, and a well-known prison escapee. Given his fame, I guess Joe could also have been classified as a public figure – in certain circles – at that time.

The same goes for Robert Bardo (page 158) who stalked and murdered the young actress Rebecca Schaeffer. He complained that as a result of *his* stalking, he was now being hounded by the media and countless nut jobs threatening him with harm or death, or marriage.

I think this is known as an eye for an eye.


## Harm Caused: The Toll of Stalking

Much research has been carried out into how stalking affects victims and it is clear that victims can suffer from a huge range of effects. As with so many aspects of stalking, reactions are also highly individual. Stalking behaviour that one victim shrugs off may have a shattering effect on another.

To generalise, stalking can have a profound impact on every aspect of a victim's psychological and physical health, as well as their finances, and their work and social lives. And, as some of the cases in this book show, sometimes the experience can last for years. This becomes very wearying for the victims, who may also lose their support network. And perhaps this is not surprising. Friends

**Physical Health Effects**
- Fatigue – from insomnia and the constant need to be alert
- Chronic stress – high blood pressure, headaches, exacerbation of existing problems e.g. asthma, skin issues
- Weight changes – comfort eating or *not* eating at all i.e. loss of appetite
- Sexual dysfunction
- Increased substance use – alcohol, illegal drugs, nicotine
- Heart palpitations, sweating, tummy problems
- Physical injury, due to not concentrating or being under the influence of alcohol or other substances

and family who happily rally round a victim in the early days can also become worn down by the relentless harassment – and the continual need to provide support. This, in turn, can cause them to withdraw from the victim as a form of self-preservation, leaving the victim very much isolated and just as scared and in need of support as before.

For all these reasons, it is unsurprising then that common effects of stalking include fear, depression, doubt and denial (Is this really happening to me?) as well as guilt, embarrassment and self-blame (What did I do to deserve this?).

Victims often also feel frustrated, isolated, helpless to stop the stalking, and terrified at what may happen if it continues. They may fear being alone or being shunned, and at the same time withdraw from contact with other people. Sometimes this disconnection from support networks is involuntary, as when a victim is forced to move location, change their email and phone number, appearance or even name.

Unsurprisingly, many demonstrate symptoms of anxiety, have difficulty concentrating, or may even suffer from panic attacks or agoraphobia. Nightmares, insomnia, irritability, anger and emotional numbness are other common psychological effects.

Taken to extremes, victims may actually dream about killing the stalker to remove the pain. Sadly, others may either entertain or act on suicidal thoughts for much the same reason. They see death as the only way out of the horrible situation into which they have been thrust.

But it's not just what's happening inside their minds and bodies that victims need to think about. Being stalked can also have a devastating effect on other aspects of life including work. Think about it for a minute. How well would you perform at work or school if you were being stalked? How would your manager or HR representative react – would they be supportive or judgemental? How many days could you afford to take off to deal with police, get help for any physical or psychological problems, or simply stay in bed with the covers over your head? How would you cope if you had to drop out of school or university or change an established career to escape?

And what about the financial impact? It's one thing to think about taking a few sickies to cope with the stress, but stalking also introduces a number of hidden financial costs including those associated with legal fees, repairs (should the stalker damage your property), counselling and medical treatment, removal and relocation costs … Not all of us have the financial resources to seek legal advice or take time off paid work to seek help, let alone to relocate to safer housing or a completely new environment. Without options, it's easy to feel stuck.

***

With all the negative impacts of stalking, you'd think that victims would be putting their hands up to get support straight away. But the odd thing – from my point of view – is that many people still struggle with the idea that they are being stalked, and that there *are* legal measures that can be taken.

Some simply find it hard to accept that it's happening and try

## Making It Official

If or when you decide to go down the official route to dealing with a stalker, you can either call or visit your local police station. Police officers will need to know certain things about both you and your stalker:

- Is the person subject to a current domestic violence order (DVO), police protection notice, release conditions or is an application for a protection order in place?
- Is there a pattern to the stalker's behaviour and conduct?
- Do you have a record of the stalker's vehicle details: registration number, colour, make, condition?
- Where does he/she operate: places and street names where you have seen the stalker loitering, following or watching?
- What phone numbers does the stalker use?
- Have you saved voice/text/email/photo messages?
- Have you kept a record of dates and times?
- What incidents have occurred?

They will need as much information as possible in order to help you, so they are also likely to ask:

- Is there a threat being made to you, or your children, at this time?
- Where is the offender now?
- What is your relationship with the offender?
- Are there any children involved and what are their whereabouts?
- Are the children currently with the offender?
- Are there any fears held for the welfare of you or the children?
- Does the offender possess any firearms or weapons?
- Is alcohol or are drugs involved?
- Does the person have a medical or psychiatric history?

Being prepared can help the authorities to help you better.

to pretend that it is not – the ostrich approach, if you will. Others believe they should be 'able to handle it' and hope that the stalker will come to their senses in the meantime. They may also not want to get the authorities involved if they are worried that the stalker will get into trouble – this is particularly common if the victim has had a previous relationship with the stalker, or if they have received direct threats to their safety or that of their family, friends, or even pets.

Fear of blame also plays a part in shaping the reactions of some victims. After all, if you thought that you were going to be accused of somehow *encouraging* your stalker, you might think twice about approaching police or confiding in friends about what is happening. This fear is particularly pertinent for those who know their stalker – whether they have had a brief fling, exchanged a few flirtatious words or been married for decades. The same holds true for those who have been stalked in the workplace or by a stranger.

Those who know their stalker through work have other issues that can discourage them from seeking help: fear of losing their job, or of the workplace becoming even more difficult being two key ones. And while the vast majority of organisations these days have policies in place to protect workers from unwanted harassment – including sexual harassment and workplace stalking – there's no doubt that speaking out does carry risks.

Which brings me to my final point. If a victim's previous requests for help have been ignored or downplayed – by the authorities, the workplace or family or friends – they are far more likely to feel isolated and to believe that there is nothing that can be done to help them. For this reason alone, it's important that you *listen* if someone confides in you about their stalking experience and *learn* what you can do to help.

And if it is you who is being stalked, simply don't give up. There is a plethora of useful resources out there on the internet, and widely available through domestic violence and information centres. Legal advice doesn't have to be costly, and it is not necessarily your first step in any case. There are many organisations and individuals who can help you. The police are more alert to the problem than ever before. And every victim deserves a voice. Use yours.

# Notes

1 Baum, K, Catalano, S, Rand, M and Rose, K (2009), 'Stalking victimization in the United States', Bureau of Justice Statistics Special Report, Washington DC.

2 Spitzberg, B and Cupach, W (2001), 'Paradoxes of pursuit: toward a relational model of stalking-related phenomena'. In J Davis (ed.), *Stalking, Stalkers and Their Victims: Prevention, Intervention, and Threat Assessment* (CRC Press, Boca Raton, Florida).

3 Kienlen, KK, Birmingham, DL, Solberg, KB, O'Regan, JT and Melroy, JR (1997), 'A comparative study of psychotic and non-psychotic stalking', *Journal of the American Academy of Psychiatry and Law*, 25, 317– 34.

4 McConaghy, N (1993), *Sexual Behavior: Problems and Management* (Plenum, New York).

5 Strand, S and McEwan, TE (2011), 'Same-gender stalking', *Behavioral Sciences and the Law*, 29, 209–19.

6 Strand and McEwan (2011); Kuehner, C, Gass, P and Dressing, H (2011/2012), 'Mediating effects of stalking victimization on gender differences in mental health', *Journal of Interpersonal Violence*, 27(2), 199–221; Australian Bureau of Statistics (2010), customised report, based on data from the 2005 Personal Safety Survey, Australian Bureau of Statistics, Canberra.

7 Woodlock, D (2013), 'Technology-facilitated stalking: Findings and recommendations from the SmartSafe Project', Domestic Violence Resource Centre Victoria, Collingwood.

8 Logan, TK, Leukefeld, C, Walker, B (2000), 'Stalking as a

variant of intimate violence: Implications from a young adult sample', *Violence and Victims*, 15 (1), 91–111; Hand, T, Chung, D and Peters, M (2009), *The Use of Information and Communication Technologies to Coerce and Control in Domestic Violence and Following Separation*, Australian Domestic and Family Violence Clearinghouse, Sydney; Melton, HC (2007), 'Predicting the occurrence of stalking in relationships characterised by domestic violence', *Journal of Interpersonal Violence*, 22 (1), 3–25.

9 Marshall, TC (2012), 'Facebook surveillance of former romantic partners: Associations with postbreakup recovery and personal growth', *Cyberpsychology, Behavior, and Social Networking*, 15(10): 521–6.

10 Wise, K, Alhabash, S and Park, H (2010), 'Emotional responses during social information seeking on Facebook', *Cyberpsychology, Behavior, and Social Networking*, 13(5), 555–62.

11 Chan, A and Payne, J (2013), 'Homicide in Australia: 2008–09 to 2009–10', National Homicide Monitoring Program annual report, Australian Institute of Criminology, Canberra.

12 Australian Bureau of Statistics (2006), Personal Safety Survey (reissue), Australian Bureau of Statistics, Canberra.

13 VicHealth (2004), 'The health costs of violence: Measuring the burden of disease caused by intimate partner violence', Melbourne.

14 Mouzos, J and Makkai, T (2004), 'Women's experiences of male violence: Findings from the Australian component of the International Violence Against Women Survey', Research and public policy series no. 56, AIC, Canberra; ABS (2005), Personal Safety Survey Australia 2005 (reissue), cat. no. 4906.0, ABS, Canberra.

15 Review is at www.mobilestealthreview.com (accessed 16 June 2015).

16 James, DV, Mullen, PE, Meloy, JR, Pathé, MT, Farnham, FR, Preston, L and Darnley, B (2007), 'The role of mental disorder

in attacks on European politicians 1990–2004', *Acta Psychiatrica Scandinavica*, 116(5), 334–44.

17 James, DV, Farnham, FR and Wilson, SP (2014), 'The Fixated Threat Assessment Centre: Implementing a joint policing and psychiatric approach to risk assessment and management in public figure threat cases', In: J Reid Meloy and J Hoffman (eds.), *International Handbook of Threat Assessment*, Oxford University Press, New York.

18 Park, ED and Martell, DA (1989), 'Mentally disordered offenders in pursuit of celebrities and politicians', National Institute of Justice, Washington DC, US.

19 Malsch, M, Visscher, M and Blaauw, W (2002), *Stalking van bekende personen* [Stalking of celebrities], Boom Juridische Uitgevers, Den Haag.

20 Hoffmann, JM and Sheridan, LP (2005), 'The stalking of public figures: Management and intervention', *Journal of Forensic Sciences*, 50, 1459–65.

21 Scott, AJ, Lloyd, R and Gavin, J (2010), 'The influence of prior relationship on perceptions of stalking in the United Kingdom and Australia', *Criminal Justice and Behavior*, 37, 1185–94.

22 McFarlane, J, Campbell, JC and Watson, K (2002), 'Intimate partner stalking and femicide: Urgent implications for women's safety', *Behavioral Sciences and the Law*, 20, 51–68.

23 Eyre, CB, in *R v Woodcock* (1789), 168 ER 352.

24 Mullen, PE, Pathé, M, Purcell, R (2009), *Stalkers and Their Victims*, Cambridge University Press, UK.

# Acknowledgements

I could not have completed this book without the assistance of many people, most of all, the victims of stalking and stalkers who were prepared to share their stories with me and raise awareness of this dreadful issue. For obvious reasons, I cannot name them here. I'd also like to thank all the organisations and individuals doing such sterling work to help those who have been targeted by a stalker. Particular thanks to Judy Line, Lindy Parker, Jamie Sims, Meredith Fuller, Kerryn Westhorp and Rita Erlich. Also to the wonderful team at Echo Publishing: my delightful commissioning editor, Julia Taylor, Kyla Petrilli for her eagle-eyed editing and highly sensible author queries, Luke Causby for the spooky cover and Shaun Jury for the page design. Finally, a big thanks to my family and friends who suffered my inattention and crankiness as deadline approached, and kept me fed and watered and halfway sane.